ASSOCIATION CONSISTORIALE

More Praise for *Inheritance*

"*Inheritance* offers powerful insights into the lasting multigenerational psychological effects of the Holocaust. It is a product of an incisive intellect and a compassionate heart, and embraces grief and mourning not with resentment, but with the aim of understanding and preventing further tragedies."

—Pablo de Greiff, United Nations special rapporteur on the promotion of truth, justice, reparation, and guarantees of non-recurrence

"*Inheritance* gives a human face to the story of seeking refuge from violence. As the world faces the largest crisis of forced displacement in its history, this book should be required reading. It reminds the reader that every refugee, past and present, is only seeking what we all deserve: love, safety, and a life free from persecution."

—Kerry Whigham, author of *Resonant Violence: Affect, Memory, and Activism in Post-Genocide Societies*

"Charlie Scheidt and Kat Rohrer creatively weave together threads from the lives of past generations with contemporary stories of research and discovery. What emerges is a fascinating narrative that provides vital documentation of a history that must not be forgotten now or for generations to come."

—William H. Weitzer, executive director emeritus, Leo Baeck Institute

"A remarkable, powerful tribute to family, to Holocaust studies, and to humanity. This work holds extraordinary meaning, not only for one family's survival and legacy, but for society's collective obligations toward one another and the world to ensure 'Never Again!' The courage to remember and share is inspiring in ways that ripple outward as a beacon to us all. This brilliant contribution to the world deserves to be read, taught, and cherished widely for generations to come."

—Jocelyn Getgen Kestenbaum, director, Cardozo Law Institute in Holocaust and Human Rights

"Remembering is a challenge: it requires time, demands taking winding paths, and confronts unforeseen emotions. It can also have a healing effect. While it can never close the gaps violently torn by history, it can make them tangible. *Inheritance* bears witness to this—it is a touching and impressive story about his family, but also about Charlie's own journey of remembrance."

—Angela Jannelli, curator at the Historical Museum Frankfurt

"A treasure trove of private letters, intimate memories, and decades of deep research in half a dozen countries brought into being Charlie Scheidt's beautifully written story of a German-Jewish family before, during, and after the Holocaust. A touching, honest, and meaningful book, filled with empathy, *Inheritance* is a unique history of the twentieth century that combines the personal and the political as it has rarely been accomplished before."

—Thomas Kuehne, director of the Strassler Center for Holocaust and Genocide Studies at Clark University, Worchester, MA

"Charlie Scheidt's captivating story of piecing together his family's escape from Nazi Germany casts the Holocaust as a global history of refugees. In our world of millions of refugees, *Inheritance* reminds us of the urgency of standing with those targeted by violent states today in their struggle to find refuge."

—Raz Segal, associate professor of Holocaust and Genocide Studies and founding coordinator of the Refugee Studies Initiative, Stockton University

"A remarkable achievement. Combining rigorous and painstaking historical research with profound empathy, sensibility, and wit, Scheidt vividly reconstructs the lives, struggles, losses, and survivals of one family during the Holocaust. *Inheritance* masterfully weaves their unique stories into broader tapestry of millions of lives lost, saved, and transformed. The result is a book that anyone interested in the Holocaust—or families—will want to read."

—Maxim A. Pensky, codirector of the Institute for Genocide and Mass Atrocity Prevention at SUNY Binghamton

"Meticulously researched, with prose as beautiful as it is moving, Charlie Scheidt's *Inheritance* is a masterpiece. What was a story of displacement and sorrow in the shadow of the Holocaust, marked by whispered names and time cut short, becomes a story of regeneration and joy as the descendants of survivors find each other and rebuild their family. In the end, Charlie finds a new part of himself hidden in plain sight, weaving archival research with personal revelation into the broader story of a family who refused to be erased."

—Douglas S. Irvin-Erikson, director of the Genocide Prevention Program, Jimmy and Rosalynn Carter School for Peace and Conflict Resolution, George Mason University

"Tender and thoughtful, Charlie Scheidt tells the history and the story of his family, full of warmth and wisdom, hard-won over years of research and grappling with the deepest of questions. As readers, we should be grateful that he takes us along on this remarkable journey and shares a powerful inheritance with us."

—Markus Krah, executive director, Leo Baeck Institute

"Years after his parents' death, Charlie Scheidt, aided by a trove of pre-war and wartime letters, traces his family's longtime roots in Germany and uncovers what happened when they were abruptly uprooted. Scheidt draws on his own memories of those who survived and in turn, their stories of those who did not, to help reconstruct the desperate choices they made. This elegant narrative shows how he painstakingly pieced their stories together, reconstructing past choices and capturing both the power of words and the power of place. In doing so, he brings back to life their voices, and their messages resonate today."

—Annie Polland, president, Tenement Museum

Inheritance

Genocide, Political Violence, Human Rights Series

Edited by Alexander Laban Hinton, Nela Navarro, and Natasha Zaretsky

For a complete list of titles in the series, please see the last page of the book.

Inheritance

Love, Loss, and the Legacy of the Holocaust

CHARLIE SCHEIDT
with KAT ROHRER

Foreword by James Waller

Rutgers University Press
New Brunswick, Camden, and Newark, New Jersey
London

Rutgers University Press is a department of Rutgers, The State University of New Jersey, one of the leading public research universities in the nation. By publishing worldwide, it furthers the University's mission of dedication to excellence in teaching, scholarship, research, and clinical care.

ISBN 978-1-9788-4674-6 (cloth)
ISBN 978-1-9788-4675-3 (epub)

Cataloging-in-publication data is available from the Library of Congress
LCCN 2025031453

A British Cataloging-in-Publication record for this book is available from the British Library.

♾ The paper used in this publication meets the requirements of the American National Standard for Information Sciences—Permanence of Paper for Printed Library Materials, ANSI Z39.48-1992.

rutgersuniversitypress.org

To my parents, Bruno and Suse,
My uncle Max and aunt Erna,
My aunt Lilo,
My sons, their children, and future generations.

What has happened lies so far back and is yet so close. Today is also the yesterday of long ago.

—SAMSON SCHAMES (1898–1967), unpublished memoir

Contents

Foreword

Even the most restrictive of definitions estimates that at least 60 million men, women, and children were victims of genocide and mass killing in the past century alone.[1] On the upper end, political scientist Rudolph Rummel argues that close to 170 million civilians were murdered in the twentieth century.[2] Unfortunately, the first decades of the twenty-first century have brought little light to the darkness as a variety of international watchlists suggest that close to twenty countries are currently "at risk" for genocide.

The massive scale of the numbers of people killed, or at risk of being killed, by genocide can become an abstraction and, even, a form of dehumanization. They obscure the reality that embedded within these numbers are individuals—people who loved someone and were loved by someone else; who had hopes, dreams, and aspirations that would never be fulfilled. Not because of anything they did as individuals, but because of a group identity they held—racial, religious, ethnic, tribal, national, political, and so on—that the perpetrators deemed necessary to eliminate.

So, it is essential that we open space for, and hear, the voices that rehumanize the experience of those who have been victimized by and survived genocide and mass atrocity. First-person accounts are textual spaces that not only humanize the darker sides of our collective history but also offer the opportunity to put a face to the people who were ostracized and persecuted and killed because of their group identity.

Charlie Scheidt's remarkable memoir provides us with deep insights into the personal, familial, and collective life of his family before, during, and after the Holocaust. The book, particularly as it deals with the reverberating consequences of Jewish life after the Holocaust, is a powerful undertaking of active witnessing. As Charlie describes, however, nothing about the meticulous research and absorbing writing of this book, taking place over decades and in many countries, was easy. He was torn between the need to know and a sometimes equally compelling need to *not* know. A need to confront his family's past clashing with an emotional need to bury it. A need to ask unanswered questions or to simply let them lie.

I suspect that this powerful memoir—knowing that the Ballin and Scheidt family stories have been told and will live on—was a point of self-liberation for Charlie and his family. It also is a point of self-liberation for its readers. Even though most of us have not lived through the specific types of experiences recounted in *Inheritance*, reading this memoir opens for us a critical bridge of empathy and, if we so choose, compassionate action.

As Haig Manuelian, a second-generation survivor of the Armenian genocide, says, "We must know each other's stories. We must consider ourselves one constituent element of a symphony."[3] While, at points, the symphony of suffering described in the Ballin-Scheidt family tree is certainly hard on the ears, and even harder on the heart, it is part of our collective story. And to know these stories is to reach beyond ourselves to a more expansive awareness of the world in which we live.

If we allow empathy and compassion to be handcuffed by our own self-absorption, then there remains little hope for repairing a broken world. This poignant memoir, as difficult as some of the events may be to face, can offer an antidote to self-absorption by nurturing our capability to understand the suffering of others and, more importantly, activating our responsibility for transformative compassionate action. The heroic actions, for instance, of two American officials, Myles Standish and his superior Hiram Bingham IV, at the risk of their careers, and in direct defiance of both Vichy officials and U.S. regulations, saved over 2,500 people—including members of Charlie's family. Their actions and the actions of other people in this memoir who acted compassionately in the face of the injustice surrounding them remind us that life is a matter of choices and that each of us has the power to choose compassion and inclusion over indifference and exclusion. That vital lesson, in a world reeling from a global assault on democracy and democratic institutions, is as necessary today as it has ever been.

Inheritance is a remarkable chronicle of lives lived, lives lost, and lives remembered. While portions of the memoir leave us with a palpable sense of the presence of absence, its overriding impact is to give us insight into what it means to wrestle with familial legacy, memory, displacement, trauma, and the weight of silence. Indeed, Charlie's recounting of his family's story reveals rich and complex lives that have broader meaning for each of us, and, ultimately, this is the transformative gift bequeathed by this brilliant memoir.

James Waller, PhD
Christopher J. Dodd Chair in Human Rights Practice
University of Connecticut

The Ballin Family

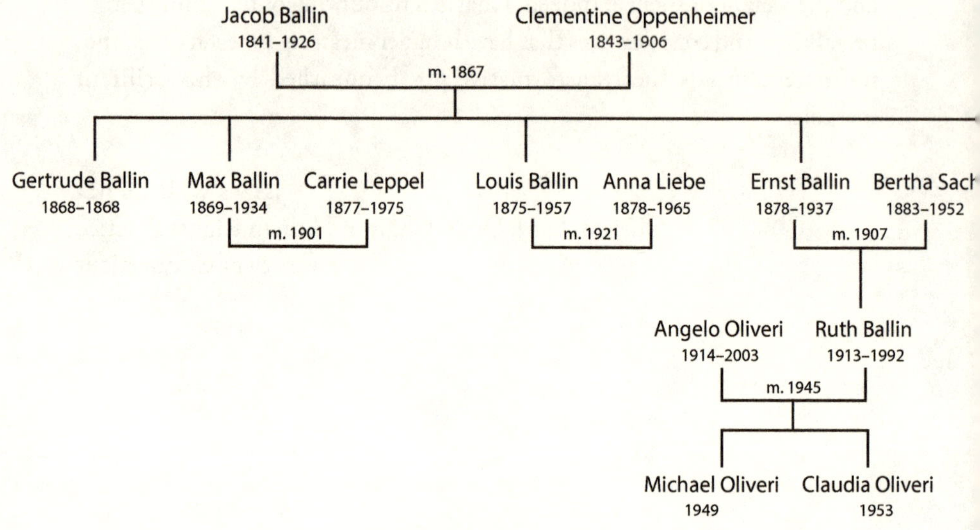

The Scheidt Family

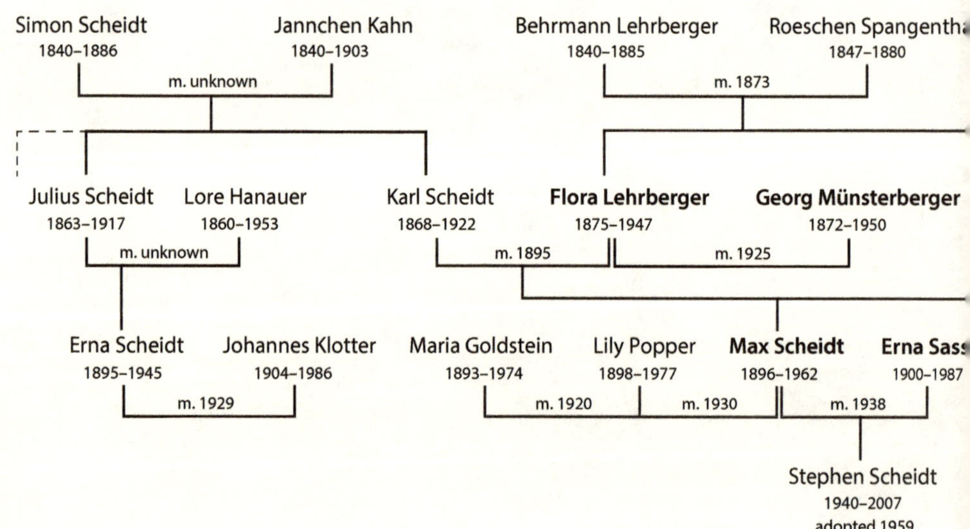

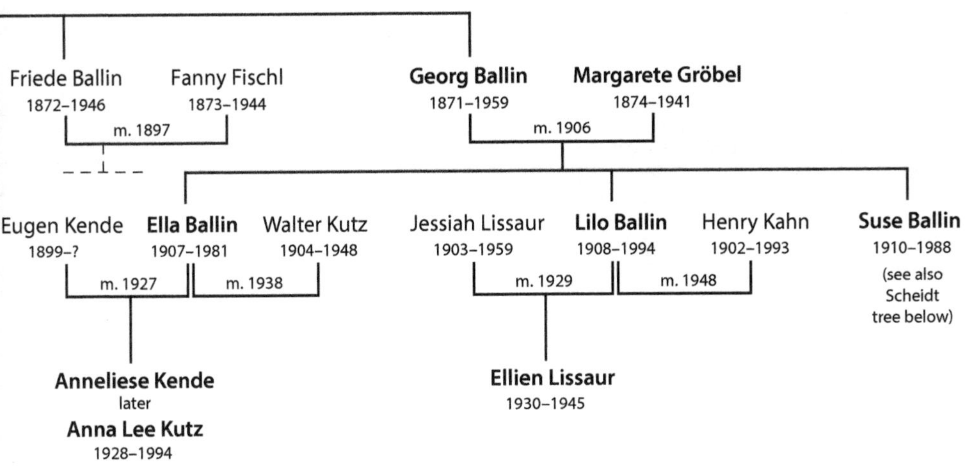
Friede Ballin
1872–1946
Fanny Fischl
1873–1944
m. 1897
Georg Ballin
1871–1959
Margarete Gröbel
1874–1941
m. 1906
Eugen Kende
1899–?
Ella Ballin
1907–1981
Walter Kutz
1904–1948
m. 1927
m. 1938
Jessiah Lissaur
1903–1959
Lilo Ballin
1908–1994
Henry Kahn
1902–1993
m. 1929
m. 1948
Suse Ballin
1910–1988
(see also Scheidt tree below)
Anneliese Kende
later
Anna Lee Kutz
1928–1994
Ellien Lissaur
1930–1945

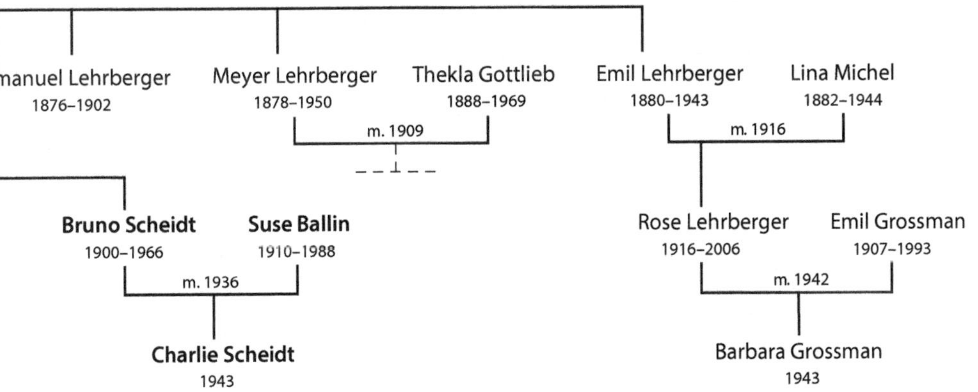
manuel Lehrberger
1876–1902
Meyer Lehrberger
1878–1950
Thekla Gottlieb
1888–1969
m. 1909
Emil Lehrberger
1880–1943
Lina Michel
1882–1944
m. 1916
Bruno Scheidt
1900–1966
Suse Ballin
1910–1988
m. 1936
Charlie Scheidt
1943
Rose Lehrberger
1916–2006
Emil Grossman
1907–1993
m. 1942
Barbara Grossman
1943

Prologue

Bruno Scheidt arrived as usual at his office in Frankfurt am Main on the morning of March 31, 1933. Two months and a day had passed since Adolf Hitler became chancellor of Germany, but Bruno was keeping his focus on doing his job and earning a living as he always did. His company, Bruno Scheidt Colonialwaren-Import, was located in a six-story building on Hanauerlandstrasse in the city's busy, bustling commercial district. This would not turn out to be an ordinary day.

Around him, the Jewish merchants in Frankfurt's Ostend were setting up for the day, readying to sell their paints, varnishes, cleaning agents, textiles, luxury items, and foods. Bruno settled himself at his desk in the large open area on the building's first floor, facing his staff's rows of desks with typewriters. The lower level of the building provided warehouse storage for his imported foods, mainly beans and legumes, waiting to be shipped to markets around the country. Bruno's desk was in front of a large set of arched windows, and he could hear the rumble and whistle of heavy freight trains pulling in and out of the Ostbahnhof train station.

Tensions in Germany were rising each day. Hitler, proclaiming that he was protecting the country from Communism, had rapidly signed several decrees that suppressed the media, outlawed political parties, and gave himself broad authoritarian powers. The Nazis had opened Dachau, the first of the Nazi concentration camps, to house political opponents of the regime. For Bruno, the danger was close to home. Just the day before, a non-Jewish friend had warned him that he was on an arrest list. That day, he must have moved around the office, spoken purposefully to his employees, and kept his focus on the tasks required to keep his business running while at the same time remaining acutely alert to his surroundings.

A Gestapo record, discovered decades later, indicated vaguely that Bruno had been accused of "stealing commercial secrets" back in 1925. He had done no such thing, and this was likely a trumped-up charge by a business competitor. But since Bruno had made no secret of his disdain for and disgust of the new regime, the Nazis used the accusation for their own purposes.

Late in the day, something outside—muffled, shouting voices; the heavy footfall of boots in the courtyard; the bark of a dog—caught his attention. He instantly sensed that the Nazis were closing in, the sound of their approach growing louder by the second. He had no time to think, no time to hesitate. He jumped up, unlocked the desk cabinet, grabbed some cash and essential papers, tucked them in a bag, and darted out the back door just as the Brownshirts reached the front entrance. Heart pounding, hardly daring to look behind him, he crossed the street and ran through a stretch of grass and over the Ostbahnhof train tracks, slipping into the crowded city streets.

He ran all the way home to the apartment he shared with his mother, Flora; his stepfather, Georg; and Georg's daughter, Lotte. Entering through the back door, he startled his mother in the kitchen, telling her the Brownshirts were on his trail and he had to get away. He hastily packed a few things, kissed his mother goodbye, and raced on foot to the city's main train station. He boarded the first train out of the country and found himself heading to Switzerland. The next day—April 1, 1933—the Germans carried out the Boycott of Jewish Businesses, their first major action against the Jews of Germany.

In a matter of hours, Bruno was transformed from a well-established businessman in his native city to a refugee fleeing for his life. In a moment, he left behind the only city that had ever been his home.

He left his mother and stepfather, his brother, his friends, and the love of his life, a woman named Suse Ballin. He left his business, his livelihood, his language and culture, the Jewish community he knew, and the synagogue where he worshipped. He left the stores where he shopped, his doctors and barber and tailor, and the myriad familiar comforts of home. He hurtled forward into the unknown, with no plan other than to escape imminent danger.

Bruno Scheidt was my father.

Inheritance

1

The Armoire

On a crisp winter evening in 1988, I walked down Broadway in Manhattan to visit my mother at her apartment on 82nd Street, as I did every night after work. I darted into a corner market and picked up some bright, cheerful flowers, hoping to bring some color and comfort to her room. As I approached the building, I paused and tried to push away the thoughts that crowded in on me—the times I had entered this building over the decades for family celebrations, Jewish holidays, birthdays, Shabbos dinners, quiet evenings at home. Now the apartment was quiet, darkened, as my mother lay dying, wasting away from cancer.

A nurse moved silently from room to room. The elegance of the space was marred by the sterile objects of the ill—basins, wheelchairs, medical supplies. My mother had gradually stopped leaving the apartment. Then she had stopped getting up from the living room couch. Finally, over the past months, she had stopped leaving her room. She was frail and exhausted. It was just a matter of time.

It wasn't until I began sitting by my mother's bedside that I looked—*really* looked—at the family photos in frames all over the room. Some people I recognized, of course—my late father, my mother with her two sisters, and her parents, Georg and Margarete. Other faces were less familiar, peering out at me from a past I knew little about. A few times I had asked my mother to tell me about the photos and to help me construct a family tree, but almost as soon as I began, I stopped. I told myself it was because I didn't want to upset her, to confront the painful truth that she would soon not be around to answer my questions. I was engaging in my own form of magical thinking—that there was no cost or consequence to letting the past remain unexamined.

Over time, too, I sensed that my mother was preoccupied, that she had something she wanted to share with me. It may have been that night, or another one around the same time, that she gathered the strength to tell me what was on her mind.

"There is a lot of junk in there that you'll need to throw out," she said, gesturing to the large old maple armoire that stood on the opposite side of the bed. "Before you do that, I want you to know there are some family papers and letters I saved from the war years. They are behind some old clothes in the bottom. You may want to look at them and can decide for yourself what you want to do with them." She paused, then added quietly, "You're also free to throw them out. I know how busy you are."

She closed her eyes for a moment, then squeezed my hand. She was determined to stay awake during my visits, no matter how much her illness or the medication fatigued her. This time I sensed that she was unburdened, having said what she needed to say. I watched her for a moment, grateful for the rest that brought a temporary relief from her illness. It was time for me to go home to my wife and sons. I kissed her forehead and thanked her for telling me about the papers. I promised I would look at them. Then, I walked out of the bedroom, out of the living room, out of the building, into the cold night.

I grew up in a world of German-Jewish refugees in America, an only child surrounded by adults. My closest relatives in New York, my father's brother Max and his wife Erna, were childless. Most of my parents' friends, themselves refugees, did not have children either. By the time they made it to safety in America, they were too old or financially insecure to start families. With no other children around during family gatherings, I was surrounded by people of another time and place—cultivated, well traveled, and multilingual—at once admirable for their worldliness and markedly different from the Americans among whom we lived.

My parents, Suse and Bruno, 1948.

As the lone member of the next generation, I was the heir apparent, expected to carry on the Scheidt family name and ensure its legacy. This meant that even as I took advantage of all that was possible for me in America, I was never to forget where I came from. German-Jewish culture itself had nearly been extinguished in the Holocaust. My parents had managed to light a tiny sputtering flame with my birth, and it was up to me to keep it alight. In practice, this meant keeping my Jewish identity and traditions strong, honoring our family heritage, and ensuring that both survived through me.

The children of refugees always bear a particular burden—they carry the unspoken imperative to survive precisely because so much has been sacrificed and lost. We felt safe in America—as safe as refugees can ever feel—but the upheaval that led us to this country left deep scars, ones I sensed but did not understand. No one talked of the past. No one talked about Europe or the war years or how they had come here. Eyes forward on the future, on building a new life, on me. That meant my family worried not only about my physical safety but about the kind of person I would grow up to be.

Sensing that, I felt a strong pull to do as I was told, to live up to everyone's expectations, and to succeed not so much for myself but for them.

Even as a teenager—a time when most young people begin to question their parents' authority and to rebel against the pressures placed upon them—I remained respectful of my parents' wishes. When I was in college, my father instructed me not to go to civil rights demonstrations, participate in the Freedom Rides, or attend anti–Vietnam War rallies. "Don't get on the wrong side of those in power," he said, "or you just might get your skull bashed in." This was more than generic parental worry. My father's fear for my safety came from a deeper, darker place that I did not fully understand.

As I got older, I was drifting ever so slightly away from them, making the most of opportunities that they had created for me but in which they could not completely share. When I was accepted to Yale University, my father worried about losing me to the strange world of the American university. His model was the European one, where students went to the local university if there *was* one. So, even though Yale was not far from New York, he would have greatly preferred that I stay closer to home. He revealed his ambivalence through a joke that only he found funny. He would say "Yale" in an intentionally thick accent so that it sounded like "jail." I wanted him to say the name of the college I attended with pride, not to turn it into a pun whose double meaning contained a subtle, though probably unintended, barb. Then again, his own education had been truncated by World War I, and I understand better now how threatening my growing up years might have been for him. Perhaps he worried about the effect my elite and privileged education would have on my view of him.

After college, I chose Columbia Law School because it offered a joint four-year program with the School of International Affairs, allowing me to graduate with both a law degree and a master's in international affairs. I grew up speaking German at home and I had worked abroad for several summers in college, becoming fluent in French and Spanish. I also wanted to use an understanding of law, economics, and diplomacy to make the world a better place, addressing big issues of human rights, persecution, and injustice. I would chart my own path in international law while drawing on the values and skills my parents had invested in me.

Life, however, had its own plans.

I had just completed my second year of law school at Columbia when I arrived in The Netherlands to attend a summer fellowship at The Hague

Academy of International Law. I brought my suitcase upstairs at the boarding house where I was staying and began to get settled when there was a knock on the door. The proprietor told me that there was an international call for me. Calls of this kind were rare and expensive in those days. My stomach dropped.

My mother was on the phone. Her voice sounded small and far away. She told me she and my father had been at a small hotel in Lake Mohegan where they liked to spend weekends swimming and enjoying time away from the city. My father had gotten out of the water and sat down. When my mother looked over at him some minutes later, he was slumped in the chair.

At the too-young age of sixty-five, my all-powerful father was gone.

Stunned and heartbroken, I barely recall the next hours or the flight back to New York. Nothing in my life had prepared me to lose my hero and protector so suddenly. Our little family unit had always felt like a three-legged stool. I vividly remember how destabilized I felt when, every other Sunday, my father traveled for work, leaving my mother and me at home. I feared there would be an accident, and I waited eagerly for his letters, which arrived every day of his trip, sharing tales of his journey and reinforcing the close bonds between us. Before leaving, he would charge me with taking care of my mother in his absence. Even as a small boy, I felt keenly this need to fill his shoes. I was relieved when he returned by Friday night for Shabbos dinner and I could relinquish that responsibility.

My father was gregarious, charming, wise, and cultured. He presided at the head of our family table and made guests feel welcome, always engaging with them and showing his interest in them, especially my friends. He was successful in business, upstanding in his behavior, and loving to my mother. Growing up in New York, I was fascinated by the statue of Atlas with the globe on his shoulders in Rockefeller Center. To me, my father was Atlas, bearing the world on his shoulders.

I did not feel ready for the burdens and responsibilities that were suddenly handed to me. My mother was completely crushed. And no sooner had we gotten through the funeral than we learned that the bank had shut down the company's accounts. Instead of being able to mourn and absorb our loss, we were thrust into decision-making about the family business.

I faced a critical decision of my own. I certainly could not leave my mother at that point and return to The Hague, but what about the bigger picture? Should I continue to pursue a career in international law as I had planned? Or would I step into my father's shoes to carry on the business? My father had let me follow my passions, but he had also made sure that I could function in the world of commerce, involving me in his conversations with my mother about the company, taking me to meetings with customers and suppliers, and sending me for three consecutive summers to work in the offices of friends in Paris, Madrid, and Tokyo. As a result of his experience as a refugee, he wanted me to be adaptable and flexible, to be able to function in different cultures and environments, to be, like him, a "citizen of the world." He wanted to know that if I should ever find myself in danger, I would be able to leave and begin again, as he and my mother had.

As I weighed my choice, I knew my mother did not want to run the company herself, even though she was an integral part of it. No one on the staff could take over, and my decision would determine the fate of the company: If I did not commit to taking the helm, it would not survive. I felt considerable pressure. If I hesitated too long, key employees might, for their own survival, look elsewhere for work. If I took over, it would signal that the owners planned to keep the business going, which would stabilize everything.

Sightseeing with my parents the summer I worked in Tokyo for a Roland supplier, 1963.

Looking back now, I feel I was destined to follow in my father's footsteps. I could not resist the emotional pull to keep the family business alive and to grow what my parents had built. My father had founded Bruno Scheidt Inc. (BSI) and its sister company, American Roland Food Co. (Roland), within a year of his arrival in the States. Ensuring the future of BSI/Roland would not only honor my father's legacy but would provide a home and a livelihood for my mother, giving her purpose and focus, a reason to get up every day. She was needed and respected there, and she would continue supervising the billing and accounting while I focused on buying and selling, as my father had. She could also teach me what I didn't know about my father's approach to business and educate me about back-office matters I did not yet understand.

At age twenty-three, I set aside my ambitions of a career in international law. I worked part time at BSI/Roland, while at the same time completing my studies. When I had earned both an MA and a JD, and passed the bar in New York, I took the reins of the company. For the next nearly fifty years, every employee and most suppliers around the world continued to get their checks from Bruno Scheidt Inc. I kept my father's name on the door, keeping his presence close to me and holding our family, at least metaphorically, intact.

My mother and I worked together for two decades to grow what she and my father had created. She allowed me to run the company and chart its course while she provided good counsel. I always involved her in major decisions, but when we disagreed, she let me have the final say. She willingly remained in the background, as she had when my father was alive. We were enormously close; my mother prepared lunch at home for both of us—sandwiches from whatever she had made the night before, and sliced carrots, celery, and fruit—and we ate together whenever possible. She would come into my office and I'd pull out the leaf in my father's desk, which was now mine, to make a table for her. Working and spending time together every day created a safe harbor for both of us.

At the same time, I made a life of my own. I married and had two sons. Still, whenever I walked past Rockefeller Center and the statue of Atlas, I thought of my father. He had been Atlas, and now the role had been passed to me.

As the winter of 1988 turned to spring, I rarely thought about my mom's odd comment about the papers in the armoire. But her health continued to fail. The second leg in the stool would soon be gone.

Celebrating my mother's seventieth birthday, Putnam Valley, New York, 1980.

She was declining but stable, so, at her insistence, I took my sons on a ski trip to Utah. I spoke to my mother on the first night of our trip, and, thus reassured, I relaxed and tried to have fun. But early in the morning on the third day, my wife called. My mother had died in the night.

I was shattered by her death and distressed that, as with my father, I had not been there. My sons and I quickly returned to New York. On the plane ride home, I wrote a eulogy, recalling the ways her wisdom, warmth, grace, and love had shaped my life. The next day I arrived at Riverside Memorial Chapel for her funeral, uneasy and anxious that I would break down while speaking. I was struck by how many people had come to pay their respects: not only family and friends, but almost every employee of Bruno Scheidt Inc. In her quiet, modest way, my mother had touched many lives.

It wasn't until a week after her death that I was allowed to enter her apartment. It had been sealed pending a police investigation that was mandated by law when someone dies at home. A police officer removed the padlock.

As I entered her apartment, everything appeared the same, but nothing looked familiar. My eyes wandered from surface to surface, seeking, finding nothing. A dull rushing sound filled my ears like a wave at sea. I slid weakly into the living room armchair, where I had often sat when my mother was well enough to leave her bed and lie on the couch.

I pulled myself to my feet and wandered from room to room, looking for . . . what? Through the empty dining room, the empty kitchen, my old room. I ran my fingers over the books on the shelf. I opened a kitchen drawer. Her bedroom door was slightly ajar. I closed it, then opened it again, and slowly approached her bedside, where I had spent so much time. I rested my palm on her bed.

Just beyond her bed stood her old armoire.

The armoire, built from richly swirled, variegated birdseye maple, featuring elegant, clean lines, huge doors, and sturdy mahogany handles, had stood in my parents' bedroom since I could remember. When I was a child, I found it almost scary, not only because of its size but because it contained such taboo items as my mother's slips and bras. Never did I dare to open it myself. But I was an adult now, my mother was gone, and she had told me she wanted me to see what was kept inside.

I squatted down, pulling out the drawers stacked on either side of its inner shelves, one by one. There were no papers there. I rocked back on my heels and surveyed the shelves, crammed full of uneven stacks of old clothing. I impatiently pulled them out. As they tumbled to my feet, I saw behind them a pile of yellowed manila folders. I got on my hands and knees and dug them out.

When I had pulled out every last folder, I spotted something in the back of the armoire: an antique silver box, ever so slightly tarnished, with a key. I pulled it toward me and unlocked it. Inside was a stack of old passports and official documents from the Nazi German Reich, the French Republic, the United States, a marriage license in French, a birth certificate in German. I sat cross-legged surrounded by the pile of papers and slowly opened the passports, running my fingers over border-control stamps from all over the world. I set the silver box to the side and began opening the stained manila folders.

There must have been a thousand pages: letters in German, in French, in broken English—yellowed, wavy, brittle; return addresses from hotels, boarding houses, and various ports of call; identity cards, residency permits, and police registrations; corporate documents and court records in French and German; letters addressed to government offices, bank statements, refugee visas; transit documents with stamps from Paris, Marseille, Port-au-Prince, and Havana; postcards and business cards and address cards; and a baby's autopsy report.

I pulled out one letter and the next and the next, and, as I read, dozens of voices bubbled up, speaking over each other; some I recognized and some I'd never heard. They quibbled about furniture and the weather and family politics on the eve of impending doom; they scoffed at the thought of moving someplace hot even while hearing that more and more countries were closing their borders; and, finally, they clamored to be rescued from prospects too frightening to contemplate. They told stories I'd never heard—about how my parents and most of their families had made it to safety in the United States.

I sat back and took a breath. How long had I been sitting there? My shoulders were stiff, my eyes were burning, a dull ache had settled in the pit of my stomach. Why had my mother held on to this cache of records from their painful past? Why had she hidden them for all these years? And if she had wanted me to know this history, why didn't she just *tell* me, rather than leaving me with a pile of documents I couldn't make sense of or understand? Whatever I might learn from these records, some questions would never be answered. Only my parents could have told me why they did what they did, or what these documents meant, and they were both gone.

Exhausted, I shoved the letters back inside the folders, the folders back into the drawer, and closed the armoire firmly. My mother had bequeathed these stories to me, and the voices of the dead were waiting to be heard. But my heart was overfull with aching. And I had sons to raise, a business to run, and a life to lead. I was not ready to sit still and listen to those voices. Later, I thought. *Later.*

For the next twenty years, I swung between pushing the documents out of sight and peering into their depths. I carried that box with me, moving it first from the armoire to my home, then to a filing cabinet in my office, and then to my new home when I moved. From time to time, I looked inside and got lost for an hour or two. Every time, grief for my long-dead loved ones swirled together with curiosity, uncertainty, and confusion. I worried that if I dared to enter that dark, unknown territory, I might not get back out again. What secrets and pain lay waiting to be uncovered? I had been taught to live in the present, to avoid dwelling on the past. Our family's unspoken mantra had been *forward motion*. Something about looking backward was anathema to me.

In 2009, BSI/Roland was celebrating its seventy-fifth year. We were making a commemorative video about the company's history that was an ode to my parents, connecting them to the present-day company and its employees. That's how I met Kat Rohrer, who was on the crew that interviewed me.

After we finished my interview, I wandered into a darkened room, where the director, lead cameraman, and Kat were bent over a sheaf of documents, deciding what to shoot next. The director held out an old piece of paper, and Kat quickly translated *Pfifferlinge*, the German word for chanterelles. She was from Austria. It was the first time I really saw her face, her thin eyebrows slightly arched over her intelligent brown eyes, an ironic smile on her lips. Her dark, curly hair swept back from her high forehead, falling just to the line of her square jaw. I spoke to her shyly in German, embarrassed that mine was rusty, and we chatted lightly for a few moments.

Some months later, in early May, I found myself pulling out the letters yet again. This time, Kat came to mind. Something about her—maybe her open and curious manner, or maybe the fact that she spoke German—made me wonder if she might be a kindred spirit. On an impulse, I wrote to her, giving her a brief outline of what I knew of my family history and telling her about the trove of letters. There was a story there, and I had the sense that she might be able to help me find it.

I was not wrong. She replied almost immediately, saying she had a personal interest in that time in history and the stories of that generation. It would take time for me to learn just what she meant.

A decade or so earlier, in the mid-1990s, through a mutual friend, I met Feli Gürsching, a German woman who volunteered at the Historical Museum Frankfurt. She was the first of many non-Jewish Germans I encountered who were committed to documenting Germany's past in order to give something back to Jewish families that had lost so much. Feli dug into old files in German archives to find my family's records. She rode her bike around the city to take photographs of buildings connected to our story. She taped the photos to pieces of paper, captioned them, and mailed them to me. Over time, she translated parts of our family's documents and helped me make sense of it all.

Feli visited me in New York every few years, and each time she nagged me relentlessly to visit Frankfurt. She insisted that my family's refugee story was worthwhile, not only for me but for German and Jewish historians and the public. Sometimes I grew enthusiastic and hopeful about this undertaking, but these periods were buffered by ambivalence. I was too busy with life and family to delve into this seemingly never-ending project.

Every other year, I would go to Cologne to attend the Anuga Trade Fair, the largest international food and beverage exhibition in the industry. In fall of 2009, I agreed to stop first in Frankfurt because Feli had arranged for me to donate a beautiful, melancholy painting titled *Frankfurt Opera Square* to the Jewish Museum of Frankfurt. It was painted by a childhood friend of my father, Samson Schames, who had also escaped Germany and eventually landed in New York, where he and my father reconnected. Schames was a gifted and successful artist who struggled to re-establish his career after the war. He'd fled to England, where, as a German, he was interned as an enemy alien. The fact that he was Jewish didn't matter. In exile, without art supplies, Schames had made his own rich, deep black paint out of soot mixed with condensed milk. He had incorporated broken glass, nails, and fragments of stone and pottery shattered in the Blitz into his art. My parents often purchased Schames' paintings and periodically hired him to design logos for the business.[1]

After the donation ceremony, I spent a few days with Feli and my mother's Swiss cousin Claudia. Feli was eager to introduce us to the city, take us to some archives, and visit our relatives' schools, workplaces, and homes. I must admit that during the first few days, I was mostly bored and disengaged. Perhaps I wanted to keep my emotional distance. As Feli walked us along the Frankfurt streets, I dutifully took pictures of buildings that meant nothing to me. She took us to archives where we held the original documents she had researched. Still, nothing. At my mother's childhood primary school, we saw her and my aunt's enrollment forms and report cards. Aside from surprise that these bits of paper had survived the war, the fragments of my parents' life didn't affect me.

One of our last stops was Hanauerlandstrasse, my father's office. We were shown to an elevator that came to an abrupt halt on an empty floor. The concierge drew back an accordion-style metal gate and in we walked. To get my bearings, I walked slowly across the cavernous space to the tall industrial, top-opening windows with arched windowpanes above. Everything was coated in dust. I peered out and saw a set of railroad tracks.

I had grown up hearing a pared-down version of how my father had slipped out the back door of his office, crossed the railroad tracks, and fled to Switzerland. I had heard the story so often it seemed almost like a myth. Now, suddenly, I realized I was looking out the window at the tracks he crossed that day. It was not a fable or a legend. I could almost see the shadow of my father fleeing for his life. This moment changed everything for me.

I returned from Frankfurt committed to exploring my family history and telling their story. During the trip, I had begun to think that Kat could be the partner I needed. I reached out to her again and we began working together in earnest. Meanwhile, I had never forgotten Kat's veiled allusion to her own family's past. What I didn't know was that she was terrified to tell me about it. One day, six months after we began working together, an email from Kat landed in my inbox. She had decided the time had come to tell me the story of her family who were haunted by the same patch of ash and dust that haunted mine.

Kat's forebears had for generations farmed a plot of land outside a picturesque town called Klagenfurt in the Austrian forest, ringed by Italy and Slovenia. This lovely town, looking like an antique woodblock come to life, hid a virulent pro-Nazi sympathy—and it still does to this day.

Kat's maternal grandfather was indoctrinated at a young age, and by the time he was fifteen years old, he'd become active in the pro-Nazi underground. He became a full-fledged member of the Nazi party back when it was still illegal in Austria. Eventually, after the Anschluss, the German annexation of Austria, he volunteered to join the *Wehrmacht*, abandoning his wife and family. A true believer, he died in battle one month after his youngest daughter, Kat's mother, was born.

When Kat's grandmother died, her only sister—whom Kat called Tante Willy—returned to Klagenfurt to help take care of Kat. Separated by seventy years, Kat and Tante Willy were soulmates. Tante Willy spent every summer in Klagenfurt caring for Kat while her mother, a prominent and formidable political journalist, worked. Months before her death in 1993, Tante Willy pulled out her own box of weather-beaten documents from under her bed. Although her family's story had never been secret, the papers filled out the details of her marriage to a Jewish lawyer and their panicked flight in 1938 to escape the Nazis in Austria. At the time, Tante Willy told her sister she was going on vacation and would return in two weeks, but instead she, her husband, their infant son, and his parents fled to France. From there, they crossed the channel to England

and then traveled by boat to New Zealand. Finding no asylum there, they finally landed in Australia.

Kat's complicated past mirrored aspects of my own family's experiences as refugees, but the silences she grew up with were blanketed with inherited shame about her grandfather's role in the Nazi movement. She later told me that almost immediately after she replied to my first email offering to help, she began to worry how I would feel about working with the granddaughter of a Nazi. I was touched by her frankness and reassured her that I could never hold her accountable for the actions taken by relatives long before she was born. To the contrary, I felt her past helped her understand mine. We had much to learn from each other.

We met in my office, amid my family photographs, memorabilia, and personal collectibles. Some might say we were an unlikely pair: a man from a proud Jewish family in the dusk of his life, descended from refugees who escaped one of the twentieth century's defining tragedies, and a woman at the beginning of hers, raised by free-thinking women, descended from a war criminal who shared responsibility for enacting that tragedy on the world. But in each other, we found more relevant qualities—an obsessive absorption in uncovering the truth about the past, a relentless drive to complete a thing started, and an enthusiasm for solving mysteries. Most of all, in our own ways, we had borne witness to the trauma unleashed by Nazi Germany on those we loved most.

Kat began reading the digitized letters, groping for a thread that tied together the disparate and confusing files. The document numbers were based on the order in which they'd been scanned, but the letters inside followed no discernible timeline or pattern. It was difficult to decipher the dynamics between correspondents or the context of their discussions. Many of the letters had no replies—reading them felt like overhearing only half a conversation—and the overall picture was confused by nicknames and multiple people named Georg, Erna, and Hans. Kat started sketching out a family tree, trying to connect the names to each other, to my parents, and to me.

I also told Kat about another important source, one that had nothing to do with the armoire. In 1991, when my mother's older sister Lilo was eighty-four, I encouraged her to give testimony about her experiences during the Holocaust. She did so at the Martyrs Memorial and Museum in Los Angeles. The video interview lasted three and a half hours—a long time by any standard and surely an exhausting endeavor for a woman her age. I was relieved she had done it and that her story was preserved.

Lilo died in 1994. Several years later, I realized with dismay that no one in the family had a copy of her video testimony or a transcript of it. In the years since, the Martyrs Memorial had been dismantled, and after multiple calls and inquires, I was lucky to find a woman who discovered a copy of it lying untouched in a drawer. It seemed like something of a miracle. Still, at the time, I wasn't ready to see Lilo on screen; it was enough just to know that her testimony was safely in my possession.

In time, I found the strength to watch it a little at a time. It wasn't easy; I felt that I was always bracing myself for what I might hear. Then again, seeing my aunt onscreen felt like being reunited with her, basking in her warmth even if only for a few short hours. When Kat came along, first I shared the letters with her, and eventually I felt ready to share the testimony with her as well. We agreed that it was a critical element in reconstructing the family story.

A turning point in my ability to focus on this book came in 2014 after I sold my father's company and retired as the CEO of BSI/Roland. It had been a difficult decision, fraught with emotion, to let the company go and to do so with care and consideration for the employees who had made it what it was. It was the end of an era, time to relinquish the deep sense of responsibility I had always felt to carry on my father's professional legacy. In the wake of the sale, after decades of a demanding career, I found myself with time on my hands. I began to support work on behalf of refugees and in the service of genocide prevention. The tiny flame that my parents, as refugees, had kindled decades before had yielded enough success that I could support those who were struggling now as they had then. At the same time, the years of preliminary work on my family's story coalesced into an imperative to seek the answers to the questions it raised. With Kat whispering in my ear—well, she doesn't really whisper—it was time to face the past.

Over the next several years, Kat and I inched forward. What began as a spare-time project soon became all-consuming, a conversation between us that would last over a decade and take us to places we couldn't yet imagine. While Kat had always known her family's past, mine was so thickly shrouded in the silence of my parents' generation that I didn't even know I *had* questions, let alone which ones to ask. With Kat's help, I was beginning to wonder aloud for the first time: What happened to my family in Nazi Europe?

Kat and me in 2016 at Schumannstrasse 10, my maternal grandparents' last home in Frankfurt.

How did they come to America? And how did their escape and the establishment of a new life create an indelible impact on them and me?

This book is the result of Kat's and my journey. It tells two stories: first, that of my family's harrowing escape as refugees fleeing the Nazis, and second, the story of my research and travels with Kat, and the hard-won insights into how my family's trauma shaped my own childhood and life. It took fifteen years, four trips to Europe, dozens of people in Europe and America, and countless hours to untangle the story and make sense of it.

The core of this story comes from the papers my mother left me. She had kept everything—not just letters she'd received, starting with her and my father's departure from France in 1939, but nearly every page of correspondence that passed through the various branches of the family. I'm so grateful for Kat's doggedness, commitment, and emotional distance, which helped me fill in gaps in the narrative and identify threads to pursue. At one point, we were so overwhelmed by the morass of names, people, and places that we felt we would never make sense of it. We made lists, datelines, maps, and spreadsheets to try to keep track of the various family members and friends, their whereabouts, and their movements through time and space.

But gradually we began to make order of the chaos. We began to see the shape of each family member's journey, to follow recurring themes that appeared across letters, and to untangle threads that had seemed impossibly snarled.

The letters eventually provided a spine for the story. They helped us see and understand nuances that would have otherwise eluded us. They brought to life tiny details of family life—health issues, financial worries, yapping little dogs, the joy of sitting under an ancient apple tree in a beautiful garden, the misunderstandings, forgiveness, expressions of love and care—across thousands of miles and the chasm of time. Most of all, they helped me hear the voices of my loved ones—my father's calm, measured tone; Uncle Max's emotional ups and downs; Aunt Erna's humor and competence; my mother's quiet strength; my grandmother Flora's concern for her children; my grandfather Georg's determination. The magic of primary sources is that they contain traces of life as it was lived in the moment, helping us touch its texture and nuance. And then there are the physical letters—frayed, yellowing pages that held the imprint of my parents' hands, cellular traces of who they were at that time.

Finally, these letters preserve names of people once dear to my family, names I had never heard. These were friends and relatives my parents tried to help but couldn't, people who were caught in the Nazi snare, never to escape. Bits of their stories—evidence of how loved these lost souls once were—survives in my family's letters. I have devoted several pages at the end of this book to their stories.

Some of my questions about what happened to my family may never be answered. But in the decades that I spent on this work, I have found that it is the asking of the questions, the process of facing the past and reconstructing as much of it as possible, that matters most. In that sense, this is a book about my family and a very specific past. And it is also a story that reaches far beyond the particular, touching on the challenges that face anyone who struggles to understand their family and make sense of the world that shaped them.

2

Jewish and German

The Scheidts

In all refugee stories, origins matter. And though much of this story takes place during the years of Nazi rule in Germany, Holland, and France, the strands that attenuated and ultimately snapped reach far back into history. For this reason, it's worth going back in time to describe my family's beginnings.

Bruno's mother, Flora, was born in 1875 in a small German town called Borken. She was the first child and only daughter of Behrmann, a merchant, and Roeschen Lehrberger. Snapshots of Borken at the time show modest buildings clad in the half-timber framing that is traditional throughout Germany. In my grandmother's day, the town was rural, heavily reliant on farming, and economically modest, at best. In one photo, probably taken around the turn of the century, a family poses for a portrait outside their home, a cluster of chickens at their feet.

Flora was not an only child for long; three younger brothers—Emanuel, Meyer, and Emil—were born in quick succession. When Flora was just five years old and her youngest brother not yet six months old, their mother died. As was so often the case at the time, Flora had to grow up quickly, taking responsibility for her young siblings and helping her father manage the household. When she was ten, he died too, leaving the children orphans.

The three young boys were sent to live with their father's brother Ephraim (who had his hands full with ten of his own children).[1] Flora was dispatched to her aunt Regine in Frankfurt, as opportunities for her in rural Borken were few. Regine lived and worked in the home of Jacques Snatich, scion of a Dutch Jewish family, an unmarried banker and poet who used his considerable wealth for charitable purposes. He supported the Philanthropin, the nearly century-old Jewish school for poor children in Frankfurt. Most notably, he started a foundation in his parents' names, the David and Rosine Snatich Stiftung, which granted study stipends for young Jews and paid dowries for orphaned or impoverished Jewish women as long as they married observant Jewish husbands. Although Flora's uncle Ephraim remained her legal guardian, Snatich took her into his elegant home, providing for her education and upbringing under Regine's care.

When Flora was twenty, she met and fell in love with Karl Scheidt. Jacques Snatich provided the dowry that allowed them to marry. A photo of young Karl from that time shows a handsome young man with a full mustache, wearing the elegant clothing of the day—a starched white collar, tails, and a waistcoat with a visible chain for his pocket watch. He is poised and confident, looking not at the camera but off into a promising future. The young couple were wed in Flora's hometown, Borken, in November 1895, followed a month later by a second ceremony in Frankfurt. They set up house in Frankfurt's Ostend, home to a thriving Jewish community, where Karl ran a wholesale business supplying furniture, linens, and accessories for hotels. Their first son, Max, was born in 1896, and Bruno, my father, followed in 1900.[2]

When Snatich died in 1903, Regine moved in with the family. Snatich remembered Flora and Regine in his will, providing generous monthly stipends for both of them. My father and my uncle Max spoke often about Snatich's generosity, especially his care for my grandmother, an orphan child who was no relation but who needed financial protection and help. She survived and thrived because a stranger helped her; Bruno and Max's very existence was a consequence of that magnanimity. They internalized that story, its lessons taking a place in the brothers' constellation of values and sense of moral obligation.

When Kat and I embarked on our first research trip to Europe in 2016, we went to Borken, seeking information about my grandmother's past. We spent a day with two local historians, Hans-Peter and Ingo, non-Jewish descendants of people who lived during the war, who had taken it upon themselves to help reconstruct and preserve their country's Jewish history. They worked quietly and reverentially, as if it were their own small part in Germany's postwar redemption. They met us at a local museum bearing a thick file of my family's records from the local archive. As I paged through these documents, I saw the sketchy details of my grandmother's past and sensed how deeply the family was rooted in this small town.

It wasn't the first small town we had visited or the first Germans we met who approached the labor of commemoration with such personal dedication. Feli Gürsching had been the same way. Kat reflected on how very unusual this was; Germany stands as a rare example of a country that has embraced the effort to come to terms with its wartime culpability. This national commitment has trickled to regular citizens—ones we met during our many travels—who see it as their personal mission to document and preserve what is left of Jewish life in Germany. Not so in Austria, Kat told me. There, it has been a difficult process to acknowledge the Nazi strain in the country and to recast its status as victim of Nazism to one of shared responsibility for it. I fully understood what she meant. The United States, too, has fallen short of acknowledging the original sin of slavery and genocide against native peoples. It was a moment of understanding between Kat and me; though we are from two totally different worlds, we each carry the burden of our nation's histories and failures.

Before we left town, Hans-Peter and Ingo took us to Borken's old cemetery. It sits in a forest clearing, the graves clustered together in uneven groupings, following no visible pattern. There are no paths, tidy sidewalks, or trimmed hedges. Instead, drooping evergreens and ivy-clad tree trunks create a cathedral of deepest green, light shooting through in shafts here and there, illuminating the Hebrew lettering on the stones and patches of brittle, dried leaves that scatter over the grass. The markers lean this way and that, streaked with downy, dark green moss or a pale green lichen, nearly white in places. Everything about the place feels as if it magically appeared in the forest, untouched by human hands. If I believed in ghosts, I would believe they dwelt in this mystical, mysterious place.

As Hans-Peter and Ingo bounded around the cemetery checking names and trying to locate my relatives, they seemed more curious about my family's past than I was. Suddenly, they called me over, and I found myself standing in front of the graves of my paternal great-grandmother Roeschen and great-grandfather Behrmann. I hoped to feel a connection to these ancestors but, somehow, I didn't. Still, I dutifully followed the Jewish tradition of placing a few stones on their graves to signify that someone had been there. I said the Kaddish prayer of mourning in their memory, feeling little connection to the words I was reciting. But in Jewish tradition, the imperative is *zachor*, to remember. In fact, we are taught to do it even if we do not feel it. And so, I fulfilled my obligation toward my ancestors. For now, that would have to be enough.

Bruno and Max's childhood in Frankfurt was comfortable and secure. Regine lived with the family, helping to bring up the boys and providing a sense of continuity. Their neighborhood in the Ostend boasted not only religious and social institutions, such as Torah schools, soup kitchens, and hospitals, but also elegant townhomes, a famous city library established in 1825, a music conservatory, and a beloved zoo, the second oldest in Germany.

During the early years of their lives, the family lived on the third floor in a house owned by Karl's friend Simon Sulzbacher. The Sulzbachers had a son, David (called Dado), who became close friends with Bruno. The building still stands—an impressive five-story corner structure clad in stucco with large, elegant windows and fine moldings—with a decorative balcony jutting out at the second floor. Inside, the highly polished wood stairs and banister run the full height of the building. I can imagine the boys chasing each other up the stairs and sliding down the banister as their parents tried to read the newspaper or chatted together about daily events.

One of the few photos of my father's family was taken when they were on vacation at a holiday spot in Wildbad. They are dressed and posed to convey the image of a solidly middle-class family with the means and ability to enjoy their leisure time. Flora is seated and looking off into the distance with a serious expression. She is wearing a long, white flounced dress and a hat perched at an angle; behind her stands a notably chubbier Karl—still well dressed, still with his mustache, now in a bowler hat. Their clothing looks high-end, so much so that I wonder if they were wearing their Sunday best or if they might have rented outfits for the photograph. They appear an elegant and prosperous couple but, at the same time, they look rather uncomfortable in their stiffly posed positions.

Bruno, Flora, Karl, and Max in Wildbad, August 1906.

Max, nine, and Bruno, five, wearing matching sailor suits with short pants and straw boaters, look directly into the camera. Max's pose is confident, proud, perhaps even cocky; my father, the kid brother, seems a bit mischievous and impish. He's holding still for the photo but looks ready to run off and have fun. In that way, they remind me so much of the brothers I knew decades later.

Frankfurt's Ostend had a complex Jewish history that, in many ways, forged my family's experience and world view, and also influenced the actions they took when the Nazi threat bore down upon them. Jews had been in Frankfurt for centuries but, as elsewhere in Europe, church-supported antisemitism led to mistrust and suspicion of the Jewish population of the city. In 1462, the Frankfurt Council banished the city's Jews from their homes in the city center to a narrow strip of land at the city's edge. The *Judengasse* was Europe's first Jewish ghetto, and it lasted until 1796. Even after the Jews of Frankfurt left the physical ghetto, they still struggled against a series of social, political, and economic restrictions designed to isolate and control them. Emancipation finally came in 1864. This means that in my father's youth, the Jews of Frankfurt had been persecuted for 400 years and emancipated for only 50 years. That history hung over the streets in the Ostend even as Jews lived, married, worked, educated their children, and thrived.

In nineteenth-century Frankfurt, as elsewhere throughout Germany, gradual emancipation and the possibility of assimilation brought a new set of challenges to the Jewish community. Differences developed between Orthodox Jews, who adhered to the established traditions, and Reform Jews, who favored a more liberal approach to religious practice and the integration of Jewish life in the modern world. In 1851, Rabbi Samson Raphael Hirsch and a small group of Frankfurt's Orthodox Jews formed the Israelitische Religionsgesellschaft (IRG), which offered a third way. Rabbi Hirsch grounded his religious philosophy on the concept of *Torah im Derech Eretz*, which sought to fuse serious observance of Jewish laws and customs with integration in modern German life and society. This neo-Orthodoxy, as it came to be known, interpreted religious practice in ways that involved limited changes to ritual and liturgy, such as an all-male choir. It also encouraged Jews to be successful in all aspects of modern life.

My grandparents made this their religious and social home in Frankfurt, the universe in which my father and uncle were educated, shaped, and formed. The entire Jewish community observed Shabbos, the day of rest that falls on Saturday in Jewish tradition, walking to and from services in the synagogue and refraining from any type of labor. Meals were prepared in advance, and even carrying objects—which constituted a form of work—was forbidden. On Shabbos, following services, families took walks, strolled around the zoo, or visited with family and friends. The community observed kosher dietary laws, followed the Jewish calendar, and celebrated its own holidays, even as the great city of Frankfurt carried on a secular life around them.

For Bruno and Max, the values and culture of neo-Orthodoxy meant they were steeped in Jewish religious principles, ones that were explicitly drawn from the Torah, and also that they saw themselves as Jewish in a German world. Their sense of identity was reinforced by their education at the IRG-affiliated Jewish day school Rabbi Hirsch founded in 1853. The curriculum included mainstream secular subjects, such as math, German, French, English, literature, and the arts, and Jewish subjects, including Hebrew reading and writing, religious instruction, Bible study, and Jewish history. The school prepared students for professional lives and careers in the commercial sphere.

Beginning in 1907, the family attended the newly constructed, magnificent synagogue known as the Friedberger Anlage. One of the largest and most impressive synagogues in Germany, built to accommodate up to 1,600 worshippers, it was specifically designed to meet the ritual requirements of Orthodox practice. Women prayed in upper galleries, separated from men; the pulpit sat in the middle of the men's section; and the sanctuary was positioned three steps lower than the entrance to the building, making literal the words of Psalm 130: "From the depths, Lord, I call to you." The design for the synagogue reflected the community's complex position in Frankfurt. Though it was grand and beautiful, it was not so grandiose or conspicuous that it would attract negative attention or suspicion from the non-Jewish population.

My father and uncle Max's upbringing in Frankfurt's Ostend shaped their perceptions of Germany, their Jewish identity, and themselves. They came of age at a time when Jews in Germany were freer than they'd ever been, but this meant having to balance religious identity with true integration into German life, both culturally and economically. And while nothing could protect them from the persecution that followed in the 1930s, their upbringing did inoculate them to some extent against the false sense of belonging and assimilation that shaped the fate of many of their fellow German Jews.

The Scheidt family's comfortable life in Frankfurt was interrupted by the outbreak of World War I in 1914. Suddenly, they faced upheaval, separation, and chaos. Some historians say that World War I and World War II were effectively one long war, with a twenty-one-year armistice in the middle. This rings true for the story of my family. World War I was a prelude to the permanent rupture that took place when the Nazis came to power in 1933.

My paternal grandfather Karl volunteered to serve in the German army, one of nearly 100,000 Jews who fought, many out of loyalty to the fatherland. Karl felt bound by honor and dignity to serve his country. From September to December 1914, he was a clerk in a military hospital in Frankfurt. Karl was then transferred to an *Israelitisch* infirmary in Giessen for five months, a hospital that accommodated the needs of Jewish patients including observance of kosher dietary laws, and then moved to a field infirmary,

Karl and Max, c. 1915.

presumably at the front. I don't know when he was released from duty, but I do know he completed his service.

My uncle Max was a different story. Military service was mandatory for all men between the ages of seventeen and forty-five, and Max was called up and served for a time. Ultimately, though, he became disillusioned, unable to justify the violence he witnessed and unable to accept the deaths of so many comrades and friends. When I was growing up, I recall hearing the story many times that he "cooked the thermometer" to get out of returning to the front. He never shared his father's allegiance to Germany's cause and had no intention of becoming "cannon fodder." A photo of Karl and Max in uniform shows a seemingly proud father, chest puffed out, his expression calm, stoic, and resolved. His son looks more uncertain—his usually playful, twinkling, jovial demeanor undercut by unmistakable worry, even fear, on his young face.

German Jews displayed overwhelming loyalty to the fatherland during the war, even while being subjected to systemic inequality in the military ranks. Further, in 1916, the War Ministry instituted the *Judenzählung* (literally, the "Jew count"), which was designed to confirm accusations that German Jews were being unpatriotic, shirking their duty to their nation by avoiding military service, or refusing to fight on the front lines. When the count was completed, it apparently disproved those charges, but its results were never made public. Ultimately, only selective figures were leaked and used by antisemitic groups, press, and politicians, including the nascent Nazi party, which questioned Jewish motives and blamed Jews for the German defeat. This narrative—that Jews had stabbed Germany in the back in World War I—became an integral part of Nazi propaganda and rhetoric in future decades.

With Karl and Max away, and with economic conditions deteriorating, Bruno had to leave school at age fourteen to work. He took to heart his father's injunction to take care of his mother. When he reached draft age, he starved himself so he would be judged underweight during the medical review. He was in no hurry to take his place at the front, and he must also have felt a deep responsibility to provide for Flora.

The war ended in 1918 after four grueling years. As life returned to normal, Max and Bruno got a chance to sow their wild oats in the colorful, vibrant, and sensual Germany of the Weimar era. It was an intoxicating time. After the austerity of war, the country reveled in an outpouring of intellectual, creative, and artistic expression. Bruno remained close to home and family, with a brief sojourn in Düsseldorf in 1918 before returning to Frankfurt. He founded his first company in 1921, occupying a space at Kaiserstrasse 68, dealing in chemicals and then, after 1925, in imported foods.

Max, on the other hand, went to Berlin. He married Maria Algazy, née Goldstein, on February 3, 1920. One year later, in 1921, his father Karl came to Berlin. It has never really been clear why he made this move, or even how permanent it was intended to be, though I always assumed it had to do with being near Max and perhaps accepting a business opportunity. But in 1922, Karl, only fifty-four years old, died suddenly.

On the same trip as our visit to Borken, Kat and I traveled to Berlin to see the places Max had lived and where my grandfather Karl was buried. We spent half a day in Weissensee, the sprawling Jewish cemetery, hoping we could solve the small mystery of how Karl died. When we arrived, we approached the clerk at the cemetery's main office, and Kat, taking the lead, asked if he had access to the information and if he would tell us.

My father, c. 1918.

He said he did, but, "Oh no," he assured us. "No, that would be quite impossible. There are rules about these sorts of things, privacy laws, you know, and all that."

I was half amused and half annoyed that this German bureaucrat could, with a straight face, tell us that he could not disclose the cause of death of my own grandfather who had passed away nearly one hundred years before.

Kat turned on the charm, lowered her voice, and began speaking gently in German, cajoling and encouraging him. "C'mon. You can tell us. What's the harm? It's been a hundred years!"

Nothing.

"How about a hint?" She winked at him. "Just to help us with our research."

To our surprise, he winked back. "Well, it's something very common."

"Cancer!" said Kat, triumphantly.

He made a face.

I could see Kat trying to read his expression, to figure out whether it was a "yes, it was cancer" face or a "no, it was not cancer" face. Kat tried again. "Cancer?" It came out sounding a little more hopeful than she had intended.

Our poker-faced bureaucrat wasn't giving anything away.

I was standing off to the side, watching the drama unfold.

Kat gave it another try. "My friend came all this way to find out about his grandfather," she pleaded. "He's old" (thanks, Kat). "He will probably never come to Germany again" (thanks, again, Kat). "This might be his last chance to find out what happened to his grandfather, the man he was named for but never knew." I played my part to the hilt as a prop in Kat's increasingly elaborate effort, affecting a slightly doddering quality, looking helpless and frail—but to no avail. No one more jealously guards their tiny domain of power than a bureaucrat.

The clerk's boss happened to overhear the conversation, and he quickly granted the permission. I have to confess it was a bit anticlimactic to find out that Karl had died of the flu. No big secret, no big drama.

Armed with a map, Kat and I went in search of Karl's grave. In fact, it was Kat's visit to this very spot four years before that had unexpectedly shifted the trajectory of the project. Intrepid researcher that she is, she had taken it upon herself to locate my grandfather's grave in the vast sleeping world of Weissensee. When she did, she told me, she stood at his grave and sensed the weight of the decades, the history that had stemmed from his life and sprawled across Europe. It was then that she knew that the person who needed to go there, to stand at the source of the family whose story we were trying to reconstruct, was me.

Although I was reluctant at first, she won me over. She told me about her own experience researching her family, her mother's instinctive resistance to it, and what it had meant to begin to chip away at silence and fear. It was another one of the serendipities of this project—how we could have such radically divergent experiences of the war and yet share the experience of pain reverberating through the generations.

Where the cemetery in Borken had seemed mysterious and magical, a little treasure that sprang up out of the forest, Weissensee felt magnificent, grand, and vast beyond imagining. The past is heavy at Weissensee. I had trouble seeing beyond the tragic fact that this cemetery represented most of what remained of a once thriving, vibrant German-Jewish life. As Kat and I walked the wide paths in search of Karl's grave, I started to worry it might have sunk into the ground or crumbled away like so many of the others along the paths. I see now how that fear reflected something deeper than a worry for the physical state of his grave: the eternal struggle to preserve memory against time.

When at last we found the grave, it felt as close to "meeting" Karl as I will ever get. So much of him—his beliefs and values—was passed to my father, and from him to me. His marker had sat here, amid 115,000 dead Jews, unnoticed and unattended for so long. I was the first member of my family to stand there in eighty years.

Kat wandered off to give me some space and time to honor my grandfather, the aim of our visit. I cleaned off the headstone, cleared away some of the brush, and put a few stones on the marker. Kat was right; it was different this time. Unlike in Borken, I was able to—or perhaps was ready to—connect to my namesake and the past that his grave represented. This time, when I recited the Mourner's Kaddish, it was not an obligation. It was an act of remembrance and gratitude.

Max was devastated by his father's untimely death. Gradually, though, he resumed his enjoyment of interwar Berlin. He spent his time with glittering people in restaurants, cafes, and cabarets, consuming good food and drink, enjoying the diversions and entertainment the city had to offer. He first lived in Berlin's prestigious Charlottenburg district, close to the Kurfürstendamm, a main avenue running through Berlin lined with elegant shops, hotels, restaurants, and residential homes. This was the center of leisure life during the "Golden Twenties."

In business, Max succeeded as well. In 1928, he became a partner in a chemical company that was then renamed Dr. Hans Sachsse & Max Scheidt GmbH. The company focused on producing mostly *Bromsalze*, a chemical building block used in artificial colors, medicine, and pesticides. All was not rosy, however. After six years of marriage, Maria and Max divorced in February 1926. Max rebounded quickly, as he often did, and in July 1930 he married Lily Singer, née Popper, a doctor.

My uncle Max and my father looking very dapper in the 1920s.

In Frankfurt, Flora met and married widower Georg Münsterberger in 1925. They set up house together and lived with Bruno, and Georg's daughter Lotte, who was just thirteen at the time. Bruno was also enjoying his version of the high life. I am amused to see photographs of my father from those years—with many different beautiful women—including a postcard from a famous Jewish opera singer named Lotte Appel, who clearly had some sort of romance with him judging by the warm inscription.[3] But unlike Max, who played the field and married impulsively, Bruno was generally more deliberate and careful in his relationships with women. At some point—I don't know exactly when or how—he met Suse Ballin. And with that, it seems that his days of flirting with beautiful women were over.

At the same time, my father was making his own way in business. The nascent rivalry between my father and uncle grew as they competed in business and personal matters. Part of the competition came from Bruno living many years with their mother and getting to know her new husband,

Georg, who brought Bruno into the food business and then ended up working for him. Bruno would have a softer spot for Georg when things grew complicated, whereas Max was much more inclined to criticize and complain about him.

Mainly, the brothers grew and developed in divergent directions. Max was full of life, embodying a devil-may-care attitude in the face of life's hardships. He could be impulsive and explosive, though also entertaining and affectionate. Bruno was by nature more serious, bearing a strong sense of responsibility for the family. And while they never lost their deep attachment to one another, their differing styles would create considerable conflict in the turbulent years that lay ahead.

Bruno and Max must have sensed trouble in the early 1930s, but, like many German Jews, they could not have anticipated how quickly they would lose their standing in their native country. My father traveled with his childhood friend Dado to New York in 1932, possibly scouting a future safe haven should things continue to decline. In July of that same year, the Nazi party captured 37 percent of the vote in the federal elections. The newly re-elected and aging President Paul von Hindenburg, seeking to stabilize the country and placate growing Nazi support named their leader, Adolf Hitler, chancellor of Germany on January 30, 1933.

Life as Bruno and Max knew it quickly began to unravel. In February, the Reichstag building went up in flames. The Nazi party accused the Communists of an attempted coup and exploited the moment to pass the Decree for the Protection of People and State. In an instant, they gave themselves power to suppress individual liberties in the name of national security. They began arresting Communists, Socialists, labor leaders, and political dissidents. By the time Bruno heard the Nazi jackboots in the courtyard of his office building on March 31, 1933, he had a pretty good sense of what was coming. Leaving—only for the moment, he thought—his family, his business, and the woman he loved, he jumped on the first available train bound for Switzerland.

3

German and Jewish

The Ballins

When Bruno arrived in Switzerland, he quickly oriented himself. He stayed until April 20, obtaining a one-month French visa, and subsequently got a longer one enabling him to stay in France until the end of 1933. In Lausanne, and later in Paris, he kept an eye on the situation in Germany, trying to assess whether he could return, but he had no way of finding out whether the Nazis were still after him. Meanwhile, as the months ticked by, the situation for Jews in Germany grew worse. He had little choice but to leave his business in the hands of his trusted longtime employee, Georg Beckmann, and prepare for a longer-term stay outside his country. Perhaps the hardest parting was from Suse. They were not yet formally engaged, but they were committed to one another, planning their future as best they could.

Suse's family was markedly different from the Scheidts. For one thing, they were from a long and established lineage in Germany, one that stretched back centuries. In one of two books about the Ballins I inherited, author Michael Perlmann wrote, "In the middle of the 15th century, in the large Jewish community of Worms, there was one family which had distinguished itself by bearing the surname name Ballin in addition to the otherwise customary and exclusive use of Hebrew names. Such a surname is proof of an important past throughout decades."[1] The other book, written by a distant cousin, Oskar Ballin, was published in 1913 and documented that our branch of the family traced its origins to the birth of Jakob Moses Ballin in 1770.

In the 1930s, the Ballin name was widely known, thanks to the huge success and influence of Albert Ballin, a distant cousin. Albert was general director of the Hamburg America Line (HAPAG), which by 1897 was the world's largest steamship company. He is credited with inventing the modern cruise line and creating a global business that served the transatlantic needs of tourists and poor emigrants alike. The German emperor, Kaiser Wilhelm II, welcomed him at court, sought his professional counsel, and maintained a personal relationship with him over the objections of the empress and others. As a result of his exceptional status as a successful Jewish man in a still antisemitic society, Albert became known as the "Kaiser's Jew."[2]

Albert Ballin's enormous wealth and power afforded him prestige and a place in the highest circles of German society. He had a city apartment, a country house, and a villa known as "Little Potsdam," where he entertained lavishly. One aspect of Albert Ballin's professional endeavors particularly caught my attention. In 1901, Ballin created an emigration city in the Port of Hamburg occupying an area of 13.5 acres, including its own hospital, church, synagogue, and dining halls. It housed the thousands of people who arrived weekly from all over Europe, waiting to depart on one of the many Hamburg America Line steamers. Later called BallinStadt in honor of its founder, some five million emigrants leaving for North and South America passed through this small city on their way to what they hoped would be a better life.[3] It seems a particular irony that our family's most famous relative made it possible for millions to leave Europe for new opportunities abroad, given the desperate struggle his cousins would face to escape Nazi Germany decades later.

In 1954, my maternal grandfather Georg added six pages of handwritten notes about his own family to our copy of Oskar Ballin's book. From these pages, I know that Georg was born in Nordhausen in 1871, the third child of Clementine and Jacob Ballin. Like so many of this generation, his parents had already suffered the death of a child. Their firstborn, and only daughter, Gertrude, did not live to see her first birthday. Five sons followed. Georg remembered his mother, Clementine, as "very caring" and "interested in literature" until a "a severe illness" took her life in 1906. Their father Jacob was a successful bank director and an influential community figure. Georg wrote about him with evident pride: "Our father was highly respected in

Nordhausen, a board member of the Jewish congregation for many years, a member of the Grand Prussian Regional Lodge and held other honorary positions. He was most upright, a good model for his five sons, not Orthodox, yet holding fast to the Jewish faith."

This last phrase is a telling one. Although Georg, as an adult, had little interest in Jewish religious practice, he clearly wanted to affirm his father's Jewish identity. Jacob and Clementine Ballin made their home in a liberal Jewish community in Nordhausen. By this time, Jews had lived there for more than one hundred years. Relations between the Christian majority and the Jews were good—contemporary accounts show they attended special occasions at each other's houses of worship—though the town fathers insisted that the synagogue be located on a side street, in recognition of its secondary status. Jacob and Clementine belonged to the Reform congregation, which departed from strict interpretation of Jewish law and embraced modern changes such as the introduction of a choir and an organ. The congregation was so committed to its liberal approach that they dismissed their rabbi in 1875 when they felt that his old-fashioned ideas were impeding their progress.

Though the Ballins' Jewish community in Nordhausen was modern, integration did not mean a rejection of Jewishness. Jacob donated money to the synagogue and served on its board. He also ensured that his sons studied Hebrew. He always valued his Jewish identity alongside his Germanness, participating in the larger European society and culture.

Jacob and Clementine's five sons took different paths in life but got together frequently in Nordhausen and remained close all their lives. Georg met my grandmother, Karoline Margarete Gröbel, known as Margarete, in Heidelberg while visiting his favorite uncle. She was the eldest of seven children born to Victoria and Karl Friedrich, the concertmaster of the Heidelberg Orchestra. Perhaps surprisingly, the Gröbels were Catholic. I don't know what the Ballins thought about this fact, but they embraced her as their daughter-in-law. Georg and Margarete were married in Wiesbaden in July 1906 and settled in Stuttgart. Their first daughter, Ella, was born there in April 1907, a prompt nine months after their wedding. Baby in tow, they moved to Glauchau where they had two more daughters—Lilo sixteen months after Ella, in August 1908, and then my mother, Suse, in July 1910.

Among the many surviving photos, one of my favorites is of Margarete and her three daughters. In it, my grandmother is settled on a couch, as if she's just fallen back against its soft pillows, her lovely round face animated

Ella, Suse, Margarete, and Lilo, c. 1911.

by a smile on the verge of a laugh and her eyes crinkling into bright half-moons. My mother is still a baby and stands in her mother's lap, her dark, short hair tousled and her huge eyes regarding the camera seriously. To Margarete's right sits Ella, who props herself up with a hand on her mother's lap. On the other side, Lilo rests her round face in a chubby hand and snuggles into her mother's side. Margarete is the very picture of young motherhood, caught in a moment of warmth and intimacy.

By the time this photo was taken, the family of five had moved to Frankfurt. They settled in the Westend, an affluent, fashionable part of town distinguished by broad avenues and generous public squares in the Parisian style, wide parks, open spaces, and grand villas and elegant residences. It was an entirely mixed community, markedly different from the largely Jewish Ostend just a few miles away where my father was being raised.

The Ballins were comfortable in the Westend's secular environment, taking assimilation a step further than Georg's father Jacob had. Beyond their intermarriage, far from common at the time, Georg and Margarete were atypical in other ways. Politically and socially liberal, they flatly rejected religious affiliation of any kind, seeing it as divisive and preferring to locate their values in universal human ethics that they believed transcended any particular faith.

They created an entirely secular household for the raising of their daughters. On holidays, the extended family came together and celebrated with cultural rather than religious emphasis. For Christmas, they baked holiday cookies and decorated a tree that could be seen from the double doors that opened onto the balcony of their home. Their daughters' upbringing focused on literature, music, and poetry, and placed a high value on time spent in nature and engaging in physical activity and sports.

Unlike Bruno and Max, who were getting their education at the Rabbi Samson Raphael Hirsch School, Suse and her sisters attended the secular all-girls Schillerschule, named for the renowned German philosopher, historian, playwright and poet, Friedrich von Schiller. An advocate for individual freedom, human dignity, and religious tolerance, Schiller was part of the German Enlightenment, and his progressive ideas were central to the school's educational philosophy.[4] This suited the Ballins, who made a priority of providing their three daughters with a modern, liberal education. The school was also Frankfurt's only *Gymnasium* (secondary school) offering girls the courses needed to take the *Abitur* (final exams) that would allow them to enter university. Georg and Margarete were so committed to a nondenominational education that they appealed to the headmaster to exempt their daughters from any religious instruction at all. The girls' formative years in the school shaped their sense of identity as educated young women in a rapidly changing world.

When World War I broke out, Georg was called up. At forty-three, he was married with three daughters to support and a business to run, so he was far from eager to serve. In addition to his personal reasons, he was—like his distant cousin, Albert Ballin—vehemently opposed to the war, viewing it as senseless, futile, and destructive to German culture, liberal values, and the nation's middle class. Nevertheless, he was required to be part of the war effort. Like Karl and Max, he was photographed in his uniform, and the picture was sent as a postcard from Wiesbaden to his father in Nordhausen in February 1916. By this time, he had been in the service for two years. The location and battalion on the card indicate that he was in a noncombat unit, though he nonetheless saw his share of horrors. He worked in a field hospital, probably as an administrator or coordinator. In the photograph, Georg, usually so distinguished and confident, looks small and lost

My grandfather Georg Ballin, February 1916.

in his too-large greatcoat. His demeanor is stiff and uneasy, with none of the pride Karl displayed in *his* uniform.

Georg might not have believed in the war, but he did his duty. He and his brothers saw themselves as Germans who happened to be Jewish, fully part of the country and its culture, just like their fellow countrymen. Why wouldn't they? For centuries, their family had lived quite well and safely in Germany and had risen to some prominence. Like most German Jews during World War I, Georg did what was expected to help the only home he and his forefathers had known.

In the late 1890s, two of Georg's brothers, Max and Friede, had emigrated to Leadville, Colorado.[5] One consequence of this early emigration to America was that the Ballin brothers found themselves fighting on opposite sides of the Great War. Eldest brother Max, who had become a successful doctor, served as chief of surgical services and was discharged

My great-grandfather Jacob Ballin with his sons, Friede, Georg, Ernst, and Louis, early 1920s. (Max Ballin was in the United States.)

as a lieutenant colonel from the U.S. Army, while Georg, Louis (also a doctor), and Ernst all served Germany. Ernst actually fought in the infantry and was wounded in 1914. Fighting on opposing sides of this massive conflict did not harm the brothers' relationship. Loyalty to country was important, but nothing was more important than the bonds of family.

On the home front, Germany's supply of food and raw materials from neutral countries had been cut off, and, during my childhood, I remember my mother telling me how scarce food was and that her mother had to go out to the farmlands around Frankfurt to get enough to nourish her daughters. Like so many others, they experienced real hunger and deprivation. I have often wondered if this explained some of her health issues after the war and the sensitive stomach she continued to have throughout her life. Her experience trickled down to me: When I was growing up, she always insisted I eat what was on my plate and not take food for granted. She saw no excuses for being a picky eater when others were going to sleep hungry. Likewise, only truly spoiled food was thrown away; to waste food was abhorrent. I learned to appreciate food in all its variety, something that served me well in my career in the food-import business.

There was one exception for my mother. Turnips. She had the strongest, most visceral reaction at the mere sight of them. When we went to the corner produce store, she recoiled and would not go near them because they brought back miserable memories of cooked turnips or turnip soup for months on end during the war's scarce years.

The end of the war brought fresh difficulties to Germany as many found themselves struggling to survive. At the height of the country's economic woes, hyperinflation meant a single loaf of bread could cost millions of marks. My mother's sister Lilo remembered the family not being able to afford any of the luxuries they had enjoyed before the war. When their uncle Max visited from America, it was the first time she had ever seen an orange or tasted whipped cream, which she said was like eating "a cloud in the sky."

Georg and his younger brother Ernst were able to return from military service to the couture fashion company they owned, called J. Reihing-Schreiber. They sold their collections in Germany, Holland, and France, and in keeping with their unconventional ways, their wives partnered in the business, sharing not only the daily operations but powers of attorney. Described by Georg as "the heart and soul" of the company, Margarete had an outstanding eye for fashion, designing the firm's high-end women's dresses for Frankfurt's elite while simultaneously bringing up her children. Lilo remembered that they had a cook and a Fräulein to look after the girls and help with homework because Margarete was not at home when they returned from school. This was highly unusual in upper–middle class German families like the Ballins. Women of the period were expected to occupy themselves with rearing children, running a household, and providing for their family's comfort and well-being.

Margarete developed a work-from-home model for the company's seamstresses, recognizing that many women had to care for children but could sew at odd times. She and her sister-in-law, Bertha, oversaw the system that allowed women to work on their own terms and deliver their finished products to the company at regular intervals. Georg was open-minded and embraced her initiatives. They worked together for decades, setting an example of marital equity as they built a successful company.

Ella, as the eldest, was always a dominant personality among the three sisters. She was independent and strong, with no trace of submissiveness. After finishing her schooling, Ella initially went to work in the family's couture business. But in 1925, at age eighteen, she met Eugen Kende, a Hungarian Jew from a prominent family of art and book dealers and publishers

A silhouette postcard of my grandmother, Margarete, made by the artist Vokurka during the landmark aviation exhibition, 1909.

of music. I've never been able to learn how and when they met; I have only empty envelopes, saved for their stamps, that show they wrote each other frequently.

They married on October 10, 1927, in Frankfurt and moved to Vienna where, with Georg and Margarete's help, they bought a bookstore a five-minute walk from the city's famed St. Stephen's Cathedral, situated on the same street as several elegant boutiques. Ella, following her mother's example, was an equal partner with Eugen in the running of the bookstore and held power of attorney. On June 4, 1928, she gave the Ballins their first grandchild, Anneliese.

Unlike her sister Ella, Lilo was soft-spoken, sensitive, and innocent. Her family often considered her a little naïve and dreamy, lacking the organizational abilities, decisiveness, and competence of either of her sisters. Like Ella, she attended the Schillerschule, but for a shorter time. As Lilo remembered it, "My sister went to the *Gymnasium*, and I didn't want to go to there because I didn't want to have six years under our director, who was supposed—I thought—to be antisemitic." More than that, Lilo wanted to complete her education in just three years, as allowed at the *Lyceum*. "I wanted to go to my father's factory . . ." she said, "and I wanted to learn designing, and go to Paris with my parents to see the new fashions twice a year." She completed her education at age fifteen, and according to her wishes, she was able to learn the fashion-design business in the family's workshop under her mother's guidance. She spent most days over the next few years working in the business and learning the trade.

Lilo's life changed in 1928, when she joined her uncle Ernst on a business trip to Holland. There she met the young, dashing, and wealthy Jessiah Lissaur. His family was well known, with an established clothing business throughout the Netherlands. Lilo made an unforgettable impression on Jessiah, so much so that he proposed the day after they met. Lilo laughed and refused him. Later she recalled, "My uncle said, 'I'll never take you along anymore on any trips,' because he didn't enjoy this very much." Then, laughing, she added, "He probably enjoyed it very much, I thought later."

Margarete, Lilo, and Georg Ballin; Jessiah, Engeltje, and Emanuel Lissaur.

Jessiah didn't give up, and a few months later, the couple were married. Lilo was just twenty. They had two weddings: first in Frankfurt, on March 16, 1929, and then in Holland, on August 13 of the same year. The photographs of Lilo and Jessiah's Frankfurt wedding depict a lavish affair. The bride seems especially happy, surrounded by five young ladies—one of them my mother, who is wearing a different-colored dress than the others and was perhaps her maid of honor. Jessiah, a handsome man in his tuxedo, cuts a striking, sophisticated figure with his face half in shadow, a small smile playing around his lips. The second photograph shows the newlyweds surrounded by their parents, Lilo casually sitting on the armrest of Margarete's chair, looking sweetly at the camera, her arm draped affectionately over her mother's shoulder.

After the wedding, Lilo moved to Amsterdam with her new husband, where they became a fixture in the high-society scene. Years later, my cousin Anneliese remembered, "The Lissaurs were prominent and wealthy and had all that money could buy; I recall the Dutch maids in costume and the chauffeur pulling our sleds in the snowy streets of Amsterdam behind the

Lilo and Ellien, early 1931. (Courtesy of Emanuel Lissaur.)

big black Marmon." The Lissaur family was on good terms with Queen Wilhelmina and were invited as guests to the Dutch court.

The couple's first and only child, Engelina Lissaur, was born on September 2, 1930. Called Ellien or *Puppi* (little doll) by her family, she was doted upon. Lilo's life was one of luxury, leisure, and diversions. "Well, there were many wealthy Jewish families," Lilo said, "and my mother-in-law took me along in the afternoon to tea in the city . . . and she introduced me to her friends, and just sitting around, or shopping." They rented summer cottages at Zandvoort and Scheveningen, high-end seaside resorts on the Dutch coast, and spent two months every year enjoying sun and sand. "We went with the children to the *Strand*, to the beach, and swimming, and dancing in the evening, and had a good life," she wistfully recalled, many years later.

While Ella and Lilo were working, falling in love, and beginning their families in the twenties, my mother was still in school. She attended the Schillerschule from 1916 to 1924, but then her health declined, possibly as a result of food shortages during and after the war. Her parents sent her for

My mother, age twenty, Frankfurt, 1930.

a year to a boarding school called Villa Rurik, near Montreux, Switzerland. Some of the earliest family letters I have are written to my mother by her grandfather Jacob in Nordhausen, sent to her first in Frankfurt and then in Switzerland. They are warm and affectionate: He promises to drink a glass to her health on her birthday and hopes she will get the bathing suit she wants. While she was in Switzerland, her grandfather assured her that "getting to know the country and its people . . . and engaging in pleasant exercise" would be valuable for her. Upon her return, she attended the Viktoriaschule in Frankfurt, graduating in 1928. Then, like her sisters, Suse took her place working in her family's couture business. She must have been working there when she met my father, sometime around 1930.

Just over four months after Bruno's April 1933 flight from Frankfurt, he and Suse met in Switzerland. I know from the stamps in their passports that she traveled from Germany while Bruno entered from France. It was the third time they had seen each other since Bruno had fled Germany, and they had just a week together to reconnect and talk about their plans before they were parted again. While Suse returned to Germany, Bruno made plans for a life in France, with new opportunities, reunion with his family, and a glorious future with the woman he hoped would become his wife.

4

An Imperfect Reprieve

The Hotel Rochester stands on Paris' sophisticated Right Bank, a few short blocks from Boulevard Haussmann and the Champs-Élysées. Tucked in the middle of the block on Rue de la Boétie, the soft white facade is punctuated by large casement windows, wrought-iron railings, and elegant decorative masonry, all crowned by a classic Parisian Mansard roof. Built in 1928, the hotel was still relatively new when Bruno began living there in October 1933.

It was a beautiful setting, but no amount of beauty could make Bruno forget he was a refugee and his circumstances were precarious. He couldn't have stayed in Switzerland even if he'd wanted: The Swiss had enacted a policy called "transmigration," or onward migration, intended to prevent "foreign infiltration" of Switzerland by the waves of Jewish refugees at the Swiss border. The vast majority of Jews were denied permanent asylum. So, as soon as Bruno received an eight-month visa from the French consulate in Lausanne in late April 1933, he decamped for France. Like many Jews, he hoped the Nazi madness would eventually come to an end and that his German neighbors would come to their senses. The situation is poignantly described in the novella *Reunion* by Fred Uhlman, which was originally published in 1971. One of the characters, the father, answers a Zionist with the following optimistic words: "I know my Germany. This is a temporary illness, something like measles, which will pass as soon as the economic situation improves. Do you really believe the compatriots of Goethe and Schiller, Kant and Beethoven will fall for this rubbish?"[1] But in the meantime, Bruno had to ensure his own safety and financial stability as best he could.

My father was not alone in seeking asylum in France, which had long been recognized as a welcoming country having established *les droits de l'homme*—the "Declaration of the Rights of Man"—during the French Revolution in 1789. In addition to its famous motto—*Liberté, Égalité, Fraternité*—it was the first European nation to emancipate its Jewish population. Throughout the 1920s, France opened its doors to émigrés, economic migrants, and asylum seekers, perhaps in part because of its huge population losses in the Great War. In the spring of 1933, when my father sought refuge there, France was continuing to welcome people who were fleeing Hitler. By that summer, the country had absorbed about 25,000 German refugees, more than any other European nation. For the moment, it was the most logical place for Bruno to land.

That said, life in France could hardly be described as secure. While my father did not have to worry about being arrested by the Gestapo, he also could not know for sure how long he would be allowed to remain in the country. To gain a foothold there, he had to maneuver through the complex French bureaucracy, which was difficult, time-consuming, and emotionally exhausting. When I read through the surviving documentation, I see the labyrinth my family had to navigate, and I am reminded that for them, as for refugees in the present day, everything depended on those papers. It was the difference between living in the shadows, in constant fear, and being able to operate in the full light of day.

In July 1933, France's previously liberal refugee policy changed. As elsewhere, in the face of worldwide economic depression, French authorities began fearing that refugees would take jobs from needy citizens. Prime Minister Édouard Daladier's government reversed the open policies, restricted immigration, and began requiring far more stringent documentation to remain in the country. In this tense environment, my father had to keep scrambling to provide a secure foundation for his future. On August 1, he established his imported-food business with a minority partner, Joseph Gritti. He named it Établissements Roland, giving it the most French-sounding name he could to mitigate the optics of his own German name and heritage. In spite of the fact that the Nazis saw Bruno as Jewish, not German, to the French, at a time of growing xenophobia, what mattered was

Ets. Roland business card.

that he was an alien with a German surname. Further, the company name clearly invoked *La Chanson de Roland*, an eleventh-century epic poem about a heroic knight that is a foundational work of French literature and a huge source of Gallic nationalist pride.

Éstablissements Roland was located at 17 Rue du Bouloi, conveniently near Les Halles, the central Parisian food market.[2] Les Halles had been a covered market since the eleventh-century, built partially on land confiscated from exiled Jews. Parisians could go there to purchase dry goods or change money, but by the fifteenth century, it was known for sales of fish, vegetables, and meat. Companies like my father's had warehouses and offices in this area, close to the action. My father bought and sold food products there, building his business with the local vendors and making valuable contacts. True to form, he got an international driver's license, acquired a Citroën, studied French, and laid plans to secure at least a temporary future in Paris.

At the same time, he needed to protect his substantial investment in his German business. With each passing month, the Nazis made it more difficult for Jews to make a living in Germany, and, particularly relevant to Bruno, they imposed steep penalties on anyone attempting to take their hard-earned capital out of the country. The *Reichsfluchtsteuer*, established in 1931, required that those leaving the country pay a 25 percent tax on capital they sought to remove from the country. Bruno could not sell his company without losing a large part of his assets. So, in December 1933, he changed the firm from a sole proprietorship to a corporation, establishing a partnership with his longtime trusted employee, Beckmann, who was not Jewish. The agreement included a detailed inventory list fourteen pages long showing the company's impressive range of products, including rice, pasta, oats, and barley; apricot and strawberry jam; canned pears, peas, carrots, and potatoes; and pickled herring, coffee, cacao, and a variety of spices. The declared value of the inventory, however, was much less than its actual worth—a tactical move designed to lower the company's overall value. This lessened the tax burden for Bruno and let Beckmann pay less up front for his partnership. My father trusted Beckmann and planned to use the income generated by the business in Germany to help him survive as a refugee in France.

The person he relied on most, however, was my mother. In the six months after my father fled Germany, Suse traveled alone and stayed with him four times, a rather unconventional thing to do by the standards of the time. It's impossible to imagine that she would have done so unless there was a clear understanding between them about their future plans to marry. It seems they had promised themselves to each other and decided together to wait to get married until Bruno was established in France.

Meanwhile, she actively helped Bruno with the complexities of running a German business as a refugee in France. Her passport shows that from 1933 to 1935, she made a total of ten trips between Germany and France, often bringing papers and personal belongings and taking the opportunity to discuss plans for the company. In Frankfurt, she met with Bruno's lawyer to arrange all sorts of personal and business matters. She gathered cash from Georg Beckmann or his fiancée, Erika, and smuggled it into France. She relayed instructions about the business from Bruno back to Beckmann. These were risky maneuvers since they were dodging taxes and hiding information about the company from the Nazis. A letter my father wrote to my mother in 1935 shows the pressure she was under in Frankfurt to handle matters that Bruno couldn't. "Just remember," he wrote, "that what you can't save and accomplish during your short presence there is lost to us. I repeat, lost." A few lines later, he softened his tone, reassuring her of his love and devotion. "Have a good week and lots of love, stay healthy and don't take things there so seriously. In 50 years, weeks, days, hours, it will all be over."

That same year, Suse ran into trouble on one of her trips between Germany and France. As always, she had chosen to travel through the town of Saarbrücken in the Saar region, which offered the safest route. Since 1920, this region had been occupied and governed by the United Kingdom and France as part of the post–World War I League of Nations mandate. When Suse arrived at the border with cash and other small valuables on her person, she was stopped by a German official. As Suse knew all too well, there could be draconian penalties for so-called Jewish smugglers. At best, the contraband would be confiscated; at worst, the smuggler would be imprisoned or even executed, depending on the whims of the officer.

The German officer searched her and found the illegal possessions she was trying to get out of the country. I can only imagine the terror she must have felt at that moment, at the mercy of a German border official. He demanded her papers, which she quickly turned over. As the officer scanned her papers, he hesitated, noticing her famous last name, Ballin. He asked if she happened to be related to Albert Ballin. She stammered that yes, that he was her father's cousin. He paused, looking her over. He must have thought it was unwise to arrest a relative of the great Albert Ballin. But she was breaking the law, and he couldn't simply let her get away with it. After a few harrowing moments, he told her he had to confiscate the illegal property she was trying to smuggle. He told her to make haste before she was caught by someone else, who might not be as generous. He warned her against ever attempting to do this again, because next time, she might not be so lucky.

This experience was seared in my mother's memory. She recalled slipping away from the officer and drawing a long breath of relief. She periodically brought it up with me later in her life, especially in conjunction with meetings with government officials of any kind. Even in America, she could not shake the feeling of anxiety and panic when meeting with representatives of the IRS, for example. It took enormous effort—and a lot of cigarettes, before and after the meeting—to control her fear and project an air of calm, organized confidence.

My mother's trips from Germany to France and back between 1933 and 1935 coincided with the gradual deterioration of Bruno's relationship with Georg Beckmann. It was difficult enough for Bruno to control the business from France, but under Beckmann's leadership, the company foundered and lost money. My father was so frustrated that he wrote to Suse in Frankfurt to see if her business-minded sister, Ella, might step in to help. "Did you talk to Ella, and would she perhaps consider becoming business manager?" he wrote. "She certainly could represent our interests." Ella was not interested. It was not only the financial losses that pained Bruno but also the injury to his pride as he watched the business he had built fall apart.

While Bruno was laying the foundation for his future in France, Flora and Georg had to face the reality of leaving Germany. With Bruno out of the country, and both Max and Lotte (Georg's daughter) in Berlin, they had little reason to stay in their native city. Then, in July 1933, the Gestapo arrested Georg in Frankfurt on the dubious charge of having "offended the Nazi government when visiting customers" and for being "prejudiced toward German currency." There was no evidence to support these accusations, and he was released twelve hours later. He and Flora immediately left Germany for Belgium. As it turned out, their departure came not a moment too soon. Shortly after they left, the Gestapo returned to their residence in search of Georg.

Flora and Georg stayed in Antwerp, where a business opportunity with an old friend, Morris Levinstein, paved the way for a visa. Georg formed a partnership with Levinstein in a food-import company called Alima, which sold dried fruits and legumes, rice, canned foods, oils, and the like. It was fortunately an industry that Georg knew well. He and Flora struggled to stay abreast of all the documents and paperwork for a year and a half, only to be denied residency permits and forced out of Belgium in January 1935. They liquidated the company and relocated to Paris, where they lived at 2 Rue Gustave Larroumet, in the 15th arrondissement. Although their apartment was on the other side of the Seine from Bruno's current residence at the Hotel Rochester, they were at least in the same city again.

A few short months later, Max had to rethink his options as well. By all indications, Max had a good life in Berlin, though his marital situation was complicated. He was still married to Lily Singer, but, by this time, he was in love with Erna Sasse, originally his secretary in Berlin. I have not been able to establish when Max divorced Lily.[3] I do know that his marriage to Erna, his third, was the one that stuck.

The world around Max was growing more perilous all the time. Simmering tensions and escalating Nazi rhetoric against Jews exploded in July 1935. The trouble began when a mob of 200 men dressed as civilians, though suspected to be Nazi stormtroopers, attacked Jews in cafés and restaurants along Berlin's fashionable Kurfürstendamm, very near to where Max and Erna lived. In a front-page article, *The New York Times* wrote,

"Seizing men who were seated on terraces or inside cafes, they hurled them into the street and chased them, beating them as they ran. The windows of two cafes in the avenue were smashed as bottles, glasses and chairs flew through the air."[4] Dozens were injured as the rioters yelled, "Out with the Jews!" and other antisemitic slogans. The German police, unable or unwilling to tame the crowd, allowed the violence to continue. This was the most brutal and direct attack against Jews in Germany since Hitler had come to power. It was also a bellwether of the nation's mood and the ever-increasing risks to Jewish property and lives. The next month, Max and Erna left Germany for Paris.

By August 1935, the Scheidts had—couple by couple—found their way to the relative calm of France. Then, in September 1935, my parents got engaged. The previous month, the Scheidt and Ballin families had met for the first time on a vacation in the Czech spa-and-resort town of Karlsbad. The pictures from that trip show the families relaxed and happy: Max and Flora having coffee and my parents taking walks, laughing, and surrounded by friends.

Max and Flora in Karlsbad, August 1935.

Before the wedding, Suse took a huge leap of faith and devotion. My mother technically was not a Jew by birth since it is traditionally passed along matrilineally, and it was her father who was Jewish. For this reason, she formally converted through the congregation in Frankfurt, where she attended classes about Jewish history and custom. She obtained a certificate signed by the congregation's rabbi and cantor—the same cantor who would have taught my mother Jewish religion at the Schillerschule in Frankfurt, had her parents allowed her to attend. Instead, she learned about Judaism as an adult, on her own terms and for her own reasons. Bruno wrote a letter to her days before her conversion: "I am thinking a lot about you, slept badly last night. Will keep my fingers crossed for you Friday, don't worry, you'll pass."

Suse undoubtedly would have preferred to get married in her hometown, surrounded by family and friends. But returning to Frankfurt was impossible for Bruno, so they decided to marry in Paris. A month before the wedding, my parents traveled to Monaco to spend the Christmas holiday together. They stayed in the Monte Carlo Palace Hotel and dined luxuriously. My mother saved the menu—lunch included lobster Parisienne, tournedos, turkey stuffed with chestnuts, mince pie, and *Bûche de Noël*. For Christmas dinner, they had a sumptuous meal starting with chicken soup with almond milk, followed by filet of sole, lamb chops with primroses, spit-roasted pheasant with truffles, foie gras, asparagus, Christmas pudding, and *Bombe Nélusko*—chocolate mousse and praline ice cream in a chocolate shell. Dinner ended with *les plus beaux fruits* and a glass of Moët & Chandon champagne.

My parents' wedding day dawned on January 25, 1936. It was a small and simple affair, with a few friends and family gathered at the *mairie* (city hall) of the 8th arrondissement in Paris. Flora and Georg were there, as were Max and Erna. Unlike the elegant weddings of Suse's older sisters, there were no photographers, no orchestra, and no dancing. Then again, my parents' marriage lasted until death parted them, which could not be said for the unions of either Lilo or Ella.

The day didn't start auspiciously. Bruno was late to the ceremony. Everyone waited restlessly, wondering what could have possibly befallen the groom. My mother must have been a nervous wreck. Ever-jovial Max broke the tension by proposing that, since he and Bruno looked so much alike, perhaps he should marry Suse instead. That way, everyone could go out for dinner—and it would serve his brother right for being late to his own wedding! My father did, of course, show up (the reasons for his tardiness are, alas, lost to history), and my parents were married without further ado.

Suse and Bruno on holiday, Karlsbad, 1930s.

A few months later, my father acquired a two-year identity card that would allow him to remain in Paris. The die had been cast. The newlyweds would make their lives in Paris, hoping that in time the political situation would calm itself.

The following few years brought a moment of respite for my family in Paris. Beginning in 1936, my parents, grandparents, and uncle and aunt all lived near each other in the 15th arrondissement. For the first time since 1920, Flora was in the same city as both her sons, and Max and Bruno were reunited. The family was surrounded by a vibrant refugee community of many friends and acquaintances from Germany and Austria who had also settled in Paris. Among these were Max and Bruno's childhood friend Dado Sulzbacher, their cousin Hans Schwab, and Hans' wife Marie Amon, the author of *Barrières*, a scandalous bestseller based on her colorful life as a singer, model for Egon Schiele, actress, raconteuse, and "demimondiste" in

My father, Paris, c. 1936.

the avant-garde literary circles of Vienna and Berlin.[5] My father's great friend, Lucien Stern, took several wonderful photographs of my parents during this period. One that particularly tickles me is my father, well dressed as usual in a tweed suit and carrying a hat, standing in front of a wall with a sign that reads *Défense d'uriner* (no urinating). He is looking at the camera with a wry smile, sharing an inside joke with Lucien.

My father was gregarious, and people were attracted to him. My mother was introverted and shy. For this reason, life in Paris seems to have been more stressful for her than for my father. She was encircled by his family and his friends, while her family was far away in Germany and Holland. She missed them, worried about them, and periodically undertook difficult, sometimes frightening, trips to see them. In late November 1936, she went back to Frankfurt to celebrate her mother's birthday. Hours after her departure, Bruno wrote her a tender, affectionate letter on Monte Carlo Palace Hotel stationary, a reminder of their pre-wedding trip together. "My beloved Suse, dearest wife, sweetheart," he began, "I'm already looking forward to seeing you again, although you've only been gone for seven hours. When you hold this letter in your hands, it will only be ten times seven hours until we'll be together again, and that will go quickly."

The family often shared Shabbos dinners that Flora cooked, took walks, and enjoyed the rich cultural life of prewar Paris. Their closeness endured in spite of their differing personalities and various mild family tensions. Max tended to get annoyed with Georg, Max and Bruno could be competitive, and Suse and Erna didn't always see eye to eye. Some of these faint currents would erupt into larger conflicts later in life. But for now, the family lived, worked, and survived together.

In 2017, Kat and I traveled to France as part of another research trip. We'd been repeatedly stymied in our attempts to unravel the family history there—in stark contrast to our experiences in Germany, where people seemed not only willing but eager to help us. In France, in spite of repeated inquiries, we had trouble learning which archives to contact and, when we did, we did not get answers to our questions.

Then we got lucky.

I found a book written by Thierry Marchand, an avid historian whose work included information that was important to our search. We contacted the publisher, who put us in touch with him. Thierry's day job is in a bank, but he is adept and experienced at archival research and navigating the French bureaucracy to find long-buried records. He directed us to the places where we needed to go and connected us to people we needed to visit during our trip. In Paris, he joined us to visit my family's old haunts—my father's office at 17 Rue du Bouloi and the family's neighborhood in the 15th arrondissement—and traveled with us to visit Normandy, where so much of Max and Erna's later story unfolded.

On our second day in Paris, after spending some time at the *Mémorial des Martyrs de la Déportation*, we drove with Thierry to the neighborhood in southwest Paris where my family had lived. Thierry had tried on our behalf to reach the residents of the three apartments that my family had occupied, but no one responded. The best we could hope for was that we could stop into the building lobbies and, as we had done elsewhere, meet someone who would show us an apartment. I surprised even myself by how absolutely dogged and determined I became in these moments. Even when everyone else wanted to give up, or began questioning what was to be gained, I insisted on pushing forward. Where I'd once struggled to connect to this history, now I wanted to walk where my parents had walked and let the thoughts and feelings bubble up, whatever they might be.

This neighborhood was newly gentrified when my parents, aunt and uncle, and my grandmother Flora and her husband Georg settled there. As central Paris became more populated and real estate more valuable, the factories that had filled this area were torn down and replaced with residential structures. When my family moved in, they were among the first tenants. Well-established Parisians were likely not interested in this newly developed neighborhood, whereas immigrants, including my family and their friends, saw it as an opportunity. Although I knew that my family had lived near each other, it wasn't until we visited Saint-Lambert Square, a sizable park that had been created in 1933, and walked from one address to the other, that I realized just how close they had been. The three couples had lived no more than five minutes apart in buildings on three streets adjoining the park. They must have met in the park from time to time, taking evening strolls and pausing at the lovely fountain, stopping to sit on a bench, watching the world go by and listening to the sounds of the neighborhood children. On hot days, perhaps they chose a shady spot to sit and picnic, feasting on good French cheeses, fresh vegetables, wines, fruit, and pastry for dessert. Knowing my family, their baskets would have been filled with nothing but the best food; perhaps my father stopped at Les Halles after work to bring home a sampling of a delicious new product. I loved the idea of them enjoying life here. Something about Saint-Lambert touched me deeply. They had been flung from their homes and sought refuge in Paris—perhaps the park had felt like an oasis to all three families.

One of the most important stops for me was 10 Rue Peclet, the first apartment my parents shared in their married life. We were met by a very disagreeable concierge who refused to let us see any of the apartments. I did, however, notice both the nearby Chaplin Cinema—still in its Art Deco glory—and the magnificent view of the Eiffel Tower from the building. My father was a great fan of Charlie Chaplin, and I easily imagined my parents walking arm-in-arm to the cinema and stopping to admire the famous Parisian icon every time they left their apartment or came home to it.

The concierge at Max and Erna's apartment on Rue de la Croix Nivert was unavailable, and Thierry, who is polite and proper, was ready to give up and leave. He might have been unwilling to push past the limits of decorum even in the pursuit of research, but Kat is direct and determined, and I have been called stubborn. My tenacity challenged, I sat us down for lunch at a corner brasserie near the building, and to Thierry's great embarrassment, I rearranged a couple of the sidewalk tables to make sure I had optimal line of sight to anyone entering the building.

I ate my entire lunch with eyes fixed on the building's entrance, unwilling to miss any opportunity to slip inside. Each time someone seemed likely to go into the building, I was halfway out of my seat. Finally, I saw a lady at the door fishing a key out of her purse. I leapt up, ran to the door, and got there just in time to jam my foot in before it slammed shut.

At that point, I started acting like a two-bit gangster, lurking in the shadows of the darkened hallway as I followed the lady to the concierge's office. Luckily, she didn't even notice. Thierry joined me, and the concierge remembered Thierry's letter, agreeing to meet us at the Croix-Nivert address around the corner. Meanwhile, Kat was stranded back at the brasserie, in part because we had left without paying and in part because she was savoring every morsel of what she will forever remember as the world's best duck salad. Trusting that she was far too valuable to be left permanently, she sat back, Paris style, and enjoyed life and a cigarette. She told me later that she was also, somewhat diabolically, relishing the cultural differences playing out between Thierry and me. She knew I would not give up, and she knew that Thierry would not entirely approve, and she could not help but enjoy a bit of comic relief watching us navigate our differences.

We managed eventually to see the apartment adjoining Max and Erna's. The couple who lived there were Muslims, immigrants to Paris, completing the circle in my mind of past and present. Once they got over their initial skepticism, they were welcoming and kind and let us walk out on the balcony to see the view. It was breathtaking, a classic view of Parisian rooftops straight out of a French New Wave film. I imagined Max and Erna stepping onto their balcony in matching robes as they drank their morning coffee. I wondered if occasionally Max's robe might have fluttered open a bit too freely. Max lived life to the fullest and embraced all of Paris' pleasures.

Our days in Paris were full and moving for me. One evening, however, as we enjoyed dinner in a bistro near Rue du Bouloi, where Bruno's office had been, I found myself wondering why my parents had never taken me to this neighborhood. They had brought me to Paris several times. We had walked along the streets, taken in the views, and eaten in restaurants. Why had they never wanted to show me where they had lived and worked? Was the Paris of their past too painful to share? To me, this seemed like a rather happy time for them, even if it was clouded with uncertainty. I was sad and wistful that they had never told me about this time in their lives or shared the experience of these years with me, and that I was exploring this alone, long after they were gone. There were so many things we had never discussed. I will never know whether it was because they wished to put away this past for their own peace of mind or whether it was to protect me from it.

In May 1936, Joseph Gritti sold his minority interest in Établissements Roland to Max and Georg. Although Bruno remained the major shareholder and continued to run the company, he named both Max and Georg as managers. This arrangement brought several advantages. First, trusted family members could be counted upon to sign documents and protect each other's business and financial interests. Second, Bruno could help Max and Georg by making them partners in an established business before they needed to request visas and other documents to remain in France. This status established the pattern of security and financial self-sufficiency they would need. It happened that this period coincided with a brief liberalization of visa rules for refugees. With the victory of the Popular Front in the 1936 elections, socialist Léon Blum became the first Jewish prime minister of France. In the months that followed, refugees were granted identity certificates that allowed them to remain in France even if they had entered the country illegally.

Bruno's life in France might have been proceeding reasonably well, but his German business was in freefall. He needed to cut his ties with Beckmann, do whatever he could to get any of his money out of Germany, and accept that returning to Frankfurt was a fantasy. In late April 1936, unable to find any other buyer, Bruno sold his entire interest in the firm to Georg Beckmann and his fiancée, Erika Haug. I know my father was devastated that he was forced to sell his portion of the business to Beckmann for vastly less than it was worth—a mere 7,500 reichsmarks.[6] Nazi laws favored non-Jews to such a degree that no buyer paid a fair market value to a Jewish business. In addition, Bruno paid the increasingly steep *Reichsfluchtsteuer*, now at 65 percent, on the funds generated by the sale of the company.

My father felt, justifiably, that he had been cheated, and when the war was over, he sought restitution and disputed the terms of the agreement. The loss was about more than money to him. He took pride in his business acumen and his success. He had been deprived of that livelihood and was forced to accept a lower value for the business he had created. Eventually, in 1949, Beckmann agreed to pay my father a little more money. I have not been able to determine whether the transfer of funds ever happened. What I do know is that the situation rankled my father for many years.

In May 1938, Max and Erna married at the local town hall in the 15th arrondissement. Like my parents' wedding, it was a modest affair, probably followed by a dinner at a bistro. Flora recorded the wedding in the family *Stammbuch*: "On May 7, 1938, my dear son Max married Erna Sasse in Paris. On the 20th of November, 1938, my dear Erna converted to Judaism. She then received the name Ester [*sic*]. To the two, as well as dear Bruno and dear Suse, *Massel* and *Broche* [good luck and blessings] for my beloved children."

Even as my family carried on in Paris—living their lives, enjoying each other, and succeeding in business—it was impossible for them to avoid the looming war and the threat to Jewish security. In the Anschluss of March 1938, the Germans marched into Austria without opposition, incorporating it into the Third Reich. Eight months later, a young Jewish man, Herschel Grynszpan, whose parents had been expelled from Germany and were trapped in a no-mans-land between Germany and Poland, shot Ernst vom Rath, a German official in Paris, as an act of protest. When vom Rath died a few days later, Nazi Brownshirts unleashed an orgy of violence and chaos throughout Germany and Austria known as *Reichspogromnacht* (or, as the Nazis euphemistically called it, *Kristallnacht*, the Night of Broken Glass). On November 9–10, 1938, hundreds of synagogues were burned to the ground, businesses and private homes were vandalized, Jews were beaten, and tens of thousands were arrested. The shocking news of what had occurred—a clear sign that the Nazis were free to act with impunity in Germany—was reported around the world.

In France, the brief period of liberal refugee policy brought about during Léon Blum's administration came to an end. With the re-election of Édouard Daladier in 1938, there was another crackdown. As the Depression lingered and war seemed increasingly likely, the French government made moves to severely restrict refugee rights and implemented harsh penalties for those who attempted to enter the country without a valid visa. All too soon, my family would feel the effects of French anti-immigrant and anti-Jewish policies.

5

Rubble and Embers

My flight touched down in Amsterdam on a clear day in May 2016. I gathered my things and waited patiently to disembark. I was thinking about getting through passport control, collecting my bags, getting a taxi, and making my way to the hotel. I was thinking of the logistics of the trip, our itinerary, where we needed to be and how to make the most of it. I went through the familiar motions of navigating the too-narrow aisle, blinking as I stepped out of the airplane's liminal space onto the solid ground of Schiphol Airport. I was unprepared for the sudden, overwhelming sense of my aunt Lilo's presence. This city, home to many of her joys and terrible fears, had marked her. She had been gone for twenty-two years, but I was flooded with a visceral reminder of her warmth and kindness, her bright blue eyes sparkling at me, the guttural *sch* when she said Schiphol, and the lingering sense of sadness she carried with her every day of her life.

It had never occurred to me that the very air in the city would reflect Lilo back to me. I paused for a moment, letting the memory of her wash over me. It was bittersweet and nostalgic. But the airport was no place to linger. I shifted my bag on my shoulder and pressed on.

Lilo and Jessiah on the Promenade des Anglais, Nice, France, early 1930s.

The early 1930s were a happy time for Lilo. She was married to the handsome and charming Jessiah Lissaur. He was wealthy and sophisticated, and he traveled in the most elevated circles of Amsterdam society. Best of all, Lilo had her daughter Ellien to pamper and adore.

Even as the Nazis gained power in Germany, life in Holland at this time felt stable and secure. The country had a long history of religious tolerance, having welcomed Jews expelled from Spain and Portugal as early as the 1500s. In the 1600s, when a series of protracted wars with Spain finally ended, Holland established itself as a haven where Catholics and Protestants could live and do business together peacefully. The freedom to practice religion was guaranteed and codified in the early 1700s with a series of peace treaties known as the Peace of Utrecht. Jews continued to flock to the tiny nation where they could live and worship without harassment and where trading and mercantile opportunities flourished.

Further, Holland had a history of remaining neutral in international affairs, a policy dating from 1830 that continued through World War I. Most people believed it would remain so if war broke out again. The country's openness, religious tolerance, and neutrality were believed to be part of its DNA. Lilo was far from the only one lulled by this false sense of security, the notion of Holland as an island of safety next to the menacing forces in Germany.

While Lilo was reveling in marriage and motherhood, her sister Ella was suffering. In 1933, she and Eugen separated and Ella returned home to Frankfurt with her young daughter, Anneliese. Two years later, in 1935, the divorce was finalized. The complaint details considerable ugliness, stating that Eugen badly managed the business, which contributed directly to its failure, as well as badgering the Ballins for money and shirking his financial responsibilities toward Ella and Anneliese. Worst of all, he is accused of having verbally and physically abused Ella, events which were corroborated by multiple witnesses. By all accounts, Ella was fortunate to be rid of him.

Returning to Frankfurt, Ella joined J. Reihing-Schreiber, the Ballin family dressmaking business, as a designer. In March 1935, Ella all but gave up her five-year-old daughter Anneliese, sending her to live in Amsterdam with Lilo and her family. There could be any number of reasons for this, but none of them are known to me. What I do know is that Anneliese went to school in Amsterdam, learned to speak Dutch like a native, and spent the next four years with Lilo as her devoted adopted mother and Ellien as her sister. Anneliese was also very fond of her Uncle Jessiah, recalling him as a great playmate and friend. From time to time, she returned to Frankfurt to see her mother and grandparents, and they came to Holland to visit. But home for Anneliese was in Amsterdam.

A handful of photos of the girls growing up together have come down to me. In them, I see Lilo and Jessiah, Ellien and Anneliese, and occasionally my mother and grandparents Georg and Margarete, peering out from the past. In all of them, Ellien and Anneliese look remarkably alike, often dressed in matching clothes and carrying matching dolls. I notice details that might not interest others: the gap in Ellien's teeth, my aunt Lilo's elegant clothing, the way my mother frequently dips her head, shyly avoiding direct eye contact with the photographer. Ellien poses proudly with her beloved bike in one photo; in another, she is dressed in perfect tennis whites, all gangly preteen limbs, holding a racket as if about to hit a perfect shot.

None of these photographs are particularly significant historically—they are family photos, after all. But they are poignant in the way of all prewar photos: There is something haunting about the smiles of a family on a skiing holiday, in the saucy stance of the girls standing on the running board of Jessiah's huge black Marmon, in the quotidian satisfaction of the group sitting together after lunch or posing on the balcony of their apartment. These moments are meaningful exactly because they were not extraordinary. The pathos is refracted in retrospect.

Lilo with Ellien, age seven, and Anneliese, age nine, on their balcony, Amsterdam, 1938.

In Frankfurt, life was getting increasingly difficult. Georg's brother and business partner Ernst died of blood poisoning in 1937, and his wife Bertha, who had always been active in the company, became a co-owner. Despite everyone's best efforts, J. Reihing-Schreiber struggled because of the Nazis' unrelenting barrage of anti-Jewish laws and harassment.

By this time, Ella had a new boyfriend, Walter Kutz, who would be known in the family as Ella's favorite husband and the one to whom she remained married for the duration. In 1937, the duo managed to navigate the labyrinthine emigration process and secure much-coveted visas to the United States. The only hitch was that eight-year-old Anneliese could not go with them. As Ella explained it, Anneliese had Hungarian citizenship because her father was Hungarian, and the U.S. quota for that country was small and already full. Walter went first, settling in Los Angeles. On March 25, 1937, Ella followed, sailing on the SS *Washington* and leaving Anneliese in the care of her aunt Lilo. But one month later, Anneliese returned to Frankfurt to live with her grandparents.

Unfortunately, by this time Lilo's marriage was beginning to fray. Jessiah had turned into a playboy, having affairs, drinking, and gambling. Lilo, who was often ill, had exhausted herself caring for Ellien and Anneliese. This, in combination with the end of her marriage, may have contributed to the decision to send Anneliese back to Frankfurt. In July 1937, the couple divorced. Soon after, Lilo moved with Ellien into an apartment at Herculesstraat 25a, not far from Jessiah's home. Ellien attended a Montessori school nearby.

Although Anneliese and I never discussed this, I cannot help but think of the effect these years had on her. She must have felt loved by her extended family, but she was constantly being shuttled from one place to the other, never securely at home anywhere.

Ella periodically sent letters to her family in Europe with news of her life with Walter in Los Angeles. She'd found work in the clothing industry there as a designer for a blouse-manufacturing company. In February 1938, she and Walter married, and shortly thereafter, they opened a photo store in Santa Monica.

Anneliese remained with her grandparents in Germany, and her recollections of that time are mixed. In a letter to me in 1990, she wrote, "We lived in a large and beautiful flat on the Waidmannstrasse; there was a large garden and fruit trees. I went to a private school there and had to learn to read & write German. I had wonderful clothes—grandmother designed miniatures for me from her latest collection." At the same time, she seemed

Ella in Los Angeles, c. 1938.

lonely. "I recall no friends or anything about the school. I spent most of my spare time in my grandparents' factory, especially with a Fräulein Adam who taught me to embroider and appliqué." She also lived with the constant uncertainty of Jewish life in Nazi Germany. "I recall, also, the fear of the SS & SA guards in their kiosks . . . the food rations and the practice air raids. I always felt like an 'alien.' . . ."

Georg and Margarete tried valiantly to save their fashion business, and as inevitable as its failure seems in retrospect, it must have been exceedingly painful and frightening to live through. In January 1938, they had no choice but to sell at a loss. They also had to sell the office building at Hohenzollernstrasse 9, which had been owned by three of the Ballin brothers—Georg, Ernst, and Louis—since 1925.

Like so many Jews in Germany and throughout central Europe, the Ballins felt the increasing heat but adapted to it, like the frog in the proverbial pot. They told themselves that this was a passing madness, that it would abate with time. They also interpreted events through the lens of their own particular values and life experiences. First of all, Margarete was Catholic. More than that, as highly assimilated Jews on my grandfather Georg Ballin's side, who disdained religious observance in general, they found it hard to believe their negligible Jewish identity would shape their future.

They weren't blind, though. As life became increasingly difficult, their thoughts turned more and more to emigration. By 1938, about 150,000 German Jews—over one in four—had left the country. The annexation of Austria in March that year brought 185,000 more Jews under Nazi control. The pressure mounted as the Nazis made life in the Third Reich increasingly intolerable for the Jewish population. But where were the Jews to go?

In July 1938, in response to international pressure, President Franklin Roosevelt convened the now-infamous Evian Conference. Representatives from thirty-two nations gathered in the posh French resort town to discuss what to do about the Jewish refugee crisis. Roosevelt signaled American ambivalence by declining to send his secretary of state; he instead sent Myron Taylor, a friend and businessman. One representative after another stood up and hedged, offering no solutions—no easing of quotas, lessening of paperwork, or simplification of bureaucracy—but excuses and half-hearted regrets for why their country could not take Germany's Jews. It was a tragic collective moral failure. Only the tiny Dominican Republic offered to accept a larger share of the world's refugees. Lilo plaintively reflected on this in her 1991 video testimony: "I cannot forget, up to today, when they praise Roosevelt so much, that I always think, 'If you just would have enlarged that quota a little bit, how many lives would have been saved?'"

The Ballins felt an increasing urgency to get Anneliese out of Frankfurt and across the border to the relative safety of Holland. This was a perilous task because she did not have legal papers, and the borders were carefully monitored. Refugees caught crossing illegally were detained in Dutch camps. Georg came up with an ingenious, if risky, idea: One day in October 1938, he and Anneliese boarded a train to Holland. At the last stop before the Dutch border, Georg kissed his granddaughter farewell and got off the train. She would cross the border alone under the assumed identity of her younger cousin, Ellien, to whom she bore an uncanny resemblance. In her 1990 letter to me, Anneliese wrote, "As I had been programmed, I told the Dutch guards that I was eight years old and my name was Ellien as I was then traveling on my cousin's passport."

How long that trip over the border must have seemed for Anneliese. What would have happened if the border authorities had questioned her and caught her lying? I imagine her looking out the window, clutching her doll, scared and alone with a burden no child should have to bear. Thankfully, she crossed into Holland without getting caught, and Lilo boarded the train at the first stop to get her.

Anneliese might have gotten through the riskiest and most frightening part of the trip, but she was still in the country illegally. "Once in Holland," she recalled, "it took all of Uncle Jess's influence with Queen Wilhelmina to keep them from deporting me to Hungary or somewhere."

Margarete was at home on November 9, 1938, when she heard the first sounds of chaos on the streets of Frankfurt. It was the beginning of *Reichspogromnacht*. Georg was in Berlin visiting his brother when the violence erupted. He quickly boarded a train headed for Frankfurt and, since he was neither in Berlin nor at home in Frankfurt, he escaped the fate of 30,000 Jewish men and boys who were arrested and spent frightening days or weeks in Nazi concentration camps before being released. On his way home, he witnessed the damage to public property and private homes throughout the city. He also saw the magnificent Friedberger Anlage, the synagogue where the Scheidts had worshipped for decades, slowly burning over two days, reduced to rubble and embers.[1]

Reichspogromnacht was a turning point for most Jews in Germany. Yes, there had been anti-Jewish measures. Yes, people had been dismissed from their jobs and subjected to alarming curtailments of their civil rights. But never had there been such a vitriolic, terrifying display of Jewish hatred carried out by representatives of the German government. For most of the Jews who'd remained in Germany, this was the moment they understood there was no future for them in their country. The only option was to leave. That, however, was easier said than done. While the waiting list for German and Austrian visas to enter the United States in June 1938 was already shockingly high at 139,163, by January 1939 it was 240,748. It must have looked hopeless. And yet, people had no choice but to try.

Georg and Margarete were the last of the Ballin family to attempt to leave Germany. By this time, Holland had firmly closed its border to curtail the steady flow of panicked Jews and other German "undesirables" and established a small quota allowing 7,000 refugees to enter. Georg and Margarete did not have the requisite papers to enter Holland, but where else could they go?

On January 11, 1939, they got permission to leave Germany. Bringing only their hand luggage with them, they decided to cross into Holland illegally, counting on Jessiah's connections to help them once they arrived. After a lifetime of hard work and success, Georg and Margarete had to flee their native country and rely on relatives in Holland and the United States for financial support. They packed their lifetime of belongings into crates and requested that their trusted employees send them over in the coming months. They were subjected to an even more exorbitant *Reichsfluchtsteuer* (Reich flight tax) than the 65 percent Bruno had paid. The Ballins faced a surcharge of 90 percent, nearly the entire value of their possessions. The Germans were ruthlessly stripping Jews of as much of their wealth as possible before ejecting them.

On January 14, Georg and Margarete crossed into Holland. Without legal papers, they were immediately interned in a Dutch camp. Thanks to Jessiah, they were released two days later, though the fear and anxiety of that experience never left Georg. He repeatedly wrote about how he hoped never to be in such a place again. The couple moved into a small apartment at Wodanstraat 24 in Amsterdam that, unlike their sunny and spacious home in Frankfurt, was dark and cramped. When their belongings finally arrived, they found the crates had been opened and plundered by the Germans. With no recourse, they had to accept that treasures they had spent decades lovingly collecting were gone forever.[2]

Almost immediately after being granted permission to stay in Holland, Georg and Margarete began taking steps to secure visas to the United States. Bruno and Suse had already obtained U.S. visas for themselves, and Anneliese's visa had also been approved. On March 10, 1939, Suse arrived in Holland to pick up Anneliese and bring her to the States. I have a photograph of the cousins shortly before Anneliese left. The girls are lounging in a field, leaning against one another, looking up at the photographer, smiling and relaxed. They look like the sisters most people thought they were. When it finally came time to say goodbye, it was no doubt a wrenching farewell. They could only hope that the goodbye would be temporary, but there were no guarantees.

On March 15, 1939, Bruno, Suse, and Anneliese boarded the *Queen Mary* at the port of Cherbourg. Over half a century later, I found an envelope with a red wax seal and my grandmother's inscription in German: "On March 15th 1939, my dear son Bruno gave me this letter." When I finally opened it, inside was a neatly folded copy of my father's will in his beautiful and careful handwriting. It contained no financial surprises but simply provided for Suse and his mother if he didn't survive.

Anneliese had no such concerns about her safety. "What an exciting experience it was for me to roam all over this big ship," she wrote later, "the

The last photo of the cousins before Anneliese left for the United States.

fastest and most luxurious in the world at that time. I had a cabin to myself and slept in the upper and lower bunks on alternating nights."

They arrived in New York City on March 23, 1939. Free and safe at last.

In 1937, when Ella and Walter had deposited Anneliese with Lilo and sailed for the United States, Ella had told her daughter that she'd been forced to leave her behind because Anneliese had Hungarian citizenship through her father, not German citizenship like her mother. Ella said the Hungarian quota was small and already full, and that was the reason she could not get a visa for Anneliese at the same time as she secured her own. I never had cause to question this, but Kat's natural curiosity often led her to snoop around and dig into more records than I thought necessary. After all, it is one thing to seek answers. It is quite another to create questions. In the end, however, Kat's inquisitiveness and penchant for research added infinite depth, nuance, and sorrow to my family's story.

Kat had been thrown in the deep end as researcher for this project. She had begun to dig her way through hundreds of letters and documents in my possession, trying to make sense of the major and minor characters, untangling confusion, helping me see throughlines and relationships among the various threads of the story. She spotted holes, identified people whose lives and fates were unknown, recognized dynamics between family members only hinted at in the records. It was difficult for me to attend to this work myself; I often lacked a sense of why this mattered and who might benefit from rehashing old, painful events.

In 2012, Kat and I met up in Washington, DC, where I was attending the Fancy Food Show, the largest U.S. specialty-food trade show. Roland Foods had a big booth every year. Kat was filming the booth setup and some of the goings-on for a promotional video. I was in work mode, scheduled within an inch of my life with breakfast and lunch meetings, social functions, and dinners. So, when Kat asked me whether I minded if she went to the National Archives to see if she could dig up anything about my family story, I barely registered the request. I had no objection, but my mind was on other things.

We were completely unprepared for what Kat discovered. As she pored over the immigration records, Kat stumbled over the fact that Ella had applied for her visa to the United States as a Hungarian citizen. But how could that be, since her explanation for not being able to take Anneliese with her to the United States was that the Hungarian quota was full? Kat had unwittingly uncovered Ella's lie to her daughter, a secret that had been kept for seventy-five years. In fact, Ella had not even applied for a visa for Anneliese. She had deliberately left her daughter behind instead of securing her safe passage to America.

I found this discovery to be terribly distressing. After all, by 1937 it was clear that Jews were in danger. How could Ella have left her daughter? When she applied for her own visa, why didn't she apply for Anneliese as well? Could she possibly have justified it by telling herself that Anneliese would be happier with her cousin and aunt Lilo? Perhaps, considering her disastrous first marriage, Ella wanted to make sure her relationship in this new country was safe and stable before bringing her child into the mix. Perhaps she also naïvely underestimated how much risk the Nazis posed and told herself she and Walter would establish themselves financially and send for Anneliese in time. But in the end, she must have known she was doing something she could not justify to her family or her child. She did it anyway and covered it up, hoping that no one would ever find out. This secret, buried so long ago, surely explained, at least in part, the breach between Ella and Anneliese that I had always sensed but never understood.

Kat's discovery about Ella made me see how a secret could reverberate and magnify through the years. Ella's decision to leave Anneliese behind, and the lies that underpinned her actions—even the ones that no one in the family knew about—shaped the relationship between mother and daughter. But Kat's discovery had exposed more than Ella's lie—it made me wonder what other stories might lie hidden in the archival rubble of the war years. She had unearthed the possibility of a story beyond the letters and documents my mother had saved.

What had begun as uncertainty on my part slowly transformed into curiosity. I remained emotionally ambivalent about it for some time, but Kat's enthusiasm was infectious. She took me by the hand and pulled me into the past. I found that in spite of myself, I wanted to stay there for a while, to see what might be uncovered and how I might better understand my family and myself.

6

A Fateful Miscalculation

When Bruno and Suse left on the *Queen Mary*, Max and Erna stood on the dock and forlornly watched them sail away. The couples had become extremely close in Paris, and Max and Erna must have felt that they were losing their dearest friends. Over the years of the separation that would follow, they exchanged hundreds of letters that provide a window not only into their lives but also their very different attitudes toward the tensions of the moment.

On the surface, Max's view of the political situation seems in keeping with his characteristic joie de vivre. He and Erna could be romantic, reckless, and certainly less pragmatic than Bruno and Suse. For this reason, Max appears not to have wholeheartedly supported or even fully understood why Bruno and Suse felt it necessary to leave Europe. It wasn't that Max didn't understand the brewing dangers in Europe, but rather that he and Erna truly believed they were safe in France. In a letter to Bruno, Max wrote, "We won't say another word about politics today either. One can be optimistic or pessimistic. If everything were to stay calm or there were a major easing of tension, nobody would leave France and go to the U.S. I don't want to discuss it further."

In Paris, Max and Erna surrounded themselves with other German refugees, including their cousin, Hans Schwab, and friends Fritz Zuckerkandl,

Oscar Goldschmidt, and others. They entertained elegantly at their apartment, offering succor from the outside world. Max's first line of defense was always to shut out bad news and enjoy life as long as possible. "I hardly read the newspaper," he wrote, "and if I do, it's only at 3 A.M. on the toilet. At the moment, there is nothing one can do to escape, and perhaps it's not even so urgent at the moment. That's the way it is."

Erna echoed Max's determination to avoid the unpleasant thoughts of imminent war with Germany. "Once again we are not discussing politics. How long will that last? Soon enough we will again have to think about leaving and war and the like, but just want our peace and quiet at least for a few months. Mackie hardly reads the newspapers and is absolutely right—if one were to digest and then worry about each and every thing, one could never be happy again. Within a few days, one's nerves recover, a thicker skin grows, and then it can start all over again."

Nevertheless, Bruno and Suse's departure seems to have rattled Max, forcing him to think about his future options. In at least one letter, Max commented on the benefits of Bruno being stateside. "Things have turned out in such a way that by now, one can probably find family all over the world. A true blessing. And whom do we have to thank for all that? The one [Hitler] who is celebrating his 50th birthday today, this abomination of mankind, this scourge of God." Max also referred repeatedly in his letters to possible avenues for emigration, such as a business opportunity with his partner Oscar Goldschmidt in America or even a visa for Ecuador, but then ended up in a position of helplessness and resignation disguised as philosophical acceptance.[1] In a letter dated April 18, he wrote, "I am beginning to quite seriously rack my brain where to go. I see nowhere. A visa for England is limited to 8 days, and England makes no sense in any case. A visa for Switzerland is limited to circa 2 weeks at a time and from Switzerland one could never get out anymore, because Switzerland has only Germany, Italy and France for neighbors."

Bruno and Suse had urged Max and Erna to apply for visas, but Max either genuinely felt or wanted to project an image of himself as a devil-may-care lover of life, sailing above the worries that plagued his younger brother. By the time he realized he'd miscalculated, the way out was much harder. And Max's own letters show his ambivalence: He alternately tried to quell his own fears, then made efforts to plan an exit, but when he found himself helpless to see it through, he returned to telling himself and others that he didn't need to go. The letters capture this exhausting mental game: Max justified his decisions and reassured himself even as doubts and fears repeatedly bubbled up.

Erna adopted an attitude similar to Max's, though she was, by nature, a more forceful person. I remember her as tall, strong, and striking, always dressed fashionably and wearing heavy jewelry. She demanded attention, directing their (and sometimes other people's) lives with bravado and authority. She also took great care of Max, operating behind the scenes to provide him with strength and backbone when it was most needed.

While Max and Erna remained in France, Bruno and Suse were facing a number of unexpected challenges. It was far from easy getting their bearings in New York. They had landed in late March 1939, having been in contact with two Scheidt cousins there—Hans, who was nineteen years old, and his younger sister, Grete. Hans had said he would meet them at the dock and take them to a furnished apartment that had been rented for them at 241 West 101st Street. But after Bruno, Suse, and Anneliese navigated all the requisite controls—their visas and papers having fortunately passed muster with U.S. officials—they couldn't find Hans anywhere. They waited for quite some time but eventually gave up and loaded themselves in a taxi. They found their way to the new apartment, and exhausted, bewildered, and alone, they must have collapsed into their beds that night. It turned out that Hans had a good excuse. He had been rushed to the hospital for an emergency appendectomy.

Shortly after arriving, Bruno and Suse put Anneliese, whose English was rudimentary at best, on a plane bound for Los Angeles, where she would be met by her mother, whom she had not seen for more than two years. Cross-country flights in those days stopped several times to refuel, and at the age of ten, Anneliese had to navigate the complex and long journey in a new country alone.

My father and mother began to get settled in their new life. They made a deliberate choice not to live in the heart of the German-Jewish community in Washington Heights, known as Frankfurt-on-the-Hudson, where more German was spoken than English. Instead, they chose a more diverse community on Manhattan's Upper West Side, eventually joining a Modern Orthodox synagogue. Suse managed the house, cooking and providing a welcoming home for the many guests Bruno invited into their lives. Among these were a large number of German refugees who found good food and lively conversation both in the city and in summers in the nearby beach towns of Belle Harbor and Sea Gate. Bruno and Suse also became surrogate parents to Hans and Grete, who joined them for Shabbos dinners and visited them on weekends.

Bruno wasted no time starting his business. Within three weeks of arriving, he contacted a mushroom supplier, Borde, with whom he had worked in France. Despite successfully exporting wild mushrooms and truffles to Switzerland, England, Spain, and the French colonies since 1920, Borde had not yet found a foothold in America. Within weeks, Bruno was negotiating his first deal. At the same time, Bruno enlisted the help of his father-in-law, Georg Ballin, who was waiting in Amsterdam for his visa to the United States, and of his stepfather, Georg Münsterberger in France, to contact potential suppliers for the company.

Bruno and Suse were successfully creating new lives in a new country, but letters to them from Max and Erna kept up a steady stream of patronizing commentary. In May, Erna wrote to Suse, "It's up to you to make sure your husband doesn't think this is the end of the world and the two of you don't allow it to spoil your life, which you seem to have arranged very comfortably for yourselves. And see to it that you get out into the countryside, or at least into nature—also for the sake of getting away for a bit from the many people who are constantly descending upon you." This latter allusion, likely referring to Hans and Grete, shows how little Erna understood her sister-in-law.

Likewise, Max criticized Bruno for his relentless work ethic, showing little empathy for the challenges his brother was facing. "No, Bruno dear, in all frankness: you need a Roland," he wrote. "It's your life source. Then you feel good. It must fulfill you entirely, since you have no interests in life other than business and family. . . . You will work even more than here. . . . Business is and remains your favorite sport; your car is the only subsidiary. And while you long for nature, you cannot assuage this longing, because the sport of business is leaving you no time for it. It's all a matter of taste."

My father's past, in which he had repeatedly had to adapt to changing circumstances, served him well in transitioning to life in America. My mother had a more secure and established childhood, but the recent years of displacement had brought out her strengths. By the time she was twenty-nine, she had lived in two different countries, learned both French and English, and coped with being far from her family. It was not easy at first, but Suse blossomed in America. It didn't hurt that they were far away from Bruno's judgmental, if well-meaning, family. And in the United States, unlike in Paris, my mother took on a critical role in the family business, like her mother before her. She kept the books, tracked inventory, paid bills, negotiated with warehouses, dealt with customs brokers and truckers, managed invoicing, and later hired and trained the staff. She did all this while running a household and their social life.

Max seemed to recognize his sister-in-law's strengths better from a distance, expressing some slightly condescending surprise at her wisdom and insight. In a letter to her, he wrote, "Suse, I like you better and better with every line, I'm very happy to be able to tell you that so easily. I read your letters with great pleasure. I can't always write with the same intensity and coherence as I do now due to a lack of time. But: my intentions are always kind and good, then again, the two of you know that."

My father and uncle Max had a strong, brotherly bond, but there was one incident during this time that caused genuine friction between them, revealing their vastly different ways of operating in the world. Before Bruno left Europe, he had sold Établissements Roland to André Guenel, who made a partial payment when the contract was signed. Bruno deputized Max—who held a small interest in the company, together with their stepfather Georg Münsterberger—to collect the rest of the money. Guenel seems to have made a payment in April, but when the May 1 payment came due, he could not or would not pay. He said he didn't have the money, and his son, who was supposed to run the company, had been drafted. Guenel also suggested that Bruno had not made a fair deal with him; he even said he had been conned.

Bruno insisted that Max collect the payment. He had spent nearly six years building up the business, worked tirelessly to grow it, and he had made a fair deal. He could not accept that Guenel simply refused to pay. This was also the second time he was taking a significant financial hit because he was being made to leave one country for another. Forced out of Germany and then France, without status or power, he had no choice but to sell his hard-built businesses at a loss. The financial pain was one thing; the humiliation and frustration were still another. He ultimately sued Guenel for payment, a step Max vehemently protested because it entangled Max in the French legal system.

Max was in the thick of refugee stresses in Paris. In a letter scolding his brother, he made it clear he had far bigger worries than Bruno's financial ones:

> For all of us here, as *étrangers* [foreigners], it is an indescribable horror to be tied up in such an affair; it makes us feel bad both emotionally and

> physically. . . . Quite frankly, I have neither the head space nor the time for this. . . . For me this is about getting into an affair that absolutely disgusts me, that has nothing to do with me, and which I detest more than you can imagine. . . . I need my head for myself, for my affairs, for my professional advancement, and this is not something I can do easily. I cannot free myself from it, and everything that has to do with it burdens me and bears me down. . . . As a basically decent person, it must bother you how everyone here is so down, including poor, hapless Guenel, who is not managing as well as he expected.

Both Max and their stepfather, Georg, had other reasons for not wanting to push Guenel. As German refugees in France, they were in a deeply vulnerable position. Constantly under suspicion, the slightest wrong move could put them in serious trouble with the law. They had watched their cousin, Hans Schwab, and his new girlfriend denounced as spies and face serious legal and financial repercussions. Max understood that Bruno didn't want to be cheated, but if Bruno pushed him too hard, Guenel might denounce them to the authorities. Max was infuriated that Bruno was unyielding, especially in view of these potential consequences.

Bruno also constantly reminded Max that he'd agreed to sell the furniture he and Suse had left behind in Paris. Erna, who had taken charge of this task, stood with Max, telling Bruno he was being unrealistic about the value of the items. German styles were not particularly popular to begin with, and there was a glut in the market due to so many German and Austrian refugees fleeing and selling their furniture. In her characteristically blunt way, Erna also told Bruno to drop the issue with Guenel, writing, "I would recommend that you close the Guenel account both in your books and also in your head. . . . Get over it, don't occupy yourself further with this, keep your head clear for your present plans, which are much more important and can bring far greater benefit than Guenel."

For his part, Bruno was used to making deals and solving problems, and he clearly believed he would have resolved these financial matters more ably than his brother. But he didn't fully understand the situation on the ground. Max defended himself in this letter from May 1939:

> That "I fail immediately if something goes against my plans or my convenience," Bruno, is a statement you should take back. . . . Precisely because you yourself judge Guenel to be disingenuous & phony, you should

> tell yourself that he will not refrain from a denunciation if his life is in danger. I don't want to go through what Rosetta and Hans Schwab are having to deal with in spite of being innocent. I am prepared to solve this whole issue "cooperatively," meaning: not just according to your plans but also according to mine. And I mean, settle [the case]! Settle it soon! Make concessions! Don't bring him to *faillite* [bankruptcy]!

As spring turned to summer that year, the heat in Paris was stifling. The previous summer, Max and Erna had stayed as guests at the home of their friend and business partner, Oscar Goldschmidt, in a beach town called Bénerville in Normandy. Drawn back to the idyllic town and the fresh sea air, Max and Erna rented a house called La Ricoquette for the summer season. Max wrote to Bruno: "Obviously, we don't need to be told to make ourselves comfortable; we, or I, have been reproached about this for years. But you should live in such a way that you have a maximum of pleasure. Perhaps you will find a compromise solution for the apartment issue between a bit of nature and freshness on the one hand and business needs on the other. I so wish that for you."

They arrived at La Ricoquette in mid-June and stayed in the charming Norman-style masonry home with a steeply pitched gable roof, brick and stone detailing on the facade, a deep front-entry porch, and a lovely balcony. The house was dominated by large, white-trimmed double casement windows with board-and-batten shutters. "We see the sea," Erna wrote, "although the house is not directly on the beach but up on a hill; behind the house, endless meadows, green hills, in other words, everything one could wish for." Max wrote proudly to Bruno and Suse about how easily they had settled in: "Everything was fantastically organized by Erna, 10 pieces of luggage, God help us, I didn't lift a finger, and one hour after we arrived the office was already opened."

Life in Bénerville appears to have been a dream, offering a reprieve from the frightening circumstances in Europe. "My dear ones," Max wrote, shortly after they arrived, "I just finished my afternoon nap by the open window and my diary. Before I continue working, I send you my first greetings from our new earthly happiness here in Normandy." Max and Erna frequently welcomed friends to the house for a *Jause*—snack or small meal—and Max played the piano for the assembled guests. In one letter, Max described a typical afternoon: "When the two of us were lying on deck chairs on the lawn yesterday afternoon, a car honked and in walked: Mr. Stern,

Doctor Arenstein, Mr. Lorbeer with a very blond, beautiful and boring girlfriend. Later, Elisabeth and the two boys joined, and still later Zuckerkandl with his son and Mr. Goldschmidt. A total of 10 people for coffee and cake. . . . We extended the table and the gas stopped working just as the coffee was about to be made. But there were excellent cakes."

Max worked, and Erna supported him and ran a tight ship at La Ricoquette. When he was not working, he and Erna took walks on the beach, bought fish, and lived fairly cheaply—something he repeatedly mentioned to Bruno:

> Yes, my dear children, we have such an idyllic life here, we are by ourselves all day, without getting on each other's nerves even for a second. It's cold and rainy, so we heated up the fireplace with wood and coal . . . and not even the bad weather can disturb our idyll and this coziness. In the evenings we go to the seaside, and I bought three giant soles—Erna suggests they are Torbay soles—weighing about 3 pounds from a fisherman for 8 francs. In general we are amazed that we can live here so cheaply. We manage with 50 francs per day, all included.

They bought two beach chairs to place in the grass, but when the weather proved unseasonably cold, they parked them in front of the fireplace instead. When it was fine out, Max enjoyed tending to the garden. Erna described him vividly in a letter to Bruno and Suse: "In the garden, garden furniture, flowers, even roses, which my *Kater* [tomcat] has to water every evening, he enjoys it greatly and feels like a farmer, especially after having found planted parsley. You would love the meadow and the fruit trees which provide shade; I think you wouldn't ever want to leave again."

Flora and Georg, meanwhile, were crisscrossing France, sometimes together and sometimes apart, to visit family and friends. In the Bénerville letters, I could feel the low-grade tensions whenever Flora came to La Ricoquette, largely brought about because of a shift in family dynamics. She had depended heavily on Bruno ever since he was fourteen and went to work while his father and Max were fighting in World War I. Now, with Bruno far away in the United States, Flora had to rely instead on Max, who was less comfortable in this role. Max loved his mother, but he was more impatient with her and had a harder time tolerating her anxieties and needs.

The brothers were also mildly competitive in their relationship with their mother. Max felt the need to report frequently to Bruno that he was doing just fine managing Flora. Further complicating things was Flora's desire to be part of everything, repeatedly offering to help Erna manage the household at La Ricoquette. Erna's operation was shipshape and she did not want her mother-in-law interfering. Flora's dog JouJou, and JouJou's new puppy Chéri, added a sprinkle of chaos to the mix. But Flora, madly in love with them, insisted on bringing them when she visited, which in turn made Max—who could not stand the dogs—go nearly insane. "Dear Bruno," he wrote in one exasperated letter, "if you were here, I would issue the following bulletin about you: Rush of blood to the head as a result of feelings elicited by dogs, extreme agitation. Therapy: gentle kicks in dogs' asses. No offense, dear Suse, about asses."

Throughout my travels doing research and retracing my family's steps through Europe, I had sought many times to try to see their world as they had seen it. Nowhere was this more richly satisfying and meaningful than during my trip with Kat to Bénerville.

Finding La Ricoquette was not easy. I'd seen the name as part of the return address on countless letters from Max and Erna, but when Kat and I searched for it on maps of France, we could never find it. Thierry was the one who solved the puzzle, realizing that La Ricoquette was actually the name of a house, not a town. He traveled to Normandy and searched Bénerville until he located the house, but to his dismay, it was boarded up and looked abandoned. We feared it was on the verge of being sold or possibly even condemned or demolished. But Thierry didn't give up, and by what seemed like a miracle, he found the current owner, Julia, who—to our great good luck—happened to be German.

Julia first came to Bénerville as an exchange student, and her French host family lived in town over a bookstore. Julia would go with them to visit their grandmother, who owned and lived at La Ricoquette. This grandmother and her husband had built the house, and they rented it to vacationing Parisians from May through September. More than seventy-five years before our visit, this couple had rented the home to Max and Erna.

Julia fell in love with La Ricoquette on her first visit. During her teenage years and into adulthood, she stayed in touch with her "exchange sister," and on each visit to Bénerville, she gazed longingly at the house perched atop the hill. When the grandmother died in 2003, Julia discovered that the family planned to sell the house, but for legal and tax reasons, they could not do so for a few years. She took a photograph of the house, taped it to her computer screen, and resolved to make enough money in three years to cover the down payment. Sure enough, she succeeded, and in 2006 La Ricoquette became hers. Rather than modernize it, she made only the most necessary repairs. She adored the house's "old bones" and wanted La Ricoquette to keep its character, charm, and idiosyncrasies.

When Thierry reached out to Julia, we hoped that she might allow us to come and walk through the house for a few moments. When she heard the story of Max and Erna, and understood my family's deep connection to La Ricoquette, she surprised us by inviting Kat and me not only to visit but to stay over with her and her husband for a night. Like all the Germans we met on our travels, they went to great lengths to make us feel welcome and to help us understand my family's past, always giving us more than we had any right to expect.

So, on June 10, 2017, Thierry, Kat, and I drove to Bénerville, looking forward with trepidation and curiosity to visiting the place that linked me and my family with Julia and hers. We arrived to find a jumble of hills, streets at odd angles, houses perched on hillsides following no discernable pattern. As we meandered through this maze, we suddenly saw La Ricoquette on a hill perched above us. I recognized the house instantly from the postcards my mother had saved. It was almost as if it materialized mischievously, an apparition beckoning me into the past.

Julia and her husband, François, welcomed us warmly and ushered us to the backyard, where she had laid out beautiful cakes and tarts on a picnic table under a gnarled, ancient apple tree. In addition to the pastries, there were juicy, bright-red cherries picked by their sixteen-year-old son and his friends from the flourishing Bigarreau tree in the garden. I took a few deep breaths of the clean air, refreshed by breezes from the ocean down the hill, remembering a line from one of Max's letters: "We eat in the garden in the sun; and sometimes I search for the cat in the trees or in the tall grasses in the meadow where he is hard to find, which is the only thing causing nerve crises."

When we set foot inside the house, the full force of the past hit me. For years, I had imagined this place, seeing it through Max and Erna's descriptions in their letters to my parents. Suddenly, I was walking through the rooms where they had lived in that magic summer. The house felt inhabited by the echoes of my own loved ones—I saw Max's

Kat, Julia, and me in the garden of La Ricoquette, 2017.

cat curled up in his beach chair in front of the fireplace; I heard Erna's steps on the creaky, rickety stairs; I felt Max beside me in his bathrobe, coffee in hand, as I stood on the balcony, looking out at the rooftops receding down the hill and, beyond, to the vast Atlantic Ocean. My imagination of this past became my visceral, vivid reality. Never in all the years of research and travel had I felt this close to the story, this intimately connected to the shadowed, hidden life my family had lived before I was born.

I slept that night in the room on the second floor where Erna had slept. In the morning, I crept down the stairs to sit alone with my thoughts for a moment in the garden. The sunshine fell at an angle, highlighting the brickwork and vines that had grown in haphazard patterns up the side of the house. I felt Max's presence, putting worries aside and marveling at how wonderful life could be. When Julia joined me, we walked together into town for breakfast provisions, picking up baguettes, chocolate croissants, butter, apple jam, and fresh goat cheese. Walking along the shore, I felt as if I were in an Impressionist painting—it was as if I'd seen the flat, wide beach, lined with white huts, a hundred times before. Everywhere I looked it seemed as if time had collapsed in on itself. I was inhabiting the present and past, all at the same time.

After breakfast, in the glorious morning light of the garden, Kat suggested we read aloud some of the letters Max and Erna had written from La Ricoquette. Once again, Kat brought an instinctive sense of what I needed to the moment. Just as she had pushed me, in spite of myself, to travel to Europe and walk my family's past, here she saw that it was a once-in-a-lifetime moment. We had never stayed the night where my family had lived; our time there was short and she saw and seized the moment to bring the past and present together not only for the project but also for me, so that I could feel and experience the deeper meaning of what we were doing in this work.

It was haunting, even eerie, to hear Max and Erna's words spoken in the place where they had been written so long ago. Almost nothing had changed in the intervening eight decades. Julia and François were visibly moved, recognizing the descriptions of their own home written by people they had never known. Most of all, the moment was shadowed by the knowledge that Max and Erna's Bénerville summer reprieve was just that. Upheaval and expulsion waited for them on the other side.

Before we parted, there were two matters to attend to: En route to Bénerville, I had bought a small plant, a flowering astilbe, to give to Julia. She suggested that together we plant it in the garden to mark the occasion of our visit and to hold a place in memory of Max and Erna. We also recreated the only photo I have of Max and Erna at La Ricoquette—Erna standing on the bottom step and Max, who was shorter than she, on the next step up. Kat snapped Julia and me in a similar pose and then took a group photo, all of us sharing many laughs before it was time to say goodbye.

I sometimes wondered why it seemed so important to physically trace the steps that my family had walked in those difficult years. In part, it was because my relatives had suppressed the memories and stories that would have helped me understand how their experiences shaped my own life. For too long, the surviving letters and records had been my only link to their past. In Bénerville, perhaps more than anywhere else, I could see the past before me. I could place Max in his beach chair, keeping dry by the fireplace in La Ricoquette on a cold wet day; I could visualize the living room filled with guests eating cake and drinking coffee; I could stand beside the ghosts

Photo of Erna and Max sent to my parents, inscribed on the back, "To our loved ones in the USA, a memento of our beautiful time in Normandy in the summer 1939."

of Max and Erna on that balcony as they looked out to sea, thinking of their loved ones far on the other side.

In early August 1939, Max wrote to Bruno: "First of all, here is the thunderclap: two days ago Erna received a letter from the American consulate telling her to report there urgently with a bill of health, etc. My legs are still shaking from the excitement. According to this she will be able to get the visa under the Russian quota." Erna had been born in St. Petersburg. As a Russian national, she was able to get a visa far more quickly than Max who, born in Germany, had to apply under the German quota. Max was thrilled for his wife but also shaken. He was dependent on Erna and feared the idea

François, Thierry, Julia, and me, La Ricoquette, 2017.

of being separated. He was uneasy about the paperwork involved in emigration, daunted by the idea of starting anew, in a new country, especially the United States, which he didn't trust. "Will there be peace in Europe?" he wrote, "As long as we breathe here we hope for this miracle. But others fear an increase in antisemitism in the USA, Roosevelt's disappearance, and a new king comes, *wajowau melech chodosch* [Exodus 1:8]."

Despite his anxieties, Max continued to press his philosophy of life on his younger brother. In a letter later in August, Max fiercely reproached Bruno for his efforts to save money:

> Why are you living frugally, you blithering idiots? Are you crazy? Why save money? And you aren't even ashamed to write me that? Me? So that I'll despise you? God forbid, four months without an income. Write me that you live grandly, that you allow yourselves this and that, because you can. But not

> that you live modestly, which in your situation would be the most ridiculous, foolish thing you could possibly do. I'm having a fit. Buy yourselves the car already, get yourselves a nice apartment, even if it costs more. . . . Buy yourselves beautiful things, plates, knives, lamps, etc. Why not?

In the context of the almost unbearable rise of tensions in Europe, I see Max's words as a reflection of something deeper than a frivolous attachment to the good life. He had a deep, existential belief that one *must* grab life and live it fully, not in spite of impending trouble but precisely because of it. What was the use of denying oneself in the present for an uncertain future? A life of war, flight, and uncertainty had turned Max into an existentialist. One must live fully and well, soaking up life and all its proximate joys, because the now was everything.

As Europe moved toward war, Max and Erna were far more vulnerable than they realized. Our research determined that without their knowledge, they were being surveilled by the local authorities. Among Max's reasons for fighting with Bruno about suing Guenel was that he didn't want to call attention to himself as a foreigner in France. Yet, merely being German in France was enough to cause the French authorities to suspect that Max and Erna might be spies. They noted that Max and Erna had rented a house near the strategic fortifications at Le Mont Canisy, Normandy's highest point. The local police checked their mail regularly and reported, "This couple receives lots of correspondence, notably registered letters, and seems to be in contact with Ets. Roland food products."

At the end of August, Flora was in Paris. Worried that war was imminent, she wanted to come to Bénerville to be with Max and Erna, but they felt she would be safer in Vichy and persuaded her to relocate there. Just two days before war broke out, Flora wrote to Bruno, "My dear ones, don't be startled, but one should definitely get away from Paris, so Max advised me to come here [Vichy]. I found a small room with use of the kitchen for 25 francs a day and will wait out the crisis here, the atmosphere in Paris was unbearable. I would much rather have gone to see Max, that's what one would like to do in these hard times, but I was advised against it, as I said before."

When I think about the net closing in around Max and Erna and of the fear they must have felt, I am reminded of a moment in the garden when Kat was reading Max's letter to Thierry, Julia, François, and me. Max captured the tension between the shelter he and Erna had created for themselves and the impending danger around them: "I implore God Almighty that the events will not prove us wrong. I remain optimistic that the very worst will be avoided; under horrible conditions, but avoided. Of course, it is unfathomable if we were to be proven wrong, and the odds, even for an optimist, are only 50:50 . . . rather, we have enough faith in God to survive unharmed whatever may come. And let's keep *sang froid* [coolheaded], which is the best thing to do."

On September 1, 1939, Hitler invaded Poland. Two days later, France declared war on Germany. The next day, notices were posted in Bénerville, as in towns and cities all over France: "All male nationals of the German empire between 17–50" had to report to various camps.

Max wrote to his mother:

> My dearest old Mutti, in the end it turns out that I wasn't all wrong when I suggested you should travel to Vichy. Just now I was notified that we are to go to the *camp de rassemblement* in Lisieux as quickly as possible. I will not make this trip alone: dear comrade Schwab is coming along, as is a nephew of Mr. Goldschmidt, a Mr. Margulies from Vienna, who also has a wife. . . . I have no intention to become weak. . . . I thank God that I will be so much better off than millions of others.

On September 5, 1939, Max reported to Lisieux. The perfect Bénerville summer was over.

7

"Mein Lieber Bruder"

Max and his cousin Hans Schwab reported as ordered to the police in Lisieux. They had been instructed to bring with them a handful of possessions, including coats, shoes, eating utensils, a blanket, and two days' worth of food. Although the journey to Lisieux must have been sobering, they believed their internment would be short and uneventful.

German and Austrian Jewish refugees in France, like Max and Hans Schwab, found themselves in a double bind. They had overcome great obstacles to get to France, where they believed they would be safe from persecution and exploitation by the Nazis. But with France now at war with Germany, the French authorities viewed all Germans and Austrians on French soil as enemy aliens, potentially part of a "fifth column." This meant that Jews who had sought refuge from internment at the hands of the Nazis found themselves interned by the French authorities instead.

Although not much is left of the Lisieux camp, Kat, Thierry, and I traveled from Bénerville to see it and the surrounding area. Thierry grew up in this part of the country and wrote a book, *Exils Normands*, about the camps in Normandy, including Lisieux. He was the ideal guide for our visit, knowing more than perhaps anyone about this camp and its place in the context of the French internment camp system.

Thierry showing us where the former Lisieux camp stood, 2017.

The camp was built in what was once a textile factory; today, all that remains is a small piece of the façade. As we stood there, Thierry pulled out his book to show us old photographs and postcards of the buildings in this area, including the one used for the detainees. He explained that the unheated building where the prisoners were held sat adjacent to a rail line, surrounded by other small factories in a low-lying, damp, and impoverished part of town.

The area had hardly changed. As we walked around the neighborhood, we saw dozens of brick buildings similar to the factories that once surrounded the prison. They date back at least a hundred years; some were well maintained but most were not. The authorities chose to put the refugees in this undesirable neighborhood because it was empty at night and busy only when nearby factories were up and running. This kept the prisoners largely out of sight of the town's middle-class population. As we walked around, I noticed how narrow the streets were and how the buildings were crammed shoulder to shoulder. The factory workers must have been aware of the prisoners and the conditions in which they were being held. Like so many civilians in times of war, the workers in town were faced with human rights violations they either had to ignore or justify. The moral and emotional cost to the detainees and to those who bore witness without protest is an invisible and persistent price exacted by war.

The transition from La Ricoquette—the warmth of our hosts, the beauty of the house, and the sense of Max and Erna's lingering presence—to the misery and loneliness of Lisieux was painful. This juxtaposition underscored the shock Max experienced: All summer, he had been living happily in La Ricoquette, sure that he had been right to remain in France, and just a few weeks later, he was thrust into this humiliating and frightening environment.

It was difficult for me to reconcile the uncle I knew—the *bon vivant* who embraced life and its many pleasures—with this dark part of his past. Had it not been for the letters he wrote during this time, I never would have known anything of what he experienced. But now I viewed Max through new eyes. I saw traces of the trauma I had observed as a child but not understood.

Perhaps the rupture that so many members of my family experienced—from a baseline of security and comfort to the discovery that life is unpredictable and the unthinkable is possible—explains the pervasive, low-level anxiety that ran like an electrical current under the surface of that generation. It was an unconscious warning system that never quite left them, even while life was good. They were always a bit on guard, ever alert to possible danger and prepared to leap so that no one in our family would ever experience that trauma again.

During Max's early days at Lisieux, he was calm and optimistic. He was certain the French would release him and his fellow refugees quickly. Erna was able to visit on each of the first three days he was in detention and reported that he was "very well lodged in a hotel and waiting for a commission that was to decide his future fate." Then, four days after Max was interned, on September 9, the wives of the detainees were expelled from the region. Erna explained that it was "understandable because Calvados is considered a military zone." Perhaps she truly was that philosophical; perhaps she was trying to convince Bruno and Suse, and more importantly herself, that the expulsion did not bode ill for Max.

Meanwhile, Flora was alone in Vichy, where Max had insisted she go for her safety. She was suffering extreme consternation at the thought of Max's internment and Bruno being so far away. "My heart is bleeding, my brain is

My aunt Erna, c. 1939.

parched," she wrote, "On Rosh Hashanah, I will have to forget, how can I bear that? Do you remember how the six of us were together last year, did we know how fortunate we were?"

Erna soon joined her in Vichy and took charge. Right away, she wrote a letter to Bruno and described the situation:

> I did not find Mother in good condition. She worries about a lot: mainly about Max, then about you not being here or her not being with you, and then money. . . . I will support Mother with all my strength, with all my love, once she lives here [in the same boarding house]. I will be with her a lot and try everything to help her become a bit more collected and calm. I expressly promise you this, don't let it trouble you. After all, you also know me from other situations and you know that you and Mackie and Mother can rely on me.

More bad news followed. In that same letter, Erna told Bruno that after arriving in Vichy, she had learned that Max was transferred. "However, I have heard that in the meantime he has gotten away from there [Lisieux], nobody knows where to," she wrote, "About myself I probably don't have to write, I'm sure the two of you will know anyway what kind of state I'm in. I am trying to work, to pull myself together, just not to cry, and sometimes I succeed."

Max had been moved to the nearby town of Falaise. Together with Hans Schwab and 300 other men, he was crowded into a former prison constructed in the late eighteenth century, intended for just 100 people. Conditions were much worse than in Lisieux. The camp was a dismal, humid, and dark place where detainees shared just one bathroom and slept on damp straw scattered on bunk beds. Although Max wrote almost nothing about the terrible living conditions—surely in an effort to spare his family additional worries—the experience traumatized him for life.

The poet Walter Mehring, incarcerated at Falaise at the same time as Max, wrote about the experience in "Brief aus der Mitternacht V," opening with a lament about the miserable circumstances:

No day . . . no night . . . no sense of plan or place.
We are three hundred . . . I am only space.
We munch on swampy pasture through the day . . .
And find repose on rotted heaps of hay . . .

Mehring's poem reflects the emotional pain of interrogations and the helplessness of being reduced to a datum on a piece of paper.

What thoughts I own, the lines I write to you;
Am I myself, or on some masquerade . . .
The snooping guards keep at the prying trade.
While we, all mummied by the scarlet tape,
Pose before their questionings and gape.
. . . .
They stamp; they seal; they scratch a scribbled scrawl
. . . They fester and increase behind each wall . . .
And every house becomes a breeding place.
To these each of us becomes a case
For their officious games. You register . . .
This paper is your life . . . this stamp a slur
Against all dignity . . . this print reviles—
While Mankind disappears within their files . . .

Erna focused her attention on getting Max out of detention and trying to keep Flora from having a breakdown. The French government was not only imprisoning Germans and Austrians as enemy aliens; it was also freezing their possessions and bank accounts, effectively impoverishing them. Flora wrote to Bruno that, "Moreover, apparently all assets *des Allemands* [of Germans] have been seized, so that I cannot dispose of my assets. . . . I tremble at the thought of what else will be destroyed in the future." Flora's concern about money worsened as the weeks continued. She looked for cheap rooms with a kitchen so she could cook meals for herself and Georg, fretting about continuing to pay for both the Paris apartment and lodgings in Vichy.

Although France and England were at war with Germany and the Soviet Union, open hostilities had not yet begun on French soil or anywhere else in Western Europe. In France this phase of the war was known as the *Drôle de guerre* and in England as the Phoney War. Churchill called it the "Twilight War," and the Germans mockingly dubbed it "Sitzkrieg" (the opposite of blitzkrieg). It felt as though the continent was holding its breath, knowing it was only a matter of time before the fighting would begin. But as long as military action did not come to France, there remained the hope of getting to safety somewhere outside Europe.

Ten days after Max was moved to Falaise, Erna and Flora heard from him. He did his best to put on a brave face. "As you can see from this letter, I'm trying to make the best of the situation," Max wrote. "I insist, please, do not lose courage. Keep faith in God, who will help us survive this terrible separation. I constantly think about you. Dear Maman, don't worry yourself sick. I'm better off than a million other Europeans."

Erna redoubled her efforts to get him released. "I am doing everything I can to free him," she wrote to Bruno. "I've written about 20 letters; for example I asked Roche [pharmaceutical company] to request he becomes their representative. Is there a possibility you could do the same? . . . I just requested a *sauf-conduit* [safe travel pass] to go to Paris, where I want to speak with several people. . . . Let's hope one of these things is successful."

Max settled into life in the camp, and his letters reveal that he got a job working with the camp administration. This gave him a sense of purpose and focus. It also put him in favor with the guards and gave him daily access to a typewriter. He found comfort in being with Hans Schwab and other friends, and occasionally experienced a true reprieve, such as when he was allowed to take a walk in the countryside. One letter describes the profound pleasure he took in this: "Normandy is the most beautiful place one can ever imagine. It's unbelievable how much beauty there is in the coasts of Bénerville or Houlgate alone. After this incredible walk, my mood had changed completely. I am glad that we'll get to do it again this afternoon. I am telling you this so you can feel my happiness the same way you feel my depressions, which are becoming rarer. I am doing well and I have great friends, and I must say that life here is never monotonous."

In his letters, Max's moods shifted constantly from optimistic, calm, and philosophical to depressed, frustrated, and desperate. Still, he was full of awe and gratitude for Erna and her efforts to help him. "The greatness of your soul is extraordinary," he wrote her. At the same time, he also grasped for remnants of control over his situation, sometimes brusquely conveying directions that sounded like orders. His sense of helplessness spilled onto the pages, adding pressures on a woman who already felt them acutely. "I am going to end this letter because I have nothing else to tell you," he wrote in late October. "Do everything you can, and do it fast, fast."

Erna employed every ounce of her abilities to calm him, provide him with everything he needed, write to him every day as he asked, manage Flora, field suggestions from Georg, keep Bruno and Suse informed, and above all, continue to goad and entreat anyone who might be able to get Max out of the camp. She wrote to Bruno and Suse:

> As you do not read all his letters, you obviously can't picture him and the state he is in. Of course, his reports vary, which is not surprising, sometimes they are optimistic, sometimes they are dejected, but—and this makes me particularly glad—he is inwardly very strong, he is not desperate but more or less accepts things as they are. He experiences crises, he protests, his confidence in people has surely suffered a hard blow, but he writes: life, which nevertheless is beautiful, the world, which nevertheless is beautiful. I know that this time will not pass without leaving its mark on him, it has already changed him. I aim to uplift him, to tell, or rather, write him encouraging words, to assure him that I am doing everything for him, to calm him. I think it helps him. I exert all my influence so that he won't become sick at heart, not embittered and not disillusioned. That would be terrible for him. For me there is only one task, to bridge this time for him and for me and for the business, to prepare myself for him and for our new joint life that we will

> hopefully be able to begin soon. I don't have to tell you, I'm sure you know that I am not always as well as it may seem from the outside. I have to keep discipline, I have to economize with my nerves since I need them for Mackie now, for the business, for the letters to him and for him when he returns.

Max underwent a striking metamorphosis over the course of this correspondence as his easygoing, self-confident nature gave way to a far more sober and vulnerable persona. In one letter, he tried to articulate his new philosophy: "After these new lessons which life provides, I have completely changed my perspective on all the problems. I am in good health, my nerves are in excellent shape, I am not anxious. I have all the courage and cool judgment I need. I lack nothing. Nothing. I have the best comrades, which makes it easy to endure this existence. Not for a moment do I complain about my situation. It is not my focus and is not relevant."

As the months wore on, however, the simmering tensions between Bruno and Max exploded. It seems my father was writing cheerful, optimistic letters, trying to keep Max's spirits up and sharing news of life in New York as a form of distraction and perhaps an attempt to give him hope for the future. Max, in his state of disquietude and suffering, was deeply offended, even enraged, by these letters. "Bruno's letters make me ill, and he should be aware of that," he wrote to Erna in late October. Both Georg and Erna tried to explain, gently, to Bruno why his letters were having the opposite reaction than he intended. Georg wrote, "Naturally, Max's mood changes according to the prospects, sometimes he is hopeful, sometimes he is desperate, one can really understand it. Nobody is suffering, these are not German concentration camps, but the separation as such, the impossibility of free movement and the possibility of a longer duration, are discouraging often enough. Hence a request that will seem quite strange to you. Do not write overly optimistic letters. We are, of course, delighted when you are well and don't begrudge you anything, but we pass on your letters, and then the reaction is quite different."

As November arrived and Max saw no indication of impending release, he vented all his frustration and helplessness on Bruno. He surely resented that Bruno had been correct to leave for America and regretted his own choice not to emigrate at the same time. Instead of blaming himself, he turned his fury on Bruno, questioning whether his brother was doing enough to help him and attacking Bruno for thinking about business while Max was in trouble. He vented his feelings in a letter to Erna:

> What continues to be a great letdown for me as well as for Hans Ludwig [Schwab] are the very superficial letters from Bruno. He tells us stories about his business with a lot of details; you can tell that he is entirely preoccupied with such matters and that he has no idea of what's really going on. I could cry about that. The letter he wrote to the American Consulate in Paris is so weak that success is impossible. Why didn't he send a telegram? Why didn't he contact the French Consulate in New York? He asks what he can do for me? A lot, certainly a lot! But how can I advise him from here? If he was really obsessed with the idea of helping me, he would find a way; at least he would try the possible as well as the impossible.

In one particularly aggressive missive, Max turned his fury on Bruno himself:

> You are content knowing I'm in a concentration camp and it calms you, that's the most absurd thing, and it causes me great bitterness. For my birthday I received a telegram from Lily in India! Nothing from you. That too was a great letdown. But let's not dwell on that. It may well be that our current situation has hardened us. . . . I'm afraid that you will become an American businessman 100 percent while we will always be better at distinguishing what's important in this life from what isn't. . . . And I'll end with the following rumination: You were able to save yourself in America under the pretext that you could do more and better for your mother and your brother if you were out of this country. The outcome: You do nothing except worry, whenever you're not preoccupied with your business.

Years later, reading this letter, I can imagine my father's hurt and anger after all he had done to try to help Max. I can see him taking a deep breath, fighting the urge to fire off a reply to his brother—at least this time.

In mid-November, Erna was able, at long last, to visit Max in Falaise. He took great comfort in seeing her, and they were able to strategize about his situation. Until this time, the focus had been on getting him released from internment, but after Erna's visit, they shifted their attention to emigration. Erna understood that, whatever hesitations Max might continue to express, the only viable way to get him out of the camp was to secure a visa to leave Europe. "In case my current efforts should remain unsuccessful," she told

Flora, "we have decided that I should try to obtain some kind of visa, no matter for what country, in order to 1) get him out this way and 2) get away. This decision is the positive outcome of our having been together."

Erna leaned heavily on Bruno for help:

> All of us, and that includes you, Bruno, should have just one goal: that's Mackie. You must absolutely do everything possible and impossible to obtain a visa for him. That's what matters most. I don't know how, but you must do it and you will find a way. . . . Can you work on getting, or find out how to get, a visa for Mexico or Cuba? You must immediately get everything together so that you can provide an affidavit. If I need it I will send you a telegram; at that time it must be sent immediately. But not in advance.

All the while the financial strain grew worse. The family's apartments, belongings, and bank accounts were sequestered by the French government. The court-appointed bailiff hastened to create an inventory of the family's assets. On the list was Max's beloved Eibach grand piano, the value of which was about a third of their total assets. Erna had astutely removed small valuables and jewelry from their Paris apartment, probably hiding them in Vichy. Even so, the bailiff, like so many opportunists of this period, was quick to act in his own financial interest; when he discovered the brothers owned several firms, he tried to seize them and expand his role and remuneration.

Early in December 1939, Max, Hans, and the rest of internees were transferred back to Lisieux. Then, just days later, Max was released. No one quite knows why or how. What I do know is that Max was reunited with Erna, and then, one week later, they went to Vichy to see Flora and Georg. "It is pleasantly calm in Vichy," he reported to Bruno, "after a very emotional week in Paris, I've regained in Vichy my critical thinking more than ever, I am starting to sleep well and to be relaxed. But when I receive unhappy letters like the one today from our dear Schwab, who suffers tremendously from his unfortunate situation, I fall back into a depressed state. There is so, so much to be done."

The family immediately increased its efforts to get Max and Erna out of Europe. The letters are filled with details about every possible avenue—countries, paperwork, strategies, false starts, blind alleys, disappointments, and new approaches. Each country had its rules and restrictions, its requirements for visas and affidavits to guarantee that new arrivals had someone to support them so that they would not become a public charge. There were endless other hoops to jump through. No two countries' demands were the same. Regulations changed constantly, and officials often didn't know the latest rules. The émigré community added to the confusion by passing information—usually rumors, sometimes out-of-date, sometimes flat-out wrong—through their own networks.

The strain of navigating this labyrinth—in which nothing was certain and the obstacles were constantly changing—was tremendous. There was no way to know when the war would come to French soil. Max and Erna panicked that when hostilities broke out, Max would be interned again. Erna knew he would not survive that.[1]

The main hope was that Bruno, by setting up business opportunities for his brother in the United States to show he would be financially secure, could help Max get an American visa. To this end, Bruno collected letters of recommendation—such as one from their Uncle Meyer (Flora's brother) to attest to Max's reliable character—and set up bank accounts for Max to prove his financial independence. Erna had applied under the Russian quota but delayed going for her interview, because once the visa was granted, she would have a limited window of time in which to use it. If Max did not get his papers in time, she would have no choice but to leave Europe without him. As the pressure rose, even Flora lashed out at Bruno, accusing him of not doing enough to help. "You have no idea how *schwer lev* [heavy our hearts are] and how much we suffer here from the pressure, otherwise you would no longer be able to sleep and eat peacefully there."

Perhaps Bruno was not expressing well enough his concern for them and the efforts he was making, leaving them to imagine that he was blithely enjoying his life in America with no care for them. But Bruno, too, was facing changing regulations and limited options. It's clear how little my father could do in view of the United States' failure to provide sufficient visas for desperate refugees. Adding to the friction was the fact that letters took weeks to arrive, during which time circumstances could have entirely changed. Misunderstandings and frustration inevitably followed.

Another explosive exchange between the brothers occurred in December 1939. Max and Erna were in the midst of doing everything they could to arrange for their emigration and leaning heavily on Bruno to help them. They were also furious at Bruno because his lawsuit against Guenel meant that the sequester of Max's funds would not be lifted. They probably expected

Bruno to make things right by ensuring their financial security from his seemingly comfortable situation in America.

A letter from Max appears to be in response to a strategy Bruno suggested for emigration. After a patronizing explanation of why all of Bruno's suggestions were impractical and foolish, Max sniped at Bruno for not sending enough money. "As long as I don't have meaningful offers from someone else willing to pay the expenses, I will not be able to seriously consider it," he wrote. He then shifted gears to a damning accusation of Bruno's treatment of their mother:

> It's laughable that you write Maman that she shouldn't worry, that life here is so cheap, that she should go to the movies, that she should have all the fun in the world. Meanwhile you do nothing at all to help her live more comfortably. Not one franc, not a cent from you. . . . You have spent the last 4 months establishing your business. You've done well. But it's always like that: While I suffer difficult times and material losses, you have the luxury of working calmly. . . . You always made me promise to help my family first and only later to help others. I ask you: have you done enough for your family? And what is the amount you have spent for others in the last 6 months? I don't want to do an accounting, but I'm certain that the balance is significantly in my favor. . . . I feel I'm not just your older brother, but also wiser and more philosophical than you.

In fact, Bruno had been sending money to Flora as well as to Max and Erna. It was outrageous for Max to claim that his brother was living a life of ease and comfort while failing to provide for his loved ones. Bruno's response—the only surviving letter from Bruno during this period—seems entirely justified. He had clearly had enough:

> Mein lieber Bruder [My dear brother],
>
> I did not reply to your Nov. 9 letter from the camp any sooner because I felt so sorry for you. When this letter arrives, you will have been free again for three weeks and hopefully appreciate what I have to tell you. When I read your letters, I really have to think of Werfel's book about the mountain of Musa Dagh. But every time something goes wrong, when things go badly, you act up, you pounce on me, berate and insult me to your heart's content. Perhaps I will address details later. It's unbearable. This is an attitude you had towards me already as a child. I suffered from it already at that time, and perhaps it also

burdened our childhood and boyhood relationship. I cannot and will not play along with it and I ask you, if G-d forbid, difficulties arise again, you will confer or deliberate with me, or help, and I promise that I'll welcome any advice without griping and willingly be influenced by it.

How you were grandstanding in April in the Guenel lawsuit, which hit me especially hard! To use your words, you had neither head space nor time for it, the matter was none of your concern.

And now accusations after accusations, because I tried to write optimistic letters and tried but did not manage to liberate you. Tell me, did any one of the thousands here who had loved ones in the same situation achieve anything from here? No excuses, perhaps I am or was doing worse than you know. Did you really have to write me that I *sauvé* [escaped] to here under the pretext of helping you? You insisted that we leave. Since April, I constantly projected pessimism in my letters, I kept pestering you to go to Chile, Ecuador etc. In May, you were working on a N.Y. branch, visitor's visa etc., you had the possibility of getting a visa for Switzerland, Holland. Ernestos' employee went to Spain last week. Unfortunately, you did not manage to do that.—

How could you feel I was "*content*" to know you were in the camp? I really feel sorry for you. You should just realize that much of what happened here to help you did not happen on its own, but more about that another time.

Birthday. The telegram was written. After lengthy deliberation I refrained from sending it and perhaps spare you aggravation. You are mocking the *histoires de mon petit commerce* [stories about my little business]. Didn't you yourself write not too long ago that you have to work because of your obligations and the future? Unfortunately, you are in a mess and have your *considérations* [concerns]. I am 3000 miles away and have my own. Which ones are right?—

And now for your letter from last week . . .

Enough for today. Stay well, Max. If only you were here already!

Most warmly yours

These letters reveal how Bruno and Max reacted to each other from within their own confusing, ever-changing, emotionally fraught landscapes. Neither was right and neither was wrong. And yet, as decades of family dynamics played out against the backdrop of life and death, old patterns arose and reformed. Max saw his little brother as self-absorbed, obsessed with business and money, unable to conjure the necessary compassion to understand his suffering and act on his behalf. Bruno saw his big brother as patronizing, moody, irresponsible, and unfair. Each was hurt by the other.

It is a measure of the brothers' extraordinary relationship that they recovered so fully from such heated and angry words. "I always love you very much," Max wrote in December, "and evidently this may be the reason for all arising problems. . . . I am quite sure to have a perfect understanding with you as soon as we see us [each other] and speak friendly, honestly, and truly together."[2]

As time passed, the likelihood of Max getting a U.S. visa in time to sail directly for the United States dwindled. He began looking into transit visas, perhaps to Mexico, Venezuela, Argentina, Panama, or Cuba. Even so, he remained picky about his options, writing, "Venezuela: No. I don't want that, it is not a country. We must try to find something better." He feared the unknown, worried that he would not be able to work, and most of all, panicked about being separated from Erna. She wrote a frank letter to Bruno:

> You know him, as I do, well enough to be aware that everything comes to him more easily when he is pushed; and I ask you sincerely to help me push him and present him with a done deal—I can understand him so well; if he went to New York immediately and could stay there, he would leave tomorrow. But he is worried about a long stay in a transit country, from where he could not do anything, would have to interrupt his work for an indeterminate amount of time and then start all over again. . . . Brother, we must help him and handle this for him.

All the while, Flora was having her own problems in Vichy. She had developed glaucoma, which required repeated travel to Paris for treatment. And she had become so panicked about her finances that she was rationing food and refusing to throw out items that were no longer edible. (Her housekeeper became violently ill from eating a sausage Flora should have thrown away.) Flora's behavior compromised her own health as well; Max complained to Bruno that "Mother, due to her nonsensical and not in any way justifiable frugality, was completely inappropriately nourished and because of this had a blood pressure of 220, which was life-threatening."

When Flora found out about Max's letter, she wrote to Bruno defending herself: "As my dear Maxel told me, he scolded me a lot in his last letter and complained about how hard he has it with his old mother, who is dying of starvation out of stinginess, I know you will not be so foolish to believe it. . . . They don't know how insulting and devaluing it is to be treated as senile and childish."

In mid-April, Max was finally able to get a tourist visa for Cuba. It was not his ideal destination, but he took it. "Situation report;" Max wrote to Bruno, "Probably—hopefully—this is the next-to-last letter from Europe. It was impossible to get a risk-free transit visa for the U.S. for me.... We will now take the French ship to Porto Prince (or something like that) in Haiti around the 30th of this month and fly from there on a plane to Havana within a few hours."

Max and Erna originally planned to leave at the end of May, but Erna's visa required her to arrive in the United States by June 15. That became the driving force that sped up their departure since Max did not want to go to Cuba by himself. He hoped he could secure a U.S. visa at the American consulate in Havana before Erna's departure for America.

Max and Erna knew that Cuba was their best opportunity, and they had to take it, despite having to leave France with so many things unresolved: Flora was lying in a dark room in Paris recovering from a glaucoma operation; the family's possessions and bank accounts were still sequestered; and Hans Schwab, who had finally been released from Lisieux, was financially strapped and desperately trying to emigrate.

Max and Erna boarded a cargo ship, the *De la Salle*, in Le Havre on April 30 and set sail for Port-au-Prince, Haiti. They were enormously lucky they left when they did. Ten days later, on May 10, 1940, Germany invaded Belgium, France, Luxemburg, and Holland. France rapidly fell into German hands; the Wehrmacht marched triumphantly into Paris on June 14. If they had still been in Europe, their plans to emigrate would have been stymied, possibly permanently.

From the Splendid Hôtel in Port-au-Prince Max, wrote:

> As you know, we escaped this European shit as if by a miracle. The initiative for all this was with Erna, but I didn't oppose. We had to leave everything behind as it was, but that's totally irrelevant. Just imagine how lucky we are. Only 24 hours ago, everything hung by a thread because they didn't want to let us disembark here. Dear people, we have gone through a lot since September 1. But I realize I'm a real *Stehaufmännchen* [a round-bottomed toy that always rights itself when pushed over], on the first day of freedom I already feel like a new man, but the tropical heat paralyzes everything. Even though I'm sitting at the typewriter naked like a poodle, the sweat is running down my body.—If only we had the Elders [Georg and Flora] out. Are there even going to be any

ships from France to the U.S. in the foreseeable future? Almost inconceivable. We keep thinking ours was the last. It was not a comfortable crossing, we often suffered a lot. All told, the French were relatively pleasant, from their side, there was no problem leaving. But when I think of the many poor friends who are still there—oh dear God. Hopefully we will see you soon.

8

"The End of Everything"

Just as Max and Erna slipped out of Europe, my Aunt Lilo's troubles were just beginning. Throughout the late 1930s, as measures against Jews escalated, Lilo's family, like Bruno's, had scrambled to escape Europe. Even so, Lilo remained confident about her own safety. Though she applied for a visa in early 1939, it was pro forma. She had no real desire to leave Europe, and she was convinced that she'd be protected by her Dutch citizenship (by virtue of her marriage to Jessiah), Holland's history of neutrality, and the fact that she was half Jewish.

In contrast, from the moment her parents, Georg and Margarete, arrived in Holland, they began trying to leave for America. Adding to their stress, they were forced to move frequently: They left their first apartment on Wodanstraat within a few months to live in cramped quarters ("only a dollhouse," Margarete described it) with Lilo, Ellien, and Clara, a young half-Jewish refugee Lilo had employed. They relocated again to another modest apartment that at least had a small garden where they could sit, read, and write.

In part, to help Bruno start his business in the States and to avoid obsessing about their emigration status, Georg did a little work contacting suppliers of coffee, cheese, sausages, and casein. "It is difficult to get anywhere with Dutch factories directly," Georg wrote in frustration, "since even our small suppliers are wary of the immigrants." Still, he managed to win over an exporter who had good connections and was willing to supply products.

Georg tried to keep busy and productive in other ways, entertaining himself with his beloved hobbies of stamp and coin collecting, which occasionally even provided a little extra income. "I don't like to hear moaning about times past," he wrote to Bruno. Likewise, Margarete, with help from Lilo, was putting her skills as a designer to good use, making dresses and skirts for clients in Amsterdam.

Lilo, meanwhile, found a little happiness for herself. In 1939, she met and fell in love with Hans Reiss, a Jewish doctor who had fled Berlin. They planned to marry. "Hans comes for dinner almost every evening," Lilo wrote happily to Bruno and Suse, "and afterwards we take a little walk or we all stay at home together. He also gets along very well with Puppi [Ellien]." The three of them made a cozy family in uncertain times.

Georg wasn't sure about Hans. He was divorced, and Georg wanted to ensure that his interest in Lilo was genuine, not motivated by her wealth through the Lissaur family. Even though Lilo had more than proved her

Hans Reiss, Ellien, and Lilo, Amsterdam, c. 1939.

competence in caring for both Ellien and Anneliese, her family didn't trust her to make good decisions. They saw her as naïve, lacking in judgment. Perhaps she was forever viewed as needing to be protected, in counterpoint to her more commanding, more forceful elder sister. When it came to her prospective new husband, Georg went so far as to investigate him, though he sensibly kept his inquiries a secret from his daughter.

Georg acknowledged that Lilo seemed lively and happy in her relationship, but he wrote to Bruno and Suse about his efforts to check on Hans. "Through Max we received your lines concerning Dr. R. [Reiss]. One can proceed only very cautiously in the matter, since Lott is very sensitive—even more so than in the past. . . . I actually would like it best to confront Dr. R. myself, but this too Lott will take badly if she is not present for it." But the family's worries were soon put aside. Georg's queries yielded information that Hans had been a well-respected doctor in Berlin with many patients who liked him, and, in his next letter, Georg described Hans as "a refined, educated person," which was high praise indeed.

On September 1, 1939, when Germany invaded Poland, Holland predictably declared its neutrality as it had in World War I. From their precarious position as refugees in wartime Europe, Georg and Margarete expressed relief that Suse and Bruno were safe in the States. "We often say that Bruno was right yet again—how fortunate that you are no longer in P. [Paris]," Margarete wrote, adding, "We are so glad that Bruno was smart again—in spite of his preference for the pretty country [France]!" At around the same time, though, Margarete wrote wistfully to Suse (affectionately known as *Wünz* or *Wünzli*, meaning "little one"): "Last year I was with you at this time—I so often think of the lovely late summer days at the Parc de Bagatelle & on the Champs-Élysées—remember, Wünzli?"

On November 1, Georg and Margarete had a meeting at the consulate in Rotterdam, but aware of the hurdles to immigration that the United States had put in place, they tried not to get their hopes up. A few days later, they were able to share the happy news that their visas had been conditionally approved; they were to receive them in December. "We were a bit surprised that things are about to go so quickly with the visa," Margarete wrote to Bruno and Suse, "but maybe it is good this way—one has to let oneself be swept along and hope that all will be well no matter what happens. And, of course, we will be very happy to find you standing at the pier in New York to meet us."

Before they could get their visas, though, they still had one major hurdle. They had to secure a letter of credit for $4,800 (about $111,000 today), issued by a U.S. bank, and present it to the U.S. Embassy in December. The U.S. government wanted assurances that immigrants to the country were financially secure and would not become a public charge. Many impoverished refugees were not able to meet the burden of this process.

It was enormously anxiety-provoking for Georg and Margarete to round up that much capital in a short time. They wrote to Bruno and Suse for help setting up the bank account, and Georg got to work acquiring the funds. On November 5, he wrote that he was waiting for some money to be freed up by the German Ministry of Finance after paying a "5 percent fee for Jews"—yet another example of the ruthless profiteering of the Nazi government.

As the weeks ticked by, and the stress mounted, Georg sent Bruno precise instructions: "It would be of great help to us if you would now open the letter of credit for us at your bank, since, as I said before, we have to present the confirming letter from the bank (in duplicate) in order to receive the visa in December. I am enclosing a signed letter for you to fill out and hand over to your bank: 'Request for an irrevocable letter of credit for $4,800, of which after our arrival in the U.S. $100 is to be paid out to us monthly.'" In the event that Georg and Margarete should fail to reach the United States, Georg asked Bruno to verify that he and Suse would be able to access the funds. Given all they had been through, Georg wanted to make sure their assets did not become a casualty of the impossibly complex and unpredictable emigration process.

By November 22, they had transferred funds twice, but they were still short of the necessary amount. It seemed impossible to get the full $4,800 before the end of January, past their important December 1 meeting. By the end of the month, Georg had sold whatever assets he could, including his prized U.S. dollar gold coins, to free up funds and create a paper trail to show how hard they were trying and how close they were to the sum they needed. They feared that if they didn't have the money and were forced to push back the date of their meeting, they might lose their place in line.

Georg and Margarete were especially concerned because the consul handling their case was known to be inflexible and a stickler for details. Like all such officials, he held absolute power over Georg and Margarete's future. Georg wrote, "I have been strongly advised against trying to request any change with the American consul; in most cases apparently the visas are delayed if unnecessary requests are made." Margarete echoed this fear in a letter of her own:

> Dear children, I also think that we should not complicate the matter with the letter of credit. Who knows what the consul in Rotterdam will do if it is not settled? He is a very correct gentleman; he will not say a word but simply defer one. Needless to say, it has occurred to us, too, what a shame it is that we will not be earning any interest on the money for four years, but this was the easiest way. After all, we don't intend to invest money in any business over there. Better to work a little bit, and for the most important things $100 a month will suffice.

In the end, the Ballins' December 1 appointment with the consul appears to have been postponed without any dire consequences. On December 27, 1939, Georg wrote to Bruno and Suse that the letter from the bank had at last arrived. Now, it was just a matter of waiting.

We now know that officials in the U.S. Department of State deliberately created bureaucratic obstacles for those trying to get to the United States. In addition, not only did the United States refuse to increase quotas but, year after year, it also failed to fill the quotas it had established. Hundreds of thousands of Jews who might have come to the States were instead ensnared by the paperwork, slowed down by red tape, rejected for lack of sufficient funds, or made to wait years for their quota numbers to come up.

By June 30, 1939, the waiting list for Germans and Austrians had swelled to 309,782 for a total of just 27,370 visas between the two countries. "From the old homeland, SOS calls are arriving from all sides, since the prospect was held out to deport all Jews to the area of Lublin," Georg wrote. "I wrote to them that Chile (possibly Uruguay) is the only country for which one can now get a visa here, for a lot of money." Georg and Margarete were concerned about Lilo, who was far behind them in the visa process. "Lilo is well," Georg wrote to Bruno and Suse, "but it will take a while with the visa for the U.S., since she has only been registered since the beginning of this year and does not have a number." They were understandably worried about leaving her behind. "It will be hard for us to leave Lott here," they wrote, "but she too will go sooner or later with her doctor, who would prefer to go to Chile." Hans preferred Chile because German physicians could practice in South America, whereas they were unable to practice medicine in the

States without additional licensing. And though Lilo wanted to avoid even a temporary separation from Hans, she did agree that if her U.S. visa number came up, she would go with Ellien to the States.

At last, on January 2, 1940, Georg and Margarete's visas were issued. Lilo remembered, "We had to go to Rotterdam—the American consulate was in Rotterdam—and they got their visa, and it was already difficult to get passage to America. And it was in convoys—a small Dutch ship [to Antwerp] that we could get tickets for them to go. . . . It was already kind of dangerous to leave, at that time because the war had started." On March 1, 1940, Georg and Margarete bade farewell to Lilo and Ellien, leaving from Antwerp on the ocean liner *Westernland*. Before Georg left, he wisely gave Lilo documents proving she was half Jewish—a move that would be extremely helpful to her in the coming years.

They arrived in New York on March 12 and stayed for a week or two before flying to Los Angeles to reunite with Ella, Walter, Anneliese, and Georg's brother Friede and his family. Meanwhile, in the year that Anneliese had been living in the United States, she had been busy shedding her past identity. She took her stepfather's surname and Americanized her first name, noting in her 1990 letter that she "became formally known then as Anna Lee Kutz," and she was "determined to be a 100 percent American."

Holiday greeting card, early 1940s.

After Georg and Margarete left, Lilo wrote to them that her life was continuing quietly and uneventfully. She told them about bike rides in the country and the English courses she and Hans were taking. She also said ruefully that, without Margarete, she was having trouble with the dressmaking business they had established together. She couldn't seem to make a particular kind of skirt properly; several customers had returned their purchases. She was sure her skilled mother could have solved the problem if only she were there to help.

Lilo hoped to follow her parents to the United States soon, but the quota filled up swiftly. Although she had Dutch citizenship by marriage, the quota was distributed by place of birth, so she had to apply as a German. "I think, the idea was that I would be in Holland as long as they all needed me," she said in her video testimony. "My sisters had to leave first, and my parents had to leave, and then I could start to see that I would get [a] visa, because I felt safe in Holland, traveling with my Dutch passport, and my Dutch flag." With a wistful laugh, she repeated, "I felt safe."

Lilo later recalled that Ellien, as a Dutch citizen, could have had her visa "in no time," and that she could have left with Bruno and Suse, or with Georg and Margarete. But as Lilo put it, "It never occurred to me to part from her." She was devoted to her daughter and wanted to stay with her at all costs.

> I didn't know that danger, I could not imagine. I didn't know—the pogroms were in Russia, in Poland. Nothing that happened in my lifetime—nothing like that could happen in my lifetime. It didn't occur to me that something like that could happen. Even after I saw what was going on in Germany, I didn't see enough of it, I think, to really get frightened enough to let her go. Maybe if I would have seen something like the *Kristallnacht* [*Reichspogromnacht*], or the Nazis picking up the men from the street, or anything like that. . . . In the first World War, nothing happened to the Dutch, so why would it be now?

On May 10, 1940, the first German planes were seen over the skies of Holland. "It was a holiday in Germany and in Holland," Lilo remembered, "and we had packed our little suitcase, my daughter and I, to go to the resort. And, in the morning we woke up, woken up by some strange noise, and we looked at the sky, and we saw the little white clouds in the sky. . . . The Dutch were trying to shoot down the German planes, so the German planes were over Amsterdam, and that was what woke us, and we knew the Germans had [invaded] Holland. And we had the feeling it's the end of everything."

From what we could tell from the documents, Jessiah seemed to be in Holland at the time of the invasion and fled to the United States, more or less disappearing from Lilo and Ellien's life. The reality, which became clear on one of our research trips, was more complicated. Regardless, Jessiah was gone and Lilo now had the sole responsibility of caring for Ellien.

Some Dutch people, especially Jews, grabbed what they could and fled to the port town of IJmuiden and tried to cross to England. "They never thought of needing a passport in an emergency like that," Lilo said, "they just took what they thought they could take with them and left for IJmuiden. . . . Many Jews did reach England, and many never did because the ships were not safe." It was a risky move that Lilo did not attempt. She figured that she and Ellien might have been able to escape, but Hans, who had a German passport, would be stopped at the border.

"It never occurred to us—and then when we heard the roads are all clogged up with cars, then I remember that I thought, 'Oh, this is what we should have done. We should have taken the car, drive away in the morning, and leave.'" Some responded to the chaos, uncertainty, and fear by jumping into action; others hesitated. Neither course of action guaranteed anything.

The Nazi invasion of France, Holland, Belgium, and Luxembourg was swift and total. Just three days after the German invasion, Queen Wilhelmina and the Dutch government fled to London; two days later, the Dutch armed forces surrendered. With the Netherlands securely in German hands, the occupiers abolished democracy, dissolved Parliament, and quickly appointed a Reich commissar to govern the Netherlands. Normal life would soon unravel.

During the early period of the occupation, Ellien attended the First Montessori School, a traditional brick structure still standing on the quiet, tree- and hedge-lined Corellistraat in Amsterdam. Kat and I visited Amsterdam in 2016. Arriving at the school late in the afternoon, we assumed it would be closed for the night but decided to take a chance. (I had already learned in the years of work on this project that when in doubt, grab hold of every thread and pull. It usually paid off in unexpected ways.)

As we walked toward the school, we saw children romping on the playground, but when we tried the door, it was locked. Moments later, a lady carrying bags of books shouldered the door open. I got to her just before the door closed. I told her that my cousin had been a student there during the war, and she kindly let us enter. She left us in charge of her bags as she went in search of a teacher who, she said, had researched the Jewish children who had attended the First Montessori. After she left, we glanced around. Above our heads in the entrance hall was a large plaque. There was Ellien's name, alongside those of 164 other Jewish children who had once run and laughed in these halls.

Soon we were standing with Ronald Sanders, a tall, slim teacher of about sixty who had discovered a notebook in the school's attic that listed its Jewish students. He had spent years documenting their lives and fates and had written a book about them, *In verband met de vermindering van het aantal kinderen* (Due to the reduction in the number of children). He handed me a copy. As I paged through his book, I noticed a reproduction of a handwritten note from a *Poesiealbum*, a sort of friendship book children frequently exchanged and in which they wrote verses to each other. The handwriting looked vaguely familiar. When I looked closely, I was shocked to see Ellien's signature. She had written the note to a friend named Betsy when they were just ten years old. It had survived. It was one of those serendipitous moments when answers to unanswerable questions seemed close enough to touch.

Kat told me later how relieved she was that her gamble of urging me on this trip had paid off. In her role as researcher, she had sensed that I would miss out by doing the work at arm's length from America. In order to fully find the meaning of the story, she believed that I needed to travel with her back to Europe. But it was a risk to push for such a thing—she had no way of knowing what we would find, what experiences we might have, and whether our relationship would thrive or suffer under the pressure of the trip. Here, on the very first day of our first trip, we had struck gold.

Thanks to Ronald, I was able to get in touch with Betsy van der Meer after we returned home. She sent me a wonderful photo from one of her friend's birthday parties, in which a group of girls stands in a line, hands on each other's shoulders. They are dressed alike, wearing short-sleeved day dresses, several with Peter Pan collars, with their hair plaited into tight braids or secured with large bows. There, second from the left, is Ellien, her eyes crinkled into half-moons, a wide smile illuminating her face, happy and at ease among her friends.

Ellien (*second from the left*) and Betsy (*far right*), at a friend's birthday party, c. 1941. (Courtesy of Betsy van der Meer.)

Kat and I met Betsy van der Meer and her daughter when we returned to Amsterdam in 2017. Though short in height and advanced in years, she was a commanding presence. She spoke some English but had lacked opportunities to practice, so she occasionally relied on her daughter to translate. I asked Betsy what the school was like when she attended. She reflected for a few moments and rather wistfully recalled all the children being quite friendly and supportive of one another. She remembered Ellien as quiet and shy, with a warm and inviting smile. She also told us that Ellien seemed to keep to herself after school; Betsy had the impression that she was not allowed to play in the street with the other children.

There was one detail that especially stayed with me: Betsy recalled that Ellien often tilted her head to the side when talking or listening, a gesture that hinted at her curious nature. After Betsy pointed it out, I began to see that little quirk everywhere in the family photos we had. We are all made up of little attributes and characteristics that are unique to us and so easily

Betsy sharing her photos and memories, 2017.

lost in the passage of time. My many years of work on my family's story had taught me that capturing even these seemingly insignificant details is a loving gesture, a way to hold on to the individual humanity of those who are no longer here. Even this most granular labor can be infused with purpose and meaning.

By 1941, it was more difficult for Lilo to stay in contact with the family in the States. She noted that she hadn't received a letter from Suse in months, while Suse said she was writing constantly but her letters were not getting to Lilo. From Lilo's letters, a few snapshots of their daily life survive. Lilo, Ellien, and Hans shared their apartment with their friends, Berthold and Manja, and found ways to keep occupied. "We always have a good time, though, the days fly by, we always have a lot to do and sometimes we all play a game in the evening with Ellien," Lilo wrote to her parents. "She now also has a lot of homework already, all three of us practice the piano, Manja, Ellien and I, but unfortunately we are not allowed to do so in the evenings when Berthold is here. We also still take that [English] course, Manja, Hans and I, and we also read a lot, I'm sure this way we'll pick up a little."

Lilo homeschooling Ellien on their balcony, c. 1941. (Courtesy of Emanuel Lissaur.)

In the same letter, Lilo expressed her delight that she and Ellien had received news of Anna Lee. "Annele has grown up so much, the picture is so cute. . . . Ellien was so excited when we got the picture, she didn't want to put it down again at first, her little cheeks all red, and studied it very intensely." Ellien added a short note to her grandparents and cousin in Dutch: "Dear all! I was very happy with the picture of Anna Lee. Did you have a good New Year? We did. Anna Lee please write again soon. Will you send another picture soon? Lots of greetings and kisses, Ellien." Ellien clearly missed her cousin and wanted to keep the strong, sisterly bond they had shared. But Anna Lee was reveling in being an American teenager and had put the past behind her. The war and her family's troubles in Europe must have seemed far away.

On January 10, 1941, the Nazis, laying plans for more sinister moves, issued an ordinance requiring Jews to register, imprinting a large "J" on their identity cards. According to Nazi law, Jews were defined as anyone with three or four Jewish grandparents. Lilo had two on her father's side and two non-Jewish grandparents on her mother's side. She was thus designated a

Mischling, a half Jew. In a gesture of solidarity—and not, of course, imagining the consequences—she chose to register as a Jew. "I felt if the Jews have to register," she said, "I will be a Jew and register—still not seeing the danger, still not grasping what it meant. I went there of my own will. I thought I had my honor instead of finally seeing what it meant."

The first consequences came swiftly. Lilo and Ellien were forced to stay close to home, avoiding the streets because Jews were being picked up more and more frequently and sent away to destinations unknown. In mid-February 1941, the Nazis established a Jewish council composed of community leaders in Amsterdam who served as liaisons between the Nazis and the Jewish population.[1] The Germans used this strategy in cities, towns, and eventually ghettoes all over Europe, convening Jewish leaders under the guise of providing structure and support but in reality using them to enact their increasingly sinister plans.

Lilo and other German Jews were among the first to receive cards telling them to present themselves for deportation to what they were told were labor camps. "They sent out cards to the German Jews," Lilo recalled, "You had to appear on that date, at 8:00 o'clock in the morning, at Centraal Station, and you are going to *Arbeitscamp* . . . labor camps . . . in Germany. . . . And I got that card too."

The summons meant parting from Ellien. While Lilo had registered herself as a Jew both as a reflection of her sense of identity and in solidarity with the Jewish people, she now had to rethink the wisdom of that decision. She quickly chose the practical tack to protect herself and Ellien, presenting herself to the German police and vehemently explaining that she was a half Jew:

> I went to the headquarters there, again, to that school, and I said, "I'm half-Jewish, why do I get that card to go—this was only for Jews?" And he said to me, "Considering that you are half-Jewish, you got a lot from the Jewish side," you know, kind of sarcastic. But they accepted that I was half-Jewish, and they took the card away from me, and I did not have to go that day. I lived in an apartment at that time in a neighborhood where a lot of the German immigrants had rented. They all went that day. Two families—I was on the first floor, and two families above me—took that card, took their rucksack, and went. . . . They probably took the tram to Centraal Station. That's probably what they did. With their rucksack, they went to Centraal Station, and were never heard of again.

In September 1941, Jewish children were expelled from school. Ellien's friend Betsy remembered the eerie experience. The First Montessori School headmaster sent a cryptic note to the parents, stating euphemistically that the decline in the number of students necessitated a short school closure.[2] When classes resumed, all of the Jewish children were gone. Betsy and others had a sense that the Nazis had ordered the removal of the Jewish children, but nobody at school explained what had happened to their friends and classmates. In addition to Ellien, Betsy remembered that her best friend, Margrit, a Jewish girl who was in the birthday party picture, had also disappeared.

Like all Jewish children across Holland, the school expulsion meant that Ellien was increasingly isolated—cut off from her friends, social activities, and sports. Her life was getting smaller by the day.[3] Likewise, Jews had been required to register their real estate with the authorities, and by May 1942, most Jewish property was subject to expropriation. They had been forced to deposit their money in specific banks under German control and were restricted in the frequency and size of the withdrawals they could make. In every country they invaded, the Nazis employed similar measures to control, limit, and impoverish the Jewish population.

The restrictions had a drastic effect on Jewish employment. Jews were pushed out of their jobs, Dutch employers were authorized to fire Jewish employees at will, and Jews were barred from certain professions. This meant that Hans was no longer allowed to practice medicine in Amsterdam. However, he continued to work as a doctor in the Jewish community, seeing and treating patients who were rarely able to pay him. Lilo explained, "He had some kind of little practice with German immigrants, like they would sell things, so he could be a doctor to the German immigrants, clandestine—not officially, he could not be a doctor. But German immigrants that didn't speak Dutch felt naturally much more secure with a German doctor than with a Dutch doctor."

That same month, Ellien and Lilo were required to join the Jewish population in wearing a yellow Star of David on their clothing so that they could be identified as Jews everywhere they went. Lilo again protested to the authorities. Again and again, she took risks and confronted danger to try to protect herself and Ellien:

> I went to the headquarters where the Germans had taken office. And, I tried to change my position so that I would be half-Jewish, without a star, instead of half-Jewish with a star. My father gave me, before he left, documents that

> showed that I had two non-Jewish grandparents. So I went there, and I showed them the papers, that I had two non-Jewish grandparents, and that was what counted: two grandparents not Jewish. But I had been married to a Jew, and I had been in the Jewish community, and I said, "Well, I left the Jewish community right away when I had my divorce," and tried to convince them . . . then, I finally had to understand that I had to fight for it, to be half-Jewish. So, I got through with it, and I could take the star off and I had no "J," in my identification. But almost every time I walked through the streets, some of the German Nazis came up and asked for my identification, because when they saw me, they thought, "Oh, there's a Jew with a false passport."

Unlike Lilo, Ellien was considered a full Jew. She had to wear the star and carry the identity card with the "J." Lilo agonized about her safety and mostly kept her hidden away in the apartment. "I hardly let my daughter

Ellien with her beloved bike, c. 1940. (Courtesy of Emanuel Lissaur.)

go on the street. . . . She stayed in the apartment. I did not want her to go on the street, without a star—certainly not go with a star."

All too soon, in June 1942, the Germans began confiscating the private property of Jews. For Ellien, being forced to turn in her bike was a terrible blow. There was already a residential curfew, and Jews were not permitted to ride on any form of public transport. The bike was her last link to freedom and independence. Lilo remembered the painful moment for Ellien when "she went crying to deliver her bike."

Lilo's in-laws, Emanuel and Engeltje Lissaur, were the first in the family to face deportation. They were arrested and taken to the Schouwburg Theater—the collection point for deportees from Amsterdam. All their belongings were taken, but Lilo was allowed to see them and bring them clothes. "I went a couple of times to bring things to them. . . . I remember one thing, my mother-in-law had such a red face that I thought she was having a stroke. And both were yelling."

Their protests were for naught. On May 25, 1943, the Lissaurs were deported to Westerbork, the transit camp where all Jews from Holland were gathered in advance of being sent eastward. That same day, they began the long, terrible trek to the death camp at Sobibor, where they were murdered on May 29, 1943, in a gas chamber.

9

"Caught in a Mousetrap on a Powder Keg"

In the early summer of 1940, Flora's husband Georg wrote to Bruno from Vichy and said that they were trying to emigrate to the Dominican Republic. "Here a monster rages with murder and death, but now they are beginning to answer in kind. There is only one prayer . . . France and England must win." Two days later he continued the letter, saying that tickets to the Dominican Republic required extensive additional paperwork. Their efforts were also hampered by the sequester, which had limited the couple's access to their own funds, so Georg asked Bruno to send money through Western Union, rather than the bank, to ensure that it reached them. By June 10, Flora and Georg had filed their applications for visas to the Dominican Republic, and Flora's letters to her sons were quite desperate. "My dear ones," she wrote, "thank you for your nurturing, kind words but almost everything is too hard for me, and only the thought that I will perhaps see you again one day sustains me. But there are many difficulties and we are old and worn out."

Flora had understandably been shaken when Bruno suddenly fled Frankfurt in April 1933. Then in July, her husband Georg had been arrested by the Gestapo. Upon his release, he and Flora left Germany for Belgium. A year later, after being denied permanent residency, they crossed into France, where they reunited in Paris with Bruno, Suse, Max, and Erna for a peaceful interlude from 1935 to 1939. When Bruno and Suse emigrated to the United States, Flora inevitably started leaning more on Max. Whereas Bruno had always treated her with respect and courtesy, Max regarded her as needy, venting his frustration by snapping impatiently at her. He seemed to forget how exceptionally well educated she was, and how, unlike him, she was fluent in English. At the same time, Max enjoyed his new position of authority vis-à-vis their mother, lording it over Bruno when it suited his purposes. He also occasionally dragged Flora into his conflicts with Bruno, venting his resentments and grievances to her.

All of this bears on Flora and Georg's story as they found themselves stranded in France in May 1940. Flora was an unusual amalgam of strength and vulnerability, marked by a childhood in which she lost both parents in succession and was separated from her younger brothers. These years were in many ways a re-enactment of that childhood: In the face of separation and instability, she found the internal strength to risk the unknown in hopes of a better future. At the same time, nearly every aspect of her ordeal triggered memories of her past. She worried about finances and about going hungry, and she depended on her sons not only for material and logistical help but for emotional support as well.

Max was enormously troubled by Flora's anxiety. He also seemed to forget having reproached his brother for not doing enough when he was interned and resented Flora's implication that they were not doing everything to help her. In one letter, Max snapped at Flora: "Bruno is doing absolutely everything he can to get you out. He torments his head and sleeps at night no more than you or we. Stop reproaching him time and again!" At the same time, Max hid from his mother how much he feared for her. He worried that even if Flora and Georg did secure a visa, passenger ships would before long be prevented from leaving Europe. He wrote to Bruno, "I am so utterly pessimistic now that I see absolutely no hope for how they will get out. There will be no more visa, no *visa de sortie* from France, no ship; it will all get much worse and we will have to watch everything helplessly."

As the months dragged on, Flora wondered why their U.S. quota number still hadn't come up. Sensing that something might be awry, Georg requested their dossier at the U.S. embassy, but it could not be located. Max tried to ease Flora's concerns, reassuring her that Georg was capable of managing the situation: "Let's not lose our nerve completely, dearest Mama.

Keep some insight & discipline & health. Accept events that none of us can change. You need only have one thought after all: to be reunited with us, more or less quickly, as quickly as possible. But to this end you must be healthy because all the tribulations that are still to come make it a prerequisite. . . . And above all, you must see that your good, best comrade, Georg, stays healthy and keeps his nerve."

By mid-June of 1940, Nazi Germany had defeated France, and on June 22, France signed an armistice that divided the country into two zones. The Germans occupied the north and west of the country, which, in addition to Paris, included the key port towns of Le Havre and Bordeaux, crucial sites of emigration. For the time being, they did not occupy the south, which included the port city of Marseille; instead, they installed a puppet regime headquartered in Vichy run by the World War I hero-turned-collaborationist, Marshal Pétain. Since Flora and Georg were in the unoccupied zone, it was theoretically possible for them to get a visa for the Dominican Republic. Still, Bruno noted in a letter that he and the lawyer helping him agreed that the prospects looked grim.

By late June, weeks had passed without a letter from Flora or Georg. Max and Bruno were extremely worried. "I'm sure we can't picture, with all our imagination, what the poor old folks have lived through in the meantime," Bruno wrote to Max. "My fear and my prayer is that the old folks can survive this."

On June 25, Bruno wrote, "No answer to my telegram to Vichy. I dreamt so horrendously last night that I'm completely beaten today. A thousand questions, a thousand question marks. I wonder how our Mama has endured these events that have flung us 3000 miles away." Four days after that, he wrote, "What Mama is going through must be indescribable. Will she survive? . . . I pray that our good old Mama, who has to suffer so much, will survive this, and I see bad news coming. . . . We have no choice but to wait and worry."

When Bruno finally received a letter from Flora and Georg in mid-July, he learned they had relocated to Saint-Laurent-de-Céris, near Bordeaux. At least there they could help Georg's daughter Lotte, who was left alone with her children when her husband traded internment in the Braconne camp for enlistment in the French Foreign Legion. Flora and Georg were also seeking respite from the endless waiting for visas in Vichy. By this time, the family no longer cared whether Flora and Georg's escape route was convenient, only that it got them out of Europe. Now the best option appeared to be Cuba, where Max and Erna had gone. Bruno wrote detailed instructions that provide a window into what lay ahead:

> I have therefore asked Max to immediately take all the necessary steps in Cuba so that you can go to Havana. [Santo] Domingo is not working out. Reasons immaterial and [can be discussed] another time. So you will get a summons from the Cuban consul, and a tourist visa like Max did at the time. The same very reliable man will take care of it and, don't worry, Max will be there, he won't give him a moment's peace to make sure it works out. Then your problem begins. You must manage to get a transit visa through Spain and/or Portugal. The shipping companies have an interest in ships being loaded, they will also advise or assist you in booking passage. For all these problems, I think it will be better for you to be in a port or larger city. In St. Laurent you cannot learn about the daily changes. I mean Marseille or Bordeaux, where apparently only the port is occupied. I'm sure you can find out more about it there. You just have to see to it that mail is forwarded.

At the same time, Bruno exhorted them to keep trying to get U.S. visas. "Also be insistent at the American consulate. In other countries, October 1938 is already being summoned [for their interview]. If affidavit not in order, telegraph. Yesterday, Susele's birthday, we drank a toast to you, next year we will celebrate together. . . . Max will be waiting for you in Cuba. I will also come there once you are happily on your way."

At the end of July, Erna—having become the family's emigration expert—wrote to Flora and Georg that since they had not responded to Bruno's query about picking up their Cuban visas in Bordeaux or Marseille, she had decided on Marseille. Max had already applied for the visas on their behalf, and Erna instructed them that they must leave as soon as the visas were issued. She also told them to go directly to the U.S. Consulate in Marseille when they arrived, to confirm that they were indeed registered. "I reiterate," she wrote, "neither the lack of a confirmation from the American consulate nor the lack of a certificate of good conduct must prevent you from leaving as quickly as possible and at the earliest opportunity. And don't be too concerned about your luggage. If it comes along, good. If not, too bad. You mustn't let this hold you back either."

Erna's letter outlined the process, the documents, and the officials they needed to contact in Marseille. The best option appeared to be the Spain-Portugal route. It was a daunting prospect. First they had to get a French exit visa, then Portuguese and Spanish transit visas, and finally a Cuban entrance visa. Paperwork in hand, they would have to walk the hazardous route over the Pyrenees Mountains from France, cross the border into Spain, take buses and trains to Lisbon, and finally sail from there to Cuba.

Flora and Georg were sixty-five and sixty-eight years old, respectively, and not physically fit. The whole venture seemed improbable, from getting the necessary visas, to gaining passage on a boat to Havana, to managing the journey itself. Still, Erna closed her letter with a little pep talk: "What matters most is that you get out as quickly as possible. How, and how much it costs, is not so important. The main thing is that it works. And that we'll all be together soon. How happy do you think Maxl will be when he can pick you up from the ship in Havana? Just always think of Bruno and Maxl, Mutterchen [mother dear], and you'll make it, no matter how hard it is. You are intelligent and smart and you know that it is the goal that counts and not the little things."

As the family was trying to help Flora and Georg, Max continued to experience his own challenges in Cuba. When he and Erna first arrived in April 1940, he was happy and relieved to have escaped Europe and even began taking in the pleasures of Havana. "We have been getting settled more and more, are getting to know the city and its simply magical surroundings and were invited on a car ride by our landlords yesterday," he wrote to Bruno in early June. But throughout the summer and fall, as he conducted his business from Havana, Max resumed his big-brother bossiness. Max not only piled business and familial tasks on Bruno, but also did so with imperiousness and insensitivity. In one letter, he wrote, "To this end, your help as an intelligent mail carrier is indispensable."

Things reached a head between the brothers later in July, when Max wrote impatiently, "I ask you to please answer my questions, to write us and forgive me for having to make demands on you. But it's not okay not to write at all for days on end and to make me wait for your answers. Pick up all of my most recent letters and you will be amazed how much has been left unanswered." Exhausted with Max's endless orders, Bruno put his foot down, demanding not only some appreciation but also some clarity as to the terms of the business relationship:

> As for your last paragraph, it's very nice of you to apologize for putting us to work like that. But that doesn't cut it. I don't know if you can appreciate how

> much time and expense is involved here in N.Y., no matter how small the task. I am not exaggerating when I tell you that we both often spend many hours and half days in the interest of your business. I do it gladly and would gladly continue to do so. I now have very high expenses here and should use all my time and strength to open up new opportunities for myself. More than anywhere else, this requires exclusive concentration here. However, I want to continue to protect your interests, but I find myself faced with the necessity of being compensated in some way for my expenses.

In August, Erna had to travel to the United States before her visa expired.[1] She could have gone to Miami, which was closer than New York, but presumably she wanted to be near Bruno and Suse. They could help if she ran into any issues. She was worried about Max—she knew he spiraled when he was alone, waiting for his quota number to come up. "But he is so sad that my heart aches," Erna wrote to Flora, "You know him. He knows everything, all the rational reasons, tells himself everything a zillion times, and yet . . . the thing is, one gets separated, quite senselessly . . . one doesn't know for how long."

Erna arrived in New York on August 9 to stay with Bruno and Suse. They hadn't seen each other for nearly eighteen months. The threesome immediately drove to Sea Gate, where Bruno and Suse had rented a lovely cottage near the ocean to escape the summer heat in the city. Erna wrote Flora a few days later to update her on everything, from Max's state of mind to Suse's injured finger: "Bruno looks as good as ever, if anything he has become a little slimmer," she commented. "Suse is also completely unchanged, she was dealing with her finger a lot and is still struggling with it. They are both very, very kind to me and we lead a very slow-paced life. . . . I pretend to work, that is, I really work a little, and hope that it will increase and that I will be able to help Mackie from here. Mackie—that is what I miss here. He is not doing very well, as I can tell from his letters."

Max's mood deteriorated as he remained in Cuba without Erna. He became, in his own words, "severely nervous, irritable and fatigued." Jealous of others in Cuba who were getting their U.S. visas before him, he lashed out about everything: the many holidays in Cuba that delayed the mail, the sluggish pace of the consulate, the conduct of his own family—whom he accused of giving bad advice. He even complained that Erna would have been more help to him had she stayed in Cuba, conveniently ignoring the fact that she had to go to the United States for the sake of her own immigration paperwork. Max ranted to all of them: "*Eitzes* [advice]: I resent it when someone gives me this. As if I weren't able to give it all to myself, as if I weren't intelligent enough."

Although Max found company among the Jewish refugees in Havana, attending services and playing Stravinsky on the piano with a Hungarian Jewish doctor, he was worn down by the stress of arranging Flora and Georg's emigration to Cuba and managing his business from afar. In a fit of pique because a business transaction had gone awry, he lashed out at Erna: "Then you, Erna, can write private letters to me from 16 W 68 and drink cognac, and you, Bruno, can go to the brothel, if Suse allows it. But you will have nothing more to do with my business. You won't hear anything more about it. I'll arrange things for myself, it's easily done. Now, at 7:30, you haven't even cabled an answer yet. I know what to think about it."

Luckily for Max, Erna retained her sense of humor and knew how to gently tease and calm him. "So, dear Max, we received your letter. I would never dare to laugh out loud and certainly not to tell you about it, but inside I kept having to smile at your outburst, which admittedly is completely justified, including the anger, everything, but still very funny with all the true Scheidtian expressions and turns of phrase."

In October 1940, Flora and Georg relocated to the outskirts of Marseille, beginning an even more anxiety-provoking period as they traversed a city filled to the brim with frantic refugees, all trying desperately to get out of Europe before it was too late.[2] By this time, Max had learned that the plans for Flora and Georg's Cuban visas had failed, writing, "I will spare you the details. They are unreliable here, they don't keep any promises, they put you off from one day to the next, they make you wait in despair for days on end, and these two weeks are a wild chase for me, agonizing waiting, et cetera."

Bruno had discovered why Flora and Georg were having problems with the U.S. visa. Apparently their registration had never been completed; Georg was supposed to sign a specific book at the American consulate in Paris and he had not. Max quickly blamed Georg for the mistake. "I am unfortunately terribly skeptical in relation to old Georg," he wrote to Bruno, Suse, and Erna in New York. "Might anything have been omitted during registration? Did they perhaps not sign in the book there? A grievous matter and hard to think through to the end." Georg insisted that he had not been told to sign anything and that the mistake was on the part of the officials at the consulate. He was livid and wrote to HICEM, the Jewish aid organization for European refugees:

> Towards the beginning of October 1938 I was personally at the American Consulate in Paris, having previously filled out the forms at home. There a lady took both registrations—for me and my wife—from me. Not a word about the existence of a book, not a word about having to register. And so I went home in good faith that the registration was done and also told my family about the procedure.... In the meantime I repeatedly inquired in writing in Paris and later in Bordeaux when it will be our turn.... I never received an answer, which I attributed to the excessive amount of work and inquiries, otherwise they would have had to reply: But you are not registered at all. Now, after having heard that acquaintances who were registered later than we have already received their summons, we hear in response: You did not enter your names in the book in Paris, the dossier cannot be found, enter your names again.

Beginning again would be catastrophic. It could mean a wait of two years or more. With roundups increasing throughout France, only those who were far enough along in the emigration pipeline could hope to get out in time. For this reason, Georg continued to insist that he had not been the one to make the mistake. Armed with the conviction of his own rightness, he took charge of the situation, determined to fight until his last breath for the rectification of this injustice.

Daily life during the Marseille winter was miserable. It was brutally cold, and Georg and Flora were snowed in. The streetcars were not running, which meant they could not get to the city center. Newspaper and mail delivery were suspended. They barely had enough heat to avoid freezing to death, and food was growing scarce. Georg had also had enough of Max's know-it-all advice and lost his patience in a letter at the end of December:

> And now, first of all, a small speech to you, my dear Max: If everything had been known that is known today, then none of us would have gone to France at all, but we would have chosen America already at that time, and if you want to speak of clairvoyance or similar nonsense, I permit myself to remind you politely as well as modestly that I gave the signal for withdrawal [from Germany] long, long before the birth of the Third Reich.... Therefore, even if well-meant, one cannot fault me or us for having misjudged the situation or for having neglected something.

One bit of brightness lit the gloom: Erna was able to return to Cuba in time for Max's birthday. On October 24, 1940, in the middle of Max's birthday party, he got the gift he had been dreaming of: a visa for the United States. Erna wrote excitedly to the family in New York:

> Our dearest brother and dear Suse, so finally some news, and it's good news to boot: You can't imagine the type of birthday present Kater received. . . . Everything was very nice and festive, when Mackie was suddenly called away from dinner by a phone call; very indignant about this disturbance, he suddenly learned that apparently a list was published at the consulate, according to which everyone who was registered by July 12, 1938 would get their turn! . . . I have no real recollections of the turkey, or the ice cream, or Mr. Schönfeldt, that's how excited we were, and Mackie had to eat double and triple to get rid of his nervousness. And afterwards we could hardly think of sleeping either because we still didn't know: was it really true or was it again just rumors? Quick as I am, I went to the consulate early this morning, where I learned that it is true—Mr. Max Scheidt is included in the list and is to appear on November 7 with all his papers at the consulate. So! You can imagine how I feel!

As relieved as Erna was, she was leaving nothing to chance. Concerned that the letter of recommendation from Flora's brother, Meyer, might not be sufficient, she wrote to Bruno to get a letter from Suse's uncle, Friede Ballin. Both men were U.S. citizens, which she hoped would help. Erna was direct and forceful, as always, instructing Bruno and Suse to do as she asked without questions, and even stipulating whether the letters should be sent by air or sea. "No need for you to convince us otherwise, because we here are better informed about this than you there," she wrote, "Therefore, please do everything I ask of you in the best and most conscientious way."

Max wrote his last letter from Havana on November 11, in the midst of packing suitcases and preparing to leave. He looked forward to attending services with his brother in New York on the first Shabbos after arriving in the States and to giving thanks to God for their reunion. "And with this," he wrote, "we conclude for the time being this enormous correspondence. . . . Hugs to you both, yours, Mackie." After his signature, Max adds, "Yesterday I went with Meszaros to Brailowsky's piano recital, a wonderful conclusion to my stay in Cuba."[3]

Even as Bruno, Suse, Max, and Erna celebrated their reunion in New York, a cloud hung over the family. Things looked truly wretched for Flora and Georg. "Every day is the same as the one before," Georg wrote, "they all begin with the problem of emigration and end late at night with the same issue." From Flora we hear that the consulate was a nightmare: "Everything is so hard here and one doesn't know what is going on, whether one will accomplish anything or not, this consulate is hell on earth!" She added that there was now barely any food available. It was impossible to move to the hotel room they had reserved three months earlier in central Marseille because every room in every hotel was occupied by desperate refugees. Georg wrote that "ten thousand people wander the streets in Marseille," panicked because they did not have the requisite papers to flee. Flora felt she was "caught here in a mousetrap on a powder keg."

One thing that emerges clearly from the letters among Flora and Georg, Max and Erna, and Bruno and Suse is Georg's refusal, under any circumstances, to accept blame for a mistake he was sure he hadn't made. To Max he wrote:

> Perhaps one should learn from this that under these conditions, polemics of any kind whatsoever should be dropped and replaced with more concessions and understanding. This observation of mine is for you, dear Max, who always accuses, albeit clearly with love, but without having the full picture of what is actually going on here. Even if you assume, in a very human way, that our age deprives us of the necessary vigor to master the situation, you must tell yourself after some consideration that our desire to get there must be so strong that all obstacles could be overcome if it were in our power. . . . So listen to some details: Nothing, absolutely nothing has been omitted or neglected; in marked contrast to earlier times, it was mother, of all people, who wanted to sacrifice our savings up to the last cent.

At last, in March, Georg's tenacity and some good luck made the impossible happen. Two American officials, Myles Standish and his superior, Hiram Bingham IV, who were stationed at the consulate in Marseille, were inundated with refugees whose last hope for a U.S. visa was in their hands. At the risk of their careers, and in direct defiance of both Vichy officials and U.S. regulations, they took it upon themselves to speed up the emigration process by signing emergency visas (called "affidavits in lieu of passports"). Standish and Bingham saved 2,500 people, among them Marc Chagall,

That this affidavit has been executed to serve in lieu of a passport to allow **him** to proceed to the United States.

DESCRIPTION :

Height : 5' 1"
Weight : 158 lbs.
Hair : grey
Eyes : brown
Marks : ---
Complexion : dark

Georg Muensterberger

PHOTOGRAPH ATTACHED
AMERICAN
CONSULAR SERVICE

Subscribed and sworn to before me this 17th day of March 1941.

Myles Standish,
Vice Consul of the United States of America.

Georg Münsterberger's affidavit in lieu of passport.

Hannah Arendt, and Max Ernst, and many ordinary people with no fame or special connections.

Perhaps Georg's relentlessness with HICEM had worked; it must have brought him to Myles Standish's attention, and he was apparently convinced by Georg's arguments. On March 17, Flora and Georg were each granted that most precious paper—the affidavit in lieu of passport—signed in Marseille by Myles Standish.

The one hurdle left was that boats were no longer leaving from Marseille to the United States. The only ships sailing directly to New York were leaving from Lisbon, and getting there was impossible for them—a "fairytale" in Flora's words. Running out of options, Georg and Flora secured spots on a cargo ship called the SS *Winnipeg* heading to Martinique. Flora was worried they would be stuck there, and she asked Bruno to reserve places for them on a boat from Martinique to New York City. She added, "The voyage is supposed to be very hot, but I would like to be sweating already. The ship is supposed to be an old tub of 15,000 tons! It's all the same to me! I do not care! It could be 30,000 for as much as I care!" Responding to birthday wishes, she wrote, "I hope I'll celebrate mine on the high seas vomiting."

In Georg's last letter from France on May 3, 1941, he wrote to Bruno, "If nothing interferes, we'll be leaving Tuesday morning on SS *Winnipeg* via Oran-Casablanca to Fort de France—that should take about 25 days, with an interruption of 3 days each in O and C. . . . All your efforts regarding Portugal yielded no success, I'll tell you later why. . . . You did what was possible, but I decided differently, because we are now at a critical point and mother can hardly be held back. I am totally aware of the risk, but dragging it out any longer may be even riskier."

It's impossible to overstate how lucky Georg and Flora were to get on the *Winnipeg*. This was its last sailing, and the Martinique route shut down entirely at the end of May. Had they not gotten out when they did, they would have likely been trapped and almost certainly caught, rounded up, and sent to the Drancy transit camp and from there to Auschwitz. That was the fate of more than 70,000 Jews throughout France.[4]

The *Winnipeg* was a cargo vessel that had been haphazardly converted to transport people.[5] It departed Marseille for Martinique with 719 passengers—including 240 Germans, 65 "ex-Austrians," 90 who were designated as stateless, and 33 members of the Vichy military. It slipped its moorings on the evening of May 6, 1941, and sailed away from the continent. Its first stop was Oran, then Casablanca, and finally Dakar, before sailing to Martinique.

Conditions aboard were miserable. A passenger named Marie Odenheimer kept a diary and described the sleeping arrangements: "There are about 60 women in one room, two bunks above one, no daylight. No available room except in your own bunk, and the sanitary facilities are inadequate."[6] A *New York Herald Tribune* article described the lack of food, the many people suffering from food poisoning, and the majority of passengers sleeping on the decks because the holds were so unhygienic.[7] The physical privations might have been easier to bear if the passengers believed they had truly escaped danger. But Martinique was a French colony controlled by the Nazi-collaborationist Vichy government. The pro-Nazi crew on the ship repeatedly threatened that the passengers would be imprisoned in the Martinique internment camps, where refugees were being held for indeterminate periods of time.

Three weeks into the difficult journey, the *Winnipeg* was intercepted by the *Van Kinsbergen*, a Dutch warship. The captain was alerted in the middle of the night with flashing lights, followed by a warning shot across the bow. When the captain did not respond, Dutch sailors in combat gear stormed the *Winnipeg* and ordered the captain to follow their ship to Trinidad.

Georg and Flora, and their fellow passengers, were confused and terrified. Their boat had been fired upon, but they did not—at the time—know by whom or why. The engines had stopped and the ship had begun to drift in the middle of the ocean. But that was not the worst possibility: Everyone feared most of all that the ship would inexplicably and irrevocably change course, returning them to Europe and delivering them back into the hands of the Nazis.

The interception of the *Winnipeg* turned out to have little to do with its passengers. The British had begun enforcing a trade embargo on the French Caribbean route, largely to block European goods from reaching supporters of the Vichy government. The *Winnipeg* was carrying 1,500 tons of cargo, or as the British classified it, "enemy exports," including vermouth, essential oils, perfumes, gloves, wine, sardines, tires, medicine, herbs, and auto parts. The British also wanted to commandeer as many ships as they could for their own use and to control what and who was crossing the Atlantic.

The Dutch and English intelligence services were also concerned about spies on board the *Winnipeg*. A British communiqué dated May 31 reads, "We regard this cargo of Germans with deep suspicion. . . . Even if many of the Germans turn out to be genuine refugees, it seems very likely that some of them are German agents whose presence cannot be regarded as anything but threatening to the Western Hemisphere." They conjectured that some on board were making their way to Martinique to help the pro-Nazi government establish an outpost there.

Upon arrival in Trinidad, Flora and Georg, along with all the passengers and crew, were interned at Camp St. James, which the British had established in July 1940. The *Winnipeg* was confiscated by the British government.

The refugees must have been enormously relieved to find that the camp was comfortable, fully adhering to the terms of the Geneva Convention. Its nineteen huts were divided into Jewish and non-Jewish sections, each with its own kitchen, lavatory, and washing arrangements. Married persons could bunk together. There were medical and dental facilities, and internees could attend religious celebrations of their denominations, grow their own vegetables, and, at one point, even raise their own chickens.

On May 31, Trinidad's British governor, Sir H. Young, issued a communiqué to the secretary of state for the colonies verifying that most of the

A portrait of Flora taken by Ilse Bing, the well-known photographer and a fellow passenger on the SS *Winnipeg*, New York City, 1943.

passengers had been vetted and that they were "bona fide travelers with visas for USA, Cuba, Mexico and Brazil." On June 4, the internees learned that those with valid U.S. visas could depart Trinidad on June 5 on the SS *Evangeline*, heading to Martinique and then to New York. Flora and Georg were among them.

On June 13, 1941, six weeks after they had left Europe, Flora and Georg finally landed in New York, undoubtedly met at the docks by the overjoyed and relieved Bruno, Max, Suse, and Erna. At last, my family had managed the near-impossible. They were reunited safely in America.

All except Lilo and Ellien.

10

Nowhere to Turn, No One to Trust

Lilo and Ellien were stranded in Holland. By the summer of 1941, getting out of Europe was all but impossible. Their only hope was to hide, evade, and endure. In a letter to Suse, Margarete reflected on her daughter and granddaughter's predicament: "Poor Lott writes very bravely—there simply are no prospects for them. . . . One can only hope the Nazis will find their deserved end in Russia and have no time and opportunity to take revenge on Dutch Jews before that happens. In spite of this hope, the fear of the hordes lingers."

Far away in Los Angeles, at the end of August 1941, Margarete began to suffer from poor health. The diagnosis: cancer. My mother traveled from New York to care for her. Georg wrote to Bruno, "It was very fortunate for us that Suse was able to be here during those difficult weeks and that she cared for dear mother so selflessly. . . . She hardly moved from the side of Mother's bed." Margarete succumbed to her illness in early November. A few days later, Lilo received word in Holland. In the last letter we have from her until after liberation, she wrote to her father of her heartbreak at her mother's death: "My dear Papchen, one day before Mami's birthday I received your letter with the terrible news. Dear Herrchen, if only I could at least be with you to comfort you a bit. It must have been awful to see our

Georg and Margarete, Los Angeles, c. 1941.

dear Minschen suffering so much and not be able to help her. It's too terrible that Minsle didn't have a few more beautiful years there, after all the upsetting ones. I always imagined it would be so nice for me to come to you, and now I am never to see my dear Mamele again."

In 1942, the Germans began deportations from Amsterdam, determined to rid the city of Jews. A Polish acquaintance offered to take Ellien and hide her with a family in the Dutch countryside, but Lilo understood that she would not be able to accompany her. Her so-called Jewish features would be a risk to the safety of the peasants sheltering Ellien. In the end, Lilo turned down the offer, plagued by the idea that it could be a ruse and she would be apart from Ellien if something went amiss. "I could not send her away, not knowing whether—so many people fell into traps, that they said they would save the children, and they would take them into the countryside somewhere. . . . So to just let her go, without knowing where and what—I could not do it."

Lilo and Ellien were soon unable to live openly in Amsterdam. Lilo appealed for help from the Polish woman who had offered to take in Ellien.

Ellien on her apartment balcony, c. 1942.

The woman knew of an empty apartment in the city, so they went into hiding:

> I don't know exactly how long we stayed there because I always was in fear in that apartment—always in fear. I thought, "If they ring the bell, what am I

> going to do? What on earth can I tell them, why I am here?" I don't know what we did from morning till night, and through the night in that apartment for months. I have no idea. I didn't dare to show my face, even at the window. Maybe in the dark, I went down to buy food, or maybe this Polish woman brought us some food. I have no idea anymore.

Hans Reiss also remained in Amsterdam, trying to evade capture. The Germans demanded that 7,000 Jews in Amsterdam report for deportation on May 25, 1943. Only 500 showed up. The next day, the Germans sealed the city's Jewish quarter and launched raids to extract people from their apartments and roundups to seize them from the streets. They recruited and paid Dutch collaborators to inform on Jews and turn them in. Terror permeated the air. There was nowhere to turn and no one to trust.

A network of organizations began forging documents and identity papers in an effort to save Jews and members of the Dutch resistance. Hans secured a false identity card, but the day he planned to slip into hiding, he was caught in the German dragnet. Lilo saw him being taken away. "The only picture that I have is of me on my bike, driving behind that truck where they had people—an army truck that is open in the back, and I saw him sitting there, and me driving through the whole city, trying to keep up with that truck on my bike, until I lost it."

In that moment, Lilo had the presence of mind—or foolhardiness—to go to Hans' apartment, where she grabbed his false identity papers, hoping someone else would be able to use them. (Perhaps Lilo saved someone's life.) Hans was deported to Westerbork, where he was put to work as a physician. From time to time, he was able to write to Lilo, but none of those letters survived.

The most intense period of roundups and deportations lasted from May to September 1943. By the end of that period, the Germans declared the city *Judenrein*—cleansed of Jews. Of the nearly 80,000 Jews who had registered in Amsterdam in 1941, there were very few who still remained. Lilo and Ellien were among them. They briefly left their hiding place and returned to their apartment at Herculesstraat, but the Germans were raiding the neighborhood constantly: "We saw big moving trucks. . . . The name of the moving truck was taken off, and it said, *Liebesgabe aus Holland* [Gifts from Holland with love]. And those big trucks went to Germany with the furniture and everything they found in the houses after they picked people up. . . .

When we saw those trucks with 'Gifts from Holland,' I guess I felt I better go into hiding again."

In the winter of 1943, a member of the Amsterdam Jewish Council told Lilo about a place where they could hide in the countryside. She was not sure she could trust him, fearing he could be an undercover informant or a Dutch Nazi, but she felt she had to take the chance. She and Ellien boarded a train for the nearby town of Zeist. Again, she feared her "Jewish" features would give her away or endanger Ellien, so she had Ellien sit apart from her on the train. (I am reminded of my cousin Anneliese, riding the train alone from Germany into Holland with Ellien's passport—two children, both forced to take risks and bear adult burdens to survive.) "She was on one end of the train, and I was on the other," Lilo remembered. "When we went anywhere, we always went separately, because she didn't look Jewish, so I didn't want her to look suspicious with me. And we went to Zeist, and the man picked us up there, and took her to the children's home, and me to the room that he had rented for me."

Lilo remained alone in her room for months. Her only human contact was with members of the Dutch resistance bringing her food. Years later, she said she couldn't remember how she passed the time and what she did all day. She had just one memory: "One night, I dared to go to a movie. I thought in the dark, I can go."

Eventually, the Germans raided the children's home. Ellien and another girl had been tipped off and told to run quickly out the back door. They made their way breathlessly to Lilo's apartment and told her of the raid. Lilo realized Zeist was no longer safe, so she took both girls back to Amsterdam, traveling the same way they had come—separately, at opposite ends of the train car. Lilo then took Ellien's housemate to the Jewish Council offices and went with Ellien back to Herculesstraat.

The prospects for staying one step ahead of the Germans were dwindling. Lilo and Ellien now remained indoors as much as possible. One day the German Nazis, having been informed that Lilo's wealthy in-laws had a stash of diamonds in a safe, came to her apartment. "The Dutch Jews with their diamonds—we are famous, you know," Lilo drily remarked in her testimony, with a small laugh. They searched through her desk, finding nothing, and then brought her in for questioning, holding her all day, demanding that she turn over the key to the safe, which, of course, she didn't have. Perhaps because she was a half Jew, their focus was not on her "racial status" but on the possibility that she was the means to her in-laws' wealth. Lilo's concern was that Ellien was home alone. At the end of the long day, the German official had to decide how to proceed:

> He sits down at his typewriter, and he starts, "When were you born?" Tat, tat, tat. "Where were you born?" "Glauchau in Sachsen." He stops and looks at me. And he says, "Repeat this." "Glauchau in Sachsen." "I thought you were Dutch." I said, "I was Dutch by marriage. I was born in Germany, in Glauchau." He said, "That's where I am from. I'm born in Glauchau in Sachsen." And from then on, everything was easy. I didn't know where the key was, and I didn't know where my mother-in-law had her fur coats, and I didn't know where she has her jewelry, and everything went easy. And at 6:00 o'clock I was at home.

Thus ground the gears of the Nazi persecution machine. As much as the government declared its rigid adherence to racial ideology and policy, any given official, on a whim, with no reason or consequence, could easily turn a blind eye and allow someone to slip away. Arrest or release could hinge on something as superficial as a half-Jewish woman's shared birthplace with her Nazi questioner.

Lilo got involved with the Dutch underground, working for the Landelijke Organisatie voor Hulp aan Onderduikers, known as LO. The name translates to the National Organization for Aid to People in Hiding, and its primary goal was to protect so-called *onderduikers*—Jews and others who were hiding from the Germans and their Dutch collaborators. The LO supplied its network with food-ration coupons from a variety of sources: Operatives produced counterfeit coupons, stole real coupons from government agencies, and obtained coupons from Dutch civilians and resisters.

On August 21, 1944, a member of the underground came to Lilo's apartment to drop off stolen food-ration coupons for her to distribute. Unbeknownst to him, he had been followed. Soon afterward, a Nazi officer burst into Lilo's apartment. He accused her of collaborating with the resistance, arrested her and Ellien, and took them to the Schouwburg Theater, from which they were sent to the Westerbork transit camp.[1] Lilo later said, "That's one thing I can't forgive myself, ever, that I did not have the presence of mind to let her down [a rope ladder] in the back. We had people that I knew, who if I had been ready . . . I did not even prepare that. So, we were both there, and they said they had to take us in."

This episode raises a question: Lilo had papers showing that she was a half Jew, but Ellien had no such protection. She had a Jewish father and three Jewish grandparents, which, according to Nazi ideology, defined her as a full Jew. For years, Lilo had been terrified for Ellien's safety, and her choices were filtered through the lens of what she believed would be best for her daughter. Lilo had even refused to send Ellien into hiding without her, because she felt it wasn't safe. When circumstances left her with no choice, she endured a separation from her daughter and hid herself nearby. Constantly afraid that her own facial features would endanger Ellien, Lilo would not be seen in public with her. She had endured years of sacrifice, fear, and uncertainty to keep her child safe. Why, then, did Lilo willingly put herself and Ellien in danger by working for the Dutch underground? Lilo later asked herself many times what she might have done differently, but she never spoke of the choice that led to their arrest and everything that followed.

Lilo and Ellien arrived in Westerbork and were placed in Barracks 67, the "punishment" barracks, thanks to Lilo's resistance work. "We were there several nights," she recalled. "I don't know exactly how many others they had picked up—and one little boy cried all night for his mother. And there were quite a few non-Jewish young women who had worked for the underground and had Jews in their apartment, hidden. And, so that group was registered somehow a little different as *Strafprozess*, half-Jewish or non-Jewish that had worked for the underground." Lilo was arrested as a collaborator and was therefore held not as a Jew but as a criminal.

In Westerbork, Lilo saw Hans Reiss. He was afraid to speak to her, out of fear that he might compromise her slightly better status as a half Jew. But he did what he could for her and Ellien. He had fostered connections there and was able to tell those who kept the lists that Lilo and Ellien should be considered "Jewish prisoners of value." He insisted that as a relative of the legendary Albert Ballin, Lilo was important. Ellien, too, could prove useful because she had relatives in Palestine, and there was buzz about a potential prisoner swap: a thousand German Templars in the Middle East had aligned themselves with the German Nazis and were being detained by the British in Palestine, and the Nazi government was eager to get them released and back to Germany.

On September 4, 1944, Hans was deported from Westerbork to Theresienstadt. Just before he was sent away, he smuggled a letter to Lilo and Ellien. Lilo remembered, "I got a little letter from Hans Reiss, which probably was also unheard of, you know, where he writes a little letter to my daughter, and one to me, which I had in the hem of my prison gown, until the end, because I thought it gives us courage. It was mainly saying, 'Have courage, we will meet again.'"

Lilo and Ellien also faced deportation from Westerbork. They did not know their destination until the day they left:

> We were in the washroom—it was a long washroom, with the washbasins in the middle, and it was ice cold. We heard that the list was being made up between who goes to Auschwitz and who goes to Bergen-Belsen. We knew that the next morning, our names would be called up, and it would be to the one side or to the other, so we didn't dare to go and sleep. In our group was one girl that—I don't know if she was really professional—just that she learned to sing. She sang for us the whole night.

The next morning, the authorities came and called their names. Lilo and Ellien were sent to Bergen-Belsen.

They arrived in the massive camp complex, about sixty miles south of Hamburg, on September 16, 1944. Thanks to the special status Hans had managed to arrange for them, they were interned in the *Sternlager* (Star Camp) at Bergen-Belsen—so called because the prisoners did not wear camp uniforms but, rather, the Star of David on their regular clothes. The Star Camp had been established a year earlier to hold prisoners who would, in theory, be swapped for German nationals held by the Allies. There were several such exchange camps in Belsen, holding 4,000 mostly Dutch prisoners.

"They checked our hair," Lilo remembered, "and they found that we had lice. And they took us to shave, and to take our hair—pshhh . . . off . . . gone." They were housed in barracks and required to perform forced labor. Lilo and Ellien were often separated. Lilo was always the mother hen, worrying about her little chick. "I remember that I was obviously afraid when I came home, what she had done, what had happened to her in the day," she said.

"In Bergen-Belsen," she recalled, "what struck me terribly was that people that I had known a short time ago in Amsterdam were hardly recognizable. They came up to me, and said, 'Aren't you Lilo?' And I looked at them and could hardly recognize them. In a short time, in Bergen-Belsen, they had changed."

Even though Lilo and Ellien had privileges in the Star Camp, they were often treated harshly. One day, Lilo was told she hadn't made her bed well enough, and she was punished by not being given her rations for the day. But in her recounting of the episode, she added that her "Jewish" features had again gotten her in trouble. Referring to the female German camp guards, she said, "They couldn't stand me, with my Jewish face, and I think the hair was off so I must have looked very ugly, and Jewish in the way they think a Jew would look, you know, so they were always after me."

Lilo's connection to Albert Ballin wasn't powerful enough to keep them in Belsen. In mid-December 1944, they were sent to Ravensbrück, the notorious camp for women, fifty miles north of Berlin. Lilo remembered one agonizing moment en route: "One time I was close to breaking down," she said, "was when one train came by, and while they came by, they threw a few sugar cubes, and I tried to catch one for my little girl. And I didn't." Even the tiniest treat, while it would change nothing, could have provided a momentary reprieve for her daughter.

Ravensbrück was a nightmare, dramatically more brutal and terrifying than Belsen. No longer protected by even the illusion of status, Lilo and Ellien were thrown in with the general prisoner population, primarily non-Jewish women from throughout Europe. The vast majority were Poles and Soviets. They were political prisoners, criminals, the "work-shy," Jehovah's Witnesses, "asocials" (Roma and Sinti), so-called race-defilers (those who had married or had sexual relations with Jews), and a small number of Jews.

Lilo remembered her initiation into the camp:

> The thing I know for sure was that we had to undress, and there was a shower, and I knew I had heard that out of the shower comes the gas instead of the water. . . . And I looked up, and water came out. I think we got one shirt under that prison garment. I'm not even sure that we had anything under it. I had hidden the picture, and my micro document of my two Aryan grandparents and Hans' picture, and, I think 100 Gulden. I thought it might help me. That's what I had hidden in my shoe when we came out of that shower. That's all I ever had until the end of the war, in my whole possession. And I had it in the hem of my prison gown.

The conditions in Ravensbrück were barbaric. As many as four women shared a single bunk in the severely overcrowded barracks, sleeping on wood planks with a bit of straw. Many slept directly on the floor with not even a blanket to cover them. Food rations were meager and women starved. They were awakened in the morning and made to stand for hours in the icy cold for *Appell*, roll call. This was a particular form of torture for the malnourished, exhausted women who wore nothing more than a prison gown in the freezing winter. Everyone worked at slave labor. Lilo was assigned the particularly hellish job of shoveling coal from the hold of a ship docked at Lake Schwedtsee. She recalled this as "one of my—call it nightmares, where I think of at night, or very often during the day, we were shoveling coal."

Everywhere she went, her mind was preoccupied with finding a way to save Ellien, "And in that one ship," she remembered, "there was a woman, probably German. I looked at her, and I looked at her, and I thought, 'She looks like a good mother, would she take her, would she take her?' Could I trust her [enough] to say, 'Hide her and take her along in your ship when you leave?' It's one thing I'm always thinking of now."

Prisoners in Ravensbrück, like those in every camp in the Nazi system, endured punishing starvation. Once a day, they were given a small ration of bread and a watery soup with turnips. "And at one point, my daughter said she can't eat it, she can't eat it, and I said, 'Well, you have to eat it—there is nothing else. You have to eat it. You have to have something.'" Lilo remembered one small act that helped the women lift their spirits, "And there, we were very hungry. And these Dutch girls exchanged recipes to talk about food. It must have somehow satisfied them a little bit to talk about food."

Ellien's health quickly deteriorated. At fourteen, she needed extra nourishment to support her growing frame. "She got taller and taller, and thinner and thinner," Lilo recalled.

> When we went home from work, we had to march along a long road, and there were little villas where the bosses lived, you know, and we went there, and the lights were on, and maybe the Christmas tree. . . . Those miserable guys and women lived there like kings, in those villas. In the day, they were after us with a dog when we went to work. And, Ellien could hardly walk because she had the Dutch wooden shoes. And, in the evening, we walked by those villas, the lights were on, and you could tell how warm it would be inside. I didn't even have gloves for her. And we pushed that car with the coals . . . not even gloves. And we were there all winter.

On our day in Ravensbrück in 2016, Kat took this photo of one of the SS villas Lilo described in her testimony.

Some of Lilo's most painful memories of Ravensbrück were the way prisoners turned on one another. Solidarity and compassion were rare. Lilo often found herself the victim of someone else's determination to survive at any cost. When the Dutch Red Cross sent parcels for the Dutch prisoners, another woman claimed that Lilo was German—having heard her speaking to Ellien—in a bid to get a second package for herself. Lilo convinced the Red Cross that she was Dutch. "It had vitamins, and it had cans of sardines, and Ovaltine." But that night, after Lilo fell asleep, the package was stolen. "The next morning, it was gone. You almost never forget—forgive yourself for this—it's just on your mind, until your last day."

Lilo often suffered at the hands of fellow prisoners, and often blamed herself for Ellien's suffering. Perhaps Lilo wasn't ruthless enough; it wasn't in her nature to scheme or assume that others would take advantage of her. Perhaps it was not only bad luck but also a trusting nature that failed her in this heinous game of survival.

In the last months of the war, Ravensbrück grew even more overcrowded as prisoners from the East were evacuated from concentration camps and brought westward toward Germany to try to stay ahead of the advancing Red Army. The prisoner population was ravaged by epidemics of contagious diseases, such as typhus and diphtheria, and they faced dwindling food rations and appalling sanitary conditions. While the Russian advance meant the hope of liberation, it also meant more uncertainty because no one knew how far the Germans would go to prevent any Jews from surviving. Lilo recounted this frightening event:

> They started to pull people out of the group when we were lined up. And we thought that they would take some to working camps. On the other hand, sometimes we also thought that they picked those up that looked like they couldn't survive. And one day we stood in line, and they called Ellien to the side, and me to this side. What to do? What can I do? How could I not have fallen dead, I don't know . . . but she came. She had made it—when they turned around one second, she came to me. I had not made it to come to her, but she had made it to come to me. It was the closest we came to being separated.

On March 20, 1945, Lilo and Ellien were sent from Ravensbrück to Beendorf, a subcamp of Neuengamme in a rural area near Hamburg. Lilo's memories of these last weeks of the war were chaotic; in her state of exhaustion, starvation, and despair, she remembered only confused snippets of what occurred. They were moved at first by train, but then, at some point, they were taken off the trains and made to walk. Then they were again put on trains, again pulled off and forced to walk, then quartered overnight in a camp. Sometimes, they found themselves staying for a while in an open field. She remembered one agonizing day as Ellien's health was rapidly declining: "It must have been after Easter, spring, then, and it was a warm day, and we were lying there on the ground, and we were supposed to get a meal—some kind of a soup in the evening, towards evening, and we had to stand in line, and we all stood in line, and before we got there, Ellien and I, there was nothing left. So we went back without food. We hadn't had any food that day. That was it—the food was gone."

Perhaps the lowest moment came just days before liberation. Lilo heard there was water at a nearby camp. Ellien was dehydrated, exhausted, and running a fever. Lilo was determined to get her some water:

> I walked and I walked and I walked. I came to that prison camp, and we even saw prisoners, behind barbed wire, or behind a fence. And I looked, and there was a fountain, and water was running. I went to pick up my cup, and it was

> gone. And I could not take any water to her. My cup was gone. I had still not learned that you could not put down a cup for one second or it would be stolen. And I walked back without water for her. She probably was already in fever at that time. How can one survive things like that? You're surrounded only by enemies, by meanness. People get that bad if they are in a certain situation like that—that people can get that bad, I still have not learned.

Lilo and Ellien were finally liberated on May 1, 1945. They were put on cattle cars—this time by the Red Cross—and taken out of Germany to Denmark. En route, some of the most desperate, starved prisoners sought food wherever they could. "When the train stopped," Lilo recalled, "they ran out of the train to the nearest houses and stole food. They ran to those houses and went to the kitchen to get food, even though they were not in Germany anymore, and they were not in a camp anymore. But there [in Denmark], we had already gotten our first decent food.... When the train stopped in Denmark, we had gotten already something like cereal and cocoa."

Lilo described how she had been completely shut down emotionally for the entirety of their time in Ravensbrück and until liberation. Like many other inmates, she felt she could not afford the luxury of thinking or feeling. She described it vividly in her testimony, saying, "I can only describe it as *Panzer* ... a shield. You had a shield in front of your heart, your emotions are cut off behind that, and you do not let a single emotion come close to you because you would be lost if you did. We never allowed ourselves to say something like, 'Will we survive?' And, 'What will happen to us?' Never a word like that. You could not allow anything to get close to you. You were just like an island, and you could only live like a robot, like an automatic person."

With liberation, when the torment was finally over, the flood of emotions began to pour out. Lilo said, "I think the first time I remember that Ellien said anything to me, where we started to cry, was already in Denmark or in Sweden, when a well-dressed and well made-up girl walked by. She said, 'Oh, Mom, that is the way you used to look.'"

From Denmark, Lilo and Ellien were taken by boat to Sweden. Lilo was overjoyed and relieved. "To me, it was already like I was on a vacation trip," she said. "And I said, 'Ellien, we may never come here again, to go from Denmark to Sweden. Look out—look how beautiful it is!' And then we were called inside, and there were tables set for us, for a meal . . . tablecloth with silver on the table, and cups, and bowls, with cereal, probably milk." It was only in retrospect that Lilo understood just how ill Ellien was; she was far too weak to enjoy the view or take in any of the small pleasures of the journey.

When they arrived in Sweden, Lilo and Ellien were transported on Swedish Red Cross buses to Malmö. "Count Bernadotte welcomed us to Sweden, and they were trying to do what they could do for us. And that they did. . . . We were divided by the country we came from. So I was with a Dutch group in Sweden." By May 4, Lilo and Ellien were examined and housed at the Limhamns Folkskolor, a school which had been converted into a hospital. The Swedish people disinfected and quarantined the survivors, took them to pick out coats and clothing to replace what had to be destroyed, and provided medical attention and personal visits.

During the examination, Lilo was diagnosed with diphtheria in her throat, and Ellien was diagnosed with pulmonary typhoid, both of which are contagious. As a result, Lilo was sent to a nearby hospital in Malmö while Ellien was taken twenty-seven miles away to a hospital in Landskrona. Grateful that her daughter would be getting excellent medical attention, Lilo didn't hesitate to permit the separation. "So, I made no fuss that she shouldn't go, or that I should go along with her," she said. "We just thought it is wonderful that the Swedes would do that, and that they take care of them, and they get the best care possible now. And there she went."

Lilo and Ellien were able to communicate through the Red Cross. "I could write to her there in the hospital in Sweden, and there were wonderful ladies of the Red Cross, and probably other volunteers that came to the hospital, and—the one I knew already—she saw to it that I got the letters." One Swedish woman, who had been married to a Dutch man and spoke the language, made sure that mother and daughter received each other's letters. Lilo was declared well enough to be discharged from the hospital in Malmö on May 31.

Then, a few days later, on June 4, 1945, she learned the shattering news that Ellien had died of typhoid at the hospital in Landskrona. In her testimony, Lilo could not bring herself to speak about her reaction. She was haunted by her only child's death—after liberation, after *everything*—for the rest of her life.

Intake photo of Ellien, Limhamns Folkskolor, May 1945. (Courtesy of the Swedish National Archives, State Aliens Supervisory Commission.)

Intake photo of Lilo, Limhamns Folkskolor, May 1945. (Courtesy of the Swedish National Archives, State Aliens Supervisory Commission.)

Grieving, stunned, and alone, Lilo made arrangements to have Ellien buried at the Jewish cemetery in Malmö. The local rabbi at first refused to bury Ellien there, saying that she was not a Jew according to Jewish tradition. "I thought that it was the most grotesque scene that I could think of, after we had gone through that because we were Jewish, he said, 'If your mother isn't Jewish, you are not Jewish.' I think I started to laugh."

Lilo had the presence of mind to tell the rabbi that she had converted to Judaism in Holland and that Ellien was most certainly a Jew. And so, on June 5, the day after she died, Ellien was buried at the Jewish cemetery in Malmö among the many other victims who had died after liberation. The Swedish volunteer from the Red Cross who had passed the final letters between Lilo and Ellien came to the tiny funeral and stood by Lilo as she endured the unthinkable. In her testimony, Lilo recalled the emptiness of visiting her daughter's final resting place, saying, "I went a couple of times only to find out she isn't any closer to me there than she is anywhere else."

11

A Fragile Silence

Lilo had cherished her Puppi, her little doll, for nearly fifteen years. From the moment their lives were upended by the Germans, she had done everything she could, made every decision to try to protect her daughter. For Lilo, this meant staying together, even when parting might have increased Ellien's chances of survival. In the final weeks of the war, when there were no more choices to make, when everything had been reduced to simply marching along a road for an unknown destination, she held on to that single, essential goal: Stay together and survive. And they *had* survived. In the wake of Ellien's death, Lilo was left with nothing but the bitterest irony. The first and only time she let her daughter out of her sight, entrusting her to a hospital where she could recover her health, Lilo lost her forever.

Lilo faced the future in a bleak fog of grief and regret. An attack of gallstones landed her in the hospital, a turn she attributed to the shock of Ellien's death and the sudden change in her diet following liberation. On June 14, after nine days in Malmö, she was moved to a Displaced Persons (DP) camp in Gothenburg. She remembered the people there as being gentle and kind. "They treated us beautifully, and the people from the surrounding area came to visit, in order to talk to us, and they took us to families . . . to have dinner once a week or for an outing." Even so, she was only beginning to grapple, as all survivors must, with the physical and emotional aftermath of her trauma.

On top of that, she tested positive for typhoid, though she had no symptoms. The disease was highly contagious, so she had to test negative twice before she would be released from the hospital. "Therefore, [I am] once again in a striped garment and behind barbed wire," she wrote in her first letter home, "but we are doing well here. . . . Mostly lying in the garden in the sun, knitting, reading."

Her physical recovery was easy compared with the emotional devastation she faced. At last, after years of little to no contact with her family, she was able to exchange letters and share news with her father and sisters. They sent her money and photos. She learned that my parents had settled into life in New York, had built up the business, and had begun a family with my birth in New York in 1943. Lilo's essential generosity of spirit comes through in her letters from this time. With no trace of bitterness, she wrote to her father, "Wünzeli [Suse] has written me a very nice, detailed letter. Charlie is such a sweet little one, that I'm at a loss for words. I always have your letters and the photos spread out side by side on my bed, and they make me feel so rich."

At the same time, a persistent thread of self-doubt weaves through her letters, showing how she struggled not only with loss but also with the fear that perhaps she could have done something differently. Most survivors were left to contend alone with the trauma they had experienced, with no

My mother and me on Riverside Drive, New York City, February 25, 1944.

counseling or psychiatric support and little understanding of how the body and brain respond to a rupture of this magnitude. Lilo responded by reliving events and blaming herself. "Yes, dear Papa, I may have been able to bear everything," she wrote in her first letter home, "but I didn't manage to prevent them from grabbing my Puppele nor could I prevent her from tolerating the camp so badly. I tried everything, but one never knew what was the right thing to do, so you realize when it is too late that you've made mistakes. The only good thing is that now nothing can happen to her anymore."

As Lilo took the first steps toward recovery, she had to figure out how to navigate the bureaucratic channels out of Europe to reunite with her family. It was not easy. She contacted the U.S. consulate, but they did not yet have the new regulations. She could not be sure how or even whether she would be able to travel to the United States. She continued to test positive for typhoid, which kept her in the hospital. She had no choice but to wait. In response to a letter from Suse, she wrote, "Wünzli, your letter did me so much good. Now I don't feel so abandoned anymore. I'm so glad you're all well, and I've never seen anything as adorable as your Charlie (at most my Puppele was that cute). I never get tired of looking at the photo. In the meantime, better make sure to get a second Charlie, because when I come to New York, I cannot guarantee that I can leave him to you. He also has a really mischievous little face."

In early August, she received another blow: "Yesterday a gentleman from the Dutch Red Cross came to see us," she wrote her father, Georg, "and all he was able to report was that the transport Hans was put on went to Auschwitz, and this does not bode well. . . . I had always persuaded myself that I would at least get Hans back after having lost my dear child." She did not give up hope. She immediately sent a telegram to the Dutch authorities, having heard that some men were still being held by the Russians, praying that she and Hans might yet reunite.

Lilo gradually found out she would not be able to go straight from Gothenburg to America. She decided to return to Holland and attempt her emigration from there. Manja, her Polish friend, and Clara, the young refugee who had lived with her and Ellien, had invited Lilo to stay with them. They informed her that Jessiah had returned to Amsterdam and had been preparing a house on Velasquezstraat to receive Lilo and Ellien when he learned the terrible news of their daughter's death.

In mid-August, Lilo wrote from Malmö, where she had stopped to visit Ellien's grave en route to Holland. Her family—as always, worried about her perceived fragility—didn't want her to go back to Holland, the scene of so much suffering. But Lilo had been advised that she could more easily get her Dutch passport and U.S. visa there. "I hope you are not dissatisfied with me," she wrote to Georg. "I pondered at length what I should do, and this lady has the best connections one can have, and we have considered everything. I so much hope that I didn't do the wrong thing again, but I'm afraid that in the end, whatever I do is always wrong." After years of being second-guessed and underestimated by her parents and sisters, Lilo was insecure; the profundity of the losses she'd experienced during the war years made her self-criticism worse. Even when she knew what she needed to do, she read her own decisions through the lens of her family's judgment.

Lilo also had reasons other than practical ones for returning to Holland, reasons that reveal a high level of self-awareness about her own process of grieving. Something about being there and then leaving under her own terms allowed her to take a step toward acceptance of Ellien's loss and the likelihood that Hans was gone as well. From Malmö, she wrote to her father:

> I am fully aware that also from Holland there isn't much I can do to find Hans—I don't know what I am looking for there. Perhaps the remembrance, perhaps I am thinking to recover something there from all I have lost. When I'll be there alone, without my Puppele, perhaps I'll comprehend that I have lost her forever. . . . If I voluntarily leave everything behind and come to you, after having seen that there is no Puppi and no Hans, and nothing from my previous life, maybe I'll be able to start over more easily.

Soon after reaching Amsterdam, Lilo had another gallbladder attack, and this time she needed surgery. Her recovery required a three-month stay in the hospital. When she learned that Suse was expecting a second child, she wrote her a gently teasing note, asking again if she could steal me away since Suse would soon have two children. Even while acknowledging her own loss, Lilo always expressed happiness for her family's blessings.

During her time in Amsterdam, she also saw Jessiah. We have no information about their meeting. All I can do is imagine the many tears they shared over their lost daughter.

For years, Kat's and my impression of Jessiah was very poor. The information we gathered about him suggested that he was a selfish philanderer, an uncaring and absent husband, father, and son. During the course of our research, we discovered that in 1942, Jessiah was working as the director of the American Biographical Company. It seemed that he was living a comfortable, safe life in the United States after having effectively abandoned his parents, Lilo, and Ellien to their fate in Holland. Everything we learned seemed to confirm our first impression of him, and in retrospect we were too quick to judge him.

As we sought to turn over every possible stone in the course of our research, Kat—who had discovered that Jessiah had married and fathered more children after Ellien—went looking for his descendants. She managed to locate his daughter Yvonne on Facebook and called her on the phone. As it turned out, Kat was not only an impressive researcher, digging into archives and finding important elements of the story, she was also particularly good at convincing people to let us into their lives. Yvonne provided us with contact information for Emanuel, Jessiah's son from his third marriage. Yvonne warned us that Emanuel could be unreliable and difficult to reach. As far as we knew, he had no interest in learning more about his half-sister Ellien.

As a result, we were very surprised when, during our second research trip in 2017, Emanuel not only agreed to speak with us but invited us to his home in Amstelveen, an hour's drive outside Amsterdam. We nervously rang the doorbell, and Emanuel and his wife Greet welcomed us warmly. After some small talk, Emanuel gradually began to open up, slowly sharing information about his father's life during the war years and all that followed. Kat told me later that she immediately noticed that there was something fragile in Emanuel; it was hard for him to share his stories and memories about his father. They were fraught in a way we did not understand. But by then, Kat and I had learned to read each other, to communicate instinctively and without words. We both knew that we needed to tread lightly as we sought answers to our questions.

We had believed Jessiah was in Holland the day the Germans invaded and that he had made a run for safety, leaving his parents, Lilo, and Ellien behind. But Emanuel told us that Jessiah was in Italy on vacation with his second wife, Roosje Prins. Jessiah's father—a severe, controlling, and domineering parent—ordered him not to return to Holland and to find a way to get out of Europe. Jessiah did as he was told and arrived in New York about two weeks later, on May 23, 1940.

As we talked, Emanuel volunteered that he had something we might like to see. He left the room and returned with an old photo album that showed signs of having been handled frequently. It was fragile, with flaking pages, yet it was lovingly preserved. On the first page, on faded black paper, a handwritten sticker read "Ellien Lissaur," and below it was a small cutout snapshot of Ellien as a small child. Inside its pages were a wealth of images we had never seen—Ellien as a baby and toddler, surrounded by a loving family. Not only Lilo and both sets of grandparents, but also Jessiah clearly doted on her. As we carefully paged through, we saw young Ellien in her Sunday best walking down the Amsterdam streets with her paternal grandmother, playing tennis, on a skiing trip with Lilo, and enjoying a day at the beach. We also found images we had seen before—some Lilo had taken and others of Lilo and Ellien together during the war—that revealed Jessiah had remained in touch with Lilo in the years after they were separated. Jessiah had not only been an involved father when he and Lilo were together, but he tenderly preserved this album, carrying it with him as he moved from Holland to Italy to the United States to Canada and back to Holland.

Another surprise was a photograph of Jessiah in uniform. Emanuel explained that when Jessiah left the United States for Canada, he joined the Prinses (Princess) Irene Brigade, a Dutch infantry unit that was eventually mobilized to the United Kingdom. His brigade helped liberate Holland from the Nazis. Jessiah was wounded in action, though not seriously. Far from remaining comfortable and safe in America, he had volunteered to personally fight for the liberation of Holland, no doubt also motivated in part by the hope of saving his parents, Lilo, and Ellien. After liberation, around the time he heard from Lilo what had happened to Ellien, he also discovered that his parents had been deported to Sobibor and murdered there.

Jessiah had his own demons from a difficult childhood. And even before the war, he struggled with infidelity, gambling, and other risk-taking behaviors. But his parents' and Ellien's deaths wounded him in ways that haunted him for the rest of his life. He was able to reclaim his parents' valuable real estate in Amsterdam, making him a wealthy man. He married a third time and became a father again in 1947, when Emanuel was born, and again in 1949, with the birth of his daughter Helene. But he eventually lost his fortune, wasting it on an amateur football team, parties, and women. He continued to have affairs, which strained his marriage and adversely affected his children.

Emanuel told us that when he was twelve, his father died of a heart attack with just ten dollars in his pocket. But a few moments later, Greet took Kat aside to tell her the whole story. It's true that Jessiah was found with ten dollars in his pocket, but he had died not of a heart attack but by suicide, having taken an overdose of sleeping pills. Kat later reflected on this moment, saying, "It seemed Greet wanted us to know what had really happened, but she also understood that Emanuel had a lot invested in remembering his father as a hero. She was walking a fine line: bringing us into the complex reality of Jessiah's tragic life while also protecting her husband."

Meeting Emanuel, seeing the photo album, and filling in the details of Jessiah's tragic, complicated life widened the two-dimensional portrait we had of him. Now we saw a man who carried scars from childhood, who did his best to stay in touch with his family during the war, who risked his life to liberate his country and his loved ones, and who struggled to put his life back together after so much loss. We were pained by our misreading of him, ashamed that we had failed to give him the benefit of the doubt. Then again, we had relied on what we had on hand; it can be easy to forget that documents in archives don't tell the whole story. Revisiting Jessiah's character and role in the family's story during our visit to Emanuel offered us another reminder of that all-important truth. Jessiah's story also reveals, yet again, how the events of war and genocide ripple through generations, leaving lasting scars on individuals and their descendants for generations.

Knowing the odds weren't good, Lilo nonetheless continued trying to find Hans. She knew that on September 3, 1944, he was sent from Westerbork to Theresienstadt, near Prague. That was the last time Lilo had seen him. The vast majority of prisoners had been evacuated from the Theresienstadt camp on so-called death marches moving west to stay ahead of Russian liberating forces. Lilo hoped that he had survived such a march and landed in a DP camp, or that he had been liberated by the Russians and taken to the Soviet Union. Either way, as the months ticked by and she did not hear from him directly, she understood that it was less and less likely that he had survived. (During our research, Kat and I learned that on September 29, 1944, Hans was sent to Auschwitz. We can only assume he was murdered there.)

In October 1946, Lilo got her papers and returned to Gothenburg to sail for the United States. She left on October 18 on the MS *Gripsholm* and arrived in New York ten days later. Suse and Bruno met her at the pier. They had not seen each other in more than seven years.

Lilo's descent into hell—from her luxurious life in prewar Amsterdam, full of shopping and high teas with Ellien and being a guest at Queen Wilhelmina's court, to having her head shaved in Ravensbrück and spending a bitter winter with only wooden clogs on her feet and struggling to provide even a cup of water to her dying daughter—encapsulates the Nazis' attempt to destroy the Jewish people. Lilo was the only member of my family who suffered the full brunt of the Holocaust and carried its scars into her new life in America. As such, Lilo had witnessed depravity and cruelty her closest relatives could never imagine. They had slept in comfortable beds while she was hunted by the Nazis, tortured, humiliated, degraded in ways her family could barely conceive. How could anyone cross that gulf of experience and understanding?

This isn't to say that her New York family didn't suffer too, even after the war. Foremost among the sorrows: The second baby my mother had written to Lilo about never made it home with her. During her eighth month of pregnancy, Suse nearly died while giving birth to a stillborn daughter. When she returned home after several weeks in the hospital, her doctors ordered her to be shuttered away in her bedroom to heal. She was too weak and grief-stricken to take care of me, and I was told to let her rest. I was three, and I was not allowed to see her or speak with her. Her bedroom door—across the hall from mine—remained firmly closed. Only my father and the doctor were allowed to enter.

My mother eventually recovered, but none of us ever forgot that time. I had not thought much about this period until I was sifting through my mother's papers after her death, and I stumbled over a piece of thin green paper dated February 8, 1946. I was shocked to find myself looking at my sister's autopsy report. It said she died *in utero* of serious congenital lung and heart defects, including the absence of a lobe in her lungs and several holes in the walls separating the atria and ventricles of her tiny heart.

Suddenly, memories flooded me. I could see myself standing before the closed door to my parents' bedroom, confused and hurt that I was not allowed to go in. I didn't understand what had happened or why my mother was suddenly out of reach. I also remember running down the hall playing and being sharply reprimanded by my father for making too much noise. I felt lonely and afraid, barred from my mother's safe and reassuring arms. This period of abandonment felt like an eternity.

I remembered, too, speaking with my mother about that time much later. She explained to me what had happened and how physically ill and emotionally distraught she was over her loss. She said that when she finally recovered sufficiently to come out of her room, I rejected her and kept my distance. Wounded by her sudden and total disappearance, I needed time to learn to trust her again, to be sure that she wasn't going to vanish once more. She was pained by this and wanted the comfort of my affection and longed to restore the bond between us.

Lilo arrived from Europe after my mother had physically recovered, but our home was still echoing with distress and upheaval. And miraculously for me, there was Lilo, with her maternal warmth and gentleness. She doted on me, and I attached myself to her, forming a bond that lasted a lifetime. Her constancy, acceptance, and attention were healing to me. Lilo was a loving bridge that helped rebuild my trust and allowed me to connect not only with her but also with my mother.

Lilo left New York for Los Angeles in late 1946 and at last reconnected with the rest of her immediate family. Margarete had died in 1941, but her father Georg was living there with her sister Ella and her second husband Walter, as well as Anna Lee (formerly Anneliese)—whom Lilo had helped to raise in Amsterdam.

Ella and Walter had built a large, beautiful home in the early 1940s, a five-minute drive from the beach in Pacific Palisades. There were three bedrooms upstairs, each opening onto a balcony overlooking the backyard, which had a pool, badminton court, and tropical plants. Breezes coming off the ocean sometimes wafted through the house. Georg Ballin had an upstairs bedroom; a live-in maid resided in a downstairs bedroom. When Lilo arrived, she took the other upstairs bedroom and started working in Ella's photo store in Los Angeles.

As a boy, I loved going to Ella's sunny, modern home. I luxuriated in the large house and the outdoor space—I especially enjoyed swimming and playing badminton—which contrasted starkly with the crowded city streets and apartments of New York City. But even when I was young, I picked up on the tensions among Lilo, Ella, and Anna Lee. Ella and Anna Lee were not particularly close, perhaps because Ella's temperament was not particularly empathetic (her strengths were her practicality, ambition, and organization, not her tenderness), and perhaps because of the unhealed wound inflicted by Ella's leaving Anna Lee in Europe when she and Walter came to the United States. Either way, little warmth existed between mother and daughter.

More than that, I was also aware of a gulf between Lilo and the rest of the Ballin women. Although my mother could be caring toward Lilo (in particular, I was touched by a letter my mother sent in 1947 offering to help Lilo pay her rent), Ella and Suse had always been closer; Lilo was the outsider. She was the middle daughter; she spent her childhood being perceived as fragile and needy. The family questioned her decision-making, doubted the wisdom of her relationship with Hans, and, most devastatingly, privately blamed her for not getting herself and Ellien out of Europe in time. At the very least, they felt she should have sent Ellien to the United States either with my parents or with Georg and Margarete. They criticized Lilo for not being as savvy as Ella and my mother, imagining that if she had done things differently, Ellien would still be alive. Lilo's awareness of their judgment exacerbated the guilt she already felt. She could never shake the feeling that what had happened to her daughter was her fault.

I remember my mother talking with Ella and hearing them tsk-tsk Lilo's idiosyncrasies; to me, it felt like they were ganging up on her. No doubt guilt on the part of all three sisters also played a significant role, though I can parse out only some of the dynamics. Ella and my mother each had a child; their good fortune may have caused them to feel uncomfortable around Lilo's palpable grief. In addition, they did not know—and could not bear to know—what Lilo had experienced during the war. It was too difficult for them to witness her pain. Instinctively, to protect themselves they pushed her away, wounding her again and again.

The rift inside the family was not unique to the Ballins. Jewish families around the world struggled with the reverberating consequences of the Holocaust. The cataclysmic events of those years redounded on individuals, requiring them to draw on emotional resources and skills they did not have. While Ella and Suse remained close, sharing a similar past and bonding over the experience of motherhood, Lilo—the only member of the trio without a child—was the odd woman out. Sadly for all of them, neither Ella nor Suse seemed to take the steps necessary to close the gap.

Lilo's rupture with Anna Lee was perhaps the most painful. Lilo naturally reached out to the child she had loved and helped to raise, who had been so close to her own daughter. But Anna Lee had remade herself as an American. She rejected her Jewish identity and European roots, and she had little interest in renewing the close relationship with her aunt. If she grieved for Ellien, who had practically been her sister, she never showed it. She seemed to have suppressed it all and moved on with an almost aggressive desire to divorce herself from her Jewish past.

Anna Lee was immersed in preparations for high school graduation and matriculation at Stanford University. For Lilo, it would have been hard enough to watch Anna Lee growing up, always seeing the shadow of her own daughter frozen at age fourteen. Her grief might have been eased had Anna Lee let Lilo share in her life and participate in her successes and accomplishments in some way. But Anna Lee, like her mother and my mother, seemed determined to keep Lilo at a distance. The entire family seemed to be allergic to Lilo's pain.

Fortunately, Lilo was blessed by comfort from another source. In 1947, she met Henry Kahn, formerly a lawyer in Germany, who became her calm, kind, and thoughtful companion. They married on October 26, 1948, at Ella's home in the Palisades. In later years, I wondered whether the family was relieved, imagining that Lilo's marriage would allow her to move on and that her happiness could blot out the past, absolving them all of their guilt over her suffering. Of course, life does not work this way. Lilo's wartime trauma never entirely left her, but Henry provided her with much-needed stability, love, and reassurance.

Henry had a photo studio on Sunset Boulevard, where he developed, enlarged, and printed black-and-white photographs for Hollywood movie stars and directors. I loved going there. Henry taught me about photography and initiated me into the mysteries of the darkroom, a secret hideaway

Henry and Lilo during their wedding weekend, October 1948.

where magic happened. I was fascinated by the chemical process of photography and relished learning how to immerse each photo in different solutions, add the fixer, and witness the mysterious alchemy that allowed the ghostly forms to take recognizable shape on paper.

Lilo worked with Henry in the photo studio, greeting customers, answering the phone, and managing the books. She had an easy way with people and made friends more easily than my own mother. I remember Lilo striking up conversations with customers who came into the store, her gracious manner making them feel welcome and important. Though she wasn't particularly efficient, customers never seemed to mind waiting while she hunted for their prints.

Lilo had a wonderful smile and bright, beautiful blue eyes. She always made me, like the photo shop's customers, feel important. She was demonstrative and affectionate in ways that were different from my parents' more reserved style. I never understood why Ella, Anna Lee, and even my own mother were so often cold and distant toward her. Lilo was fragile and wounded: Why weren't they all kinder and more tolerant? But I never asked. I understood that like so much else in our lives, the reasons weren't mine to question.

My grandfather Georg with his daughters Lilo, Suse, and Ella, October 1948.

Instead, I quietly claimed Lilo for myself. I stopped staying at Ella's house when I went to Los Angeles, in part because Ella had married again after her husband Walter died, and I strongly disliked her new husband, Harry. (My grandfather Georg apparently felt the same way, because he, too, had moved out of Ella's home to live with Lilo and Henry, though a few years later, he moved into a nursing home.) Mainly, however, I stayed with Lilo and Henry because I treasured the cozy warmth of their home. I had a growth spurt at around age fourteen, and from then on, Lilo called me "Charlie Longlegs." In the mornings, we enjoyed leisurely breakfasts on the patio, and in the evenings, Lilo and Henry put on a long-playing record, filling their small house with classical music and opera.

When I stayed there, I slept on the pullout couch in their second bedroom. Lilo tucked me in at night, gave me a kiss, and then closed the door behind her. But I didn't go to sleep. Often, I got out of bed, tiptoed across the room, and stood before a photo collage Lilo must have made of images from before the war. There were several photos of young, smiling Ellien—one with Lilo and several with another girl, whom I didn't recognize as Anna Lee. Another photo showed Lilo smiling at the camera, standing with a man looking at her adoringly, with his arm slung around her shoulders. And a cutout circle with the words *Voor Mam van Ellien* (For Mom from Ellien)

Lilo's collage of photos and keepsakes.

had been carefully drawn in colored pencil. There was also a pastel drawing of a girl that I knew must be Ellien: rosy cheeks, light brown hair, and huge blue eyes looking out with a winsome expression. She was a beautiful child.

I was fascinated by this haunting shrine to my cousin. I knew she had died because of the Nazis' persecution of the Jews, though I knew nothing more than that. Sleeping in that room night after night, I developed my own private connection to her, partly to get close to Lilo's loss and partly as a reminder that only circumstances separated her fate from mine. But it wasn't only that. Since I had almost no relationship with my cousin Anna Lee, I couldn't help but think wistfully about Ellien and believe she would have been a part of my life had she lived.

Lilo never spoke to me about the photos or volunteered any answers to questions I might have had. I was curious about my lost cousin and confused about who was who in these photos that were clearly so important to my aunt. I would have loved to hear some stories about her, but like so much else in my young life, I didn't dare to break the fragile silence that clung to the family's past. Over the years, my questions only grew, giving rise to new ones about my family and how the war years shaped not only their lives but mine as well.

12

Making Sense of the Present

Over the years I worked on this book, Kat and I traveled to France, Holland, Germany, Switzerland, and Sweden. We stood in cemeteries, visited apartments, dug through dusty archives, and sat with historians—all in search of a past that played out almost entirely before I was born.

Although many formative events of my youth took place in Los Angeles with the Ballin family, my childhood's true center of gravity was New York. I remember Sundays, the day my father often left on his travels to see customers around the United States or suppliers in Europe and Asia. He and I took the elevator to the top floor of our building and then climbed a flight of creaky, dirty stairs, pushed open the door, and stepped out onto the black tar roof where we played catch, just the two of us. I remember quiet nights when my mother sang me German lullabies in her fine, high alto, and her cool hand on my forehead when I was in bed with the flu, mumps, and measles, soothing me and rebuilding our fractured bond. I remember Saturday afternoons after synagogue, driving with my parents to Jacob Riis Park or Jones Beach, my mother picking up my father and me several blocks away from Kehilath Jeshurun, out of respect for the more observant Jews who did not drive on Shabbos. My mother would watch and laugh with delight as my dad held my baseball bat in one hand and tossed tennis balls into air

A quick selfie with Kat, Amsterdam, 2016.

with the other, hitting them to me, never missing a swing. I'd run and dive to chase those fly balls down, invariably getting coated head to toe with sand. I marveled at his skill: In my childhood mind, I was convinced that if he'd grown up here (and cared to learn the rules of the game, which I tried to teach him multiple times), he could have been a major leaguer.

Many of my memories center on Max and Erna. We always celebrated Chanukah in their cozy living room on Manhattan's Upper West Side, taking turns spinning the dreidel, holding our breath to see if our luck would last. I particularly remember a few times when I was the last man standing against the ever-competitive Erna. On other occasions, we played Chinese checkers, Monopoly, Scrabble, and eventually, my father began to teach me chess—taking a few of his pieces off the board to give me an advantage. In spring and fall, at Max and Erna's vacation home in Upstate New York, we swam, hiked, and played tennis and croquet, again with Erna presiding and enforcing the rules.

I especially loved playing four-hand works on the piano with Max, his infectious joy spilling over as we filled the house with Mozart, Schubert, Brahms, and Beethoven. These were uncomplicated moments, fragments of memory that somehow rise to the surface even after many decades. They may

My parents and me, Belle Harbor, New York, 1948.

not be important to history, but they are *my* treasures—recollections of a sheltered childhood whose cost to my family I only now understand.

In some ways, it was as if I had four parents rather than two, and I grew up seeing the differences in style between my parents and Max and Erna. Whereas my parents assumed more or less traditional roles—my mother mostly deferred to my father, who set the tone and made most of the family decisions—Erna was the dominant force in her relationship with Max. While our lifestyle was perfectly comfortable, Max and Erna lived more lavishly, spending the money from Max's pharmaceutical company freely, not having to worry about providing for children. The two of them lived in a penthouse on 87th Street and Riverside Drive. Dinners at their home, prepared by Erna with the help of a maid, were elegant affairs, beginning with top-notch hors d'oeuvres in the living room, including the best smoked salmon and foie gras, and continuing in the dining room with a leisurely meal and dessert served on elegant china. They traveled often to Europe, sailed first class, and stayed in five-star hotels.

When I was in elementary school, I began going to Max and Erna's after school once a week. They had hired a tutor to help them improve their English; the same woman began helping me get rid of my lisp. In fifth grade, I began spending one night a week at their apartment. In the morning, we had breakfast together before I left for school. They lived in a building with a concierge and a swimming pool in the basement, and sometimes Max and I took an early-morning dip before starting the day.

Even with the closeness in our families, Erna's forceful personality took a toll. My reserved mother didn't stand a chance when Erna was around, and she refused to compete with her for attention. Tensions deepened. We visited Max and Erna at their house upstate less and less frequently; I suspect my mother simply could not tolerate the friction of being around her sister-in-law. Instead, my parents rented rooms in the summers in a modest lodge on Main Street in Tannersville, New York, and frequented hotels for weekends on Lake Mahopac or Lake Mohegan, or in Dutchess County on the Hudson. In contrast to Max, my father refused to buy a country house, always leery of real estate because it could not be quickly turned into cash if it became necessary to flee the country.

Eventually, Erna's personality affected my relationship with her as well. Although she loved me and meant well (she was particularly responsible for ensuring that I read challenging works of literature, especially the Russian masters), her domineering nature could be exhausting. Once when I slept over at their apartment, something happened between us. I can no longer remember the details, only that I was upset and when I returned home, I told my parents I wanted nothing more to do with my aunt. My father and Max must have discussed it and smoothed matters over, but I never slept at their home again. As was typical in my family, we did not address the problems openly. It was not the most emotionally healthy way to cope with issues, but I never knew any other way until I became an adult.

In the wake of my fallout with Erna, I remained close to Max. It was a special relationship, and I learned I could talk with Max about things I could not share with my own father. (For instance, I know that he advocated for me about my desire to go away to college, though my father would have preferred that I stay in New York City.) Looking back, I see that even with his carefree, exuberant persona, he carried his wartime demons with him, though of course he never once spoke to me about them. I remember hearing Erna say he used to scream and cry in his sleep. When we walked together, he often grasped my arm so tightly that it hurt—a small gesture that spoke to his lingering sense of fear and apprehension.

In fact, his charm and style covered a multitude of anxieties. He never learned to drive and was so afraid of air travel that he and Erna only crossed the ocean on transatlantic liners and traveled around Europe by train. A photo taken on one of their sea crossings in the early 1950s shows them seated at a small table for two. Erna is wearing a patterned halter dress with a large brooch at her throat; one hand with well-manicured nails and a large cocktail ring is visible. She is elegant, unsmiling, looking at the camera with a slightly quizzical expression, as if caught off guard. Max is dapper in his tuxedo, tanned and healthy, silver hair at his temples. They had clearly just finished a meal and were enjoying their coffee, two packs of cigarettes on the table. I look at the picture, seeking signs of the history that they carried. If I look hard enough, I can see it in Erna's guarded expression and in Max's pensive half smile.

There are other memories that I never thought much about until I learned more about my parents' lives. I vividly recall being with my friend Robert "Pucci" Low in the backseat of my father's Kaiser-Frazer as he and my mother took us to the beach for the day.[1] My father began his favorite

Erna and Max dining aboard ship, 1950s.

game: Name a town, city, state, or country. Then the next person had to name one beginning with the last letter of the just-named place. Each locale could only be used once. He was testing my knowledge, my awareness of the world outside my New York City home. Then he would ask us harder questions: What would it be like to live in another country? What do they eat? What language do they speak? What is the currency there? How would you adjust? Can you imagine leaving your home? If you left, where would you go? My father's questions were more than an idle game to pass the time. They were a playful yet serious way to prepare me in case things took a turn. He wanted me to be adept, alert, and ready, in case it ever stopped being safe to be a Jew in America.

In another memory, I sat in synagogue next to my father, who was next to Max. They were dozing off during the sermon, but I was listening. I heard the rabbi criticizing German Jews, accusing them of assimilating into German culture, distancing themselves from their Jewish identity, and deserting their brethren and religion in the belief they could escape antisemitism and find full acceptance in German society. Why do I recall this? Because even then, I resented the implicit critique of my own family. I now understand the warning bells that went off in my young brain, the sense that the story was more complicated than the rabbi's self-satisfied moralizing. He was pushing an agenda against assimilation at the expense of the complex truth.

Most vividly, I remember the McCarthy era and the Communist witch hunts. My family, ever on the alert for signs of danger, perceived the underlying antisemitism in the rhetoric of the time and worried it was a prelude to a rise of fascism in America. The arrest, conviction, and execution of Ethel and Julius Rosenberg as Russian spies only heightened their concerns because the event echoed past accusations of Jewish conspiracies against the state, such as the infamous Dreyfus Affair in France. I can still hear my parents and Max and Erna, who thought I was not listening, having quiet, worried conversations about possible emigration. They discussed which countries they would consider fleeing to, including Canada, Australia, and Switzerland.

As a child, I remember McCarthyism as a vague, oblique menace. But now, having learned about their experiences, I imagine my parents and Max and Erna must have felt profound fear that it was all to be replayed. Where would they go if America were no longer a safe harbor?

The combination of my family's narrow escape and my own good fortune growing up with parents who provided a very good life led me to think of myself as "the lucky one." All around me were reminders of people my own age who were either cut down in an early death or touched by parental loss. First and foremost was Ellien. Then there was my sister, who never got to live. Two of my childhood friends, Daniel and Elizabeth, had lost their fathers during the war. There was Stephen, the son of Max and Erna's friends, who was orphaned at age fifteen.[2] Most of all, there was my childhood friend Pucci, who had been a close and intimate part of my growing-up years. I'll never forget the shock I felt when my parents told me Pucci had been hit by a truck and killed at age thirteen.

This pervasive sense of good fortune translated into an ethos of looking forward, never to dwell on past hardships or feelings. But being lucky wasn't always easy. It brought pressure to live up to the adults' expectations for me and to stand in for those who had died or never got to live. I had no right to complain, no right to dwell on my losses or setbacks. The weight was even heavier for me as an only child. As so often happens in families, this was handed down in a thousand small ways that I felt but could not name. One of these was my bar mitzvah, which was a pivotal event of my childhood. I was in the eighth grade at Ramaz, the Modern Orthodox yeshiva, and I had been preparing diligently for about a year to read both the weekly Torah and Haftorah portions. At last, I was ready. I was excited and nervous that morning as we left for synagogue, probably even more so because it was the only time we ever left early enough to attend the entire hours-long service.

All eyes were on me as I read the Torah's ancient words, inscribed on the sacred scroll, a silver pointer guiding my words. My portion included the reading of the Ten Commandments, for which the entire congregation stood, making my reading feel even more momentous. I was taking my place among the men of my family, as I had always been prepared to do.

After the ceremony, it was time to celebrate. My parents hosted a catered lunch in the synagogue's social hall, not only for our family and their friends but for mine as well. It signified how far they had come in the short time they had been in America. It must have felt momentous to them. Afterward, when the family came back to our new apartment—we had moved about three months before to a larger, more beautiful one in a safer neighborhood—I snapped a picture of my father and uncle sitting together. It's not very impressively composed, as photographs go, but I must have sensed something significant in the moment. There they were, my family's patriarchs, having survived and prospered in their new life. The memory of that day is emblematic of so many things: my place as the only child in a world of refugees who sacrificed so much to remake their lives in America, the endurance of Jewish life and practice in the aftermath of the Holocaust, and my new role as an adult in the Jewish community, with its attendant privileges and responsibilities. Most of all, this day embodied the fact that I had accomplished something important, not only for myself but for the whole family. Their hopes and dreams rested on my narrow shoulders. Far from resenting or resisting that fact, I wanted to build upon that foundation, to grow up to be like them, and to continue the family legacy.

And I did, as best I could.

It would be strange to come to the end of this family memoir without reflecting on BSI/Roland, which was such an elemental part of our life and through which many of our family's values were reflected. As a child, I saw the way my father conducted his business, never leaving its success to chance. It was vital to me that I emulate his values and work ethic. He flew around the United States every two weeks and traveled every year to Europe twice and Asia once, each trip lasting two or three weeks. He always carried with him on these visits to customers and suppliers a big briefcase with the sample tins and a book with product labels (which my mother kept up to date) neatly pasted inside.

As a little boy, I sometimes took the subway with my mother to the office in Tribeca, a commercial neighborhood in those days, where she managed the staff. Roland Foods was housed in a beautiful old redbrick building at 16 Hudson Street, between Duane and Reade streets, with granite keystones and corners. When they started the company, my parents sat at two wooden desks facing each other. As time passed, my father moved into the "corner office," and my mother worked there while I was in school and at home in the evenings after I went to bed. I remember afternoons when I'd run down to visit my uncle Max at his pharmaceutical company, just a floor below my parents' office in the same building, and stepping out with my mother onto the busy Manhattan street to visit a favorite nearby cheese shop where the owner would invariably slip me a few little treats or candy.

My father hired other newcomers and refugees whenever he could, focusing on whether they could do the work, not whether they held a degree from a prestigious university or even how well they spoke English. He also believed in promoting from within. One was a young Holocaust survivor named Kurt Lang, who'd lost most of his family in the camps. Kurt was hired as a file clerk, but he was ambitious and wanted to be in sales, so my father let him try. Kurt started walking to nearby Chinatown on his lunch

Bruno leaving on a business trip to Europe, November 1958.

hour to make sales. He soon became the company's main salesman there and, eventually, for the entire country. He learned enough Mandarin and Cantonese to do business, and it's thanks to Kurt that Roland eventually imported many Asian specialties that were unknown to the American market, including sesame oil, ramen, dried lychees, and fish sauce. He was indispensable to the business and stayed at Roland for nearly sixty years.[3]

When I took over, I gradually increased the company's focus on food-service sales, importing and distributing specialty foods used by chefs and restaurateurs nationwide. We continued expanding our selections with products from all over Asia, Africa, Europe, the Caribbean, South America, and the Middle East. By the time I retired, the company was importing over 1,400 items from dozens of countries. In addition, we were selling Roland-brand products in about forty countries, mainly in Central and South America. Roland Foods was many things to our family, and I believe some of its importance lies in the fact that food brings people joy and community, and it can allow us to explore and appreciate other cultures.

Trauma reverberates. It lives in people and gets re-enacted in the most mundane, benign ways. As an only child, I observed without understanding and felt without knowing that there were stories and meanings beyond my ken. Starting with the discovery of my family's trove of letters, I embarked on a journey filled with unanticipated obstacles, struggles, surprises, joys, grief, and rewards, all in the service of closing the loop on a silenced family story and the puzzles that silence created. That was the work of this book.

Nothing about it was easy or simple. It took place over decades, in fits and starts, as I battled with myself about the need to know and not to know, wavering between the desire to confront my family's past and the desire to bury it. Was it easier for me to move forward with or without the truth? Now that I know my family's story more fully—how it began, how it unfolded, the pivot points along the way—my relationship to my relatives, to myself, and to the world around me has deepened.

I wish I'd known years ago what I know now. Everyone is gone, and buried with them are stories I'll never hear and answers to questions I never asked. My maternal grandmother Margarete Ballin died before I was born. I have only vague, pleasant memories of Flora, who passed away in 1947, and Georg, who followed in 1950. I do remember my maternal grandfather, Georg

My grandfather Georg Ballin and me, Los Angeles, c. 1948.

Ballin, from the time I spent with him in Los Angeles. He was a gentle, kind soul who died when I was sixteen. But all these characters came to vivid life for me in the letters my mother saved and through my research with Kat.

Some of my hardest losses came early. Max suffered a heart attack in 1962 while he and Erna were on holiday in the Swiss Alps. He remained there a few months, until he was strong enough to move to a hotel in Zurich. He and Erna planned to stay there for a few weeks and then return to New York. But while Erna was out on an errand, Max had a second attack. He died alone in the hotel room.

Erna never remarried. Max was the love of her life.

Losing him was unspeakably painful for my father. He never fully recovered. Their relationship was almost impossibly intense, which I can see in the letters they sent to one another—so full of fury and insult as well as the deepest brotherly love. The two of them shared memories of a harrowing time as well as an iron-willed determination to build a new life. As for me,

Max at their upstate home, Krumville, New York, mid-1950s.

I grieved too, missing my piano partner—I was unable to bring myself to play for eight years after he died—and favorite aesthete and epicurean.

A scant four years later, my father died just as unexpectedly, also of a heart attack, just shy of his sixty-sixth birthday. I was dazed as well as bereaved. My intent to pursue international law ended, and my life as steward and builder of my father's business began.[4] I married a year later. My first wife, Joanne, supported my career choice, and together we had two sons. As my life moved forward, running my father's business with my mother at my side, I tried to honor the past—conveying my parents' values to my own sons—while maintaining our family's imperative to grasp the good fortune they had created and make the most of it.

My mother's oldest sister, Ella, died in 1981. Though she and I were never close, she remained dear to my mother; they spoke on the phone at least once a week, even though they lived across the country from each other. Then, in 1988, my mother died, just weeks after telling me about the letters she had hidden for more than forty years. She bequeathed to me a precious,

Ella, Suse, and Lilo, Los Angeles, 1966.

extraordinary record, a history the family had mostly tried to forget. Its existence complicated the family imperative of always looking forward. But I believe my mother was tacitly asking me to look back, to consider the past as a way of making sense of the present.

In 1987, we said goodbye to Erna, the commanding, colorful, sometimes abrasive aunt who loved me fiercely and showered me with advice even when I didn't want it. She lived by herself for eighteen years after Max's death, moving from their apartment to one on East End Avenue, then to Zurich, and then back to New York. She spent the final seven years of her life in a nursing home with dementia. In retrospect, I see that since she stood in such stark contrast to my mother, I didn't always fully appreciate her. The research on this book helped me see her more clearly. She was able to take charge when it mattered most, to bring her total focus, determination, and wits to keeping Max's spirits up, getting him out of Falaise, and securing passage to Cuba and then to America. Had it not been for her, our family history—and my own life—would have been very different indeed.

In 1993, Henry Kahn, who had brought joy back to Lilo and who had been so kind to me when I stayed with them, passed away after years of living with Alzheimer's. The next year, my cousin Anna Lee died of cancer at sixty-six. Despite her youthful determination to keep Lilo at a distance, Lilo had stepped in at the end to care for her, reclaiming her long-ago role as surrogate mother during Ella's absence.

On a bright, sunny, cool day in December 1994, I sat in the front row of the chapel at the Jewish cemetery, twisting in my hands the written eulogy that I was soon to deliver. A few days before, I had gotten a call that Lilo—who had been diagnosed with a slow-growing blood cancer many years before—was fading. I flew to Los Angeles, hoping to see her before she passed away. But once again, as with so many of my loved ones, I arrived too late. I had missed the opportunity to be with her when she died and to hold her hand and tell her how important she had always been to me.

She was the last.

I was distraught, passing a sleepless night in my hotel. I lay in bed reflecting on my gratitude for the uncomplicated, profound relationship I'd always had with Lilo, who I now know loved me even before she'd even met me. As the next of kin, I'd had to identify her body. Now I was in a chapel surrounded by people I barely knew. As I stood to speak, I was acutely aware that I was standing in for Ellien, who should have outlived her mother and

My grandchildren, Brian, Emily, Joshua, Harry, and Noah, at my eightieth birthday celebration, New York City, 2023.

been there to memorialize her. I looked out at the faces of those who were gathered and tried my best to honor the life of a woman who endured so much suffering and loss and who had never relinquished her essential sweetness. I felt deeply the finality of that moment.

From 1994, when Lilo died, until 2009, when my German friend Feli Gürsching took me to my father's old, dust-covered office in Frankfurt, I refrained from wrestling with my family's legacy. The experience of looking at the railroad tracks over which my father had escaped helped me see the potential of my relatives' stories, showing me that their lives could have broader meaning for more people. But even then, I dragged my heels. I was more comfortable letting others take up the questions than owning them myself.

But when the time came to commit to the story, I was ready, and I have never regretted it. Perhaps it was because I was older and more reflective; because I had sold the business and my sons were grown and living their own lives; because I had remarried, and my wife, Xiomara, brought a new focus and energy to my life along with steady support and encouragement to this work; and because of Kat's enthusiasm, persistence, and questions. Surely, it was the alchemy of all those factors that provided me with a clarity I didn't have before. I resolved that the way to honor my family was to know them more fully, to brave my feelings, to document what they experienced in order to build a coherent family story that I could pass on to my children and grandchildren.

The work on this book—the travels, research, reading, and questions—became a way to end the familial cycle of silence. My parents' generation had good reasons to bury painful memories. They had to look forward to ensure a future. I, on the other hand, had the gift of time and perspective. I delved deeply into my family's story for my own sake and for the benefit of my sons and their children. I did it for my parents and for Max and Erna, and for Lilo and Ellien. I did it because nothing is more important than giving meaning to the loss and suffering; without that, the oppressors own the story. I hope others will see in my family's story the larger currents of oppression, displacement, flight, and struggle that play out among tens of millions of refugees today. Like my family, they carry their scars, look ahead, and sacrifice everything in search of a life they can bequeath to the next generation.

In Memoriam

What I didn't know during my childhood, but what surely weighed on the minds of my parents and Max and Erna in my growing-up years, were the stories of the family members who did not get out of Europe. Had it not been for the papers my mother saved, I might never have known about anyone in our family, other than Ellien, who was murdered in the Holocaust. No one ever spoke to me about these lost relatives or about my family's desperate, failed attempts to rescue them, though I'm sure that they came up in conversation among the adults. I wasn't aware of it, but their absence must have echoed through my family's postwar life. Reading the letters my mother saved, I developed an attachment to these people whose stories emerged from our research, and I felt it was important to memorialize them in a meaningful way. The Nazis attempted to erase the very existence of individuals, families, and entire communities. Briefly recounting their lives here is a small act of resistance.

Hans Schwab was Max's closest friend and most direct loss. He was Max and Bruno's cousin, Max founded a company with him (which allowed Hans to get a French visa), and he was a regular at La Ricoquette in Bénerville with Max and Erna in the summer of 1939.[1] He and Max reported for internment together in early September 1939 and endured Lisieux and Falaise together. Max often mentioned Hans in his letters,

Hans Schwab's photo on his *sauf-conduit*, 1941. (Courtesy of Archives départementales des Bouches-du-Rhône, 142 W 35 / Conseil départemental 13—Tous droits réservés.)

referring to him as his "comrade" who kept his spirits up and brought him comfort. In one of Erna's letters, she tells Max she's knitting a sweater for Hans, who didn't have warm clothing.

When Max was released, Hans remained in the camp. Max was deeply worried for him and did what he could, trying unsuccessfully to secure a job, an affidavit, and money for him from a company called Mavest in New York. He urgently enlisted Bruno's aid: "He is the primary person for whom we have to do something," Max wrote on January 3, 1940, from Vichy. "I have to send him every week between 200–250 francs. The minimum which Mavest should do is to send him money. They are big capitalists. . . . They do nothing but give vague promises. . . . You must act quickly. Money is necessary. They know how to arrange payment. I hate them from the bottom of my heart. I await your news impatiently, and I thank you in the name of our poor friend."

Hans was finally released on January 29, 1940. By the end of February, he was ordered to report to an assembly center in Limoges, from which he was transferred to the Braconne camp, near Angoulême. He failed a physical exam on March 4, at which point he was declared unfit and released with an authorization to live and work in Ambazac. He quickly helped establish and run, for a pittance, a factory there that employed more than a hundred workers.

At the beginning of August 1940, Hans was ordered to report to the small Saint-Germain-les-Belles camp near Limoges. From there, on November 4, he was sent to Gurs, the notorious internment camp located at the foot of the Pyrenees, near the Spanish border. Both camps were in the so-called Free Zone of France. Conditions in Gurs were particularly horrific. Prisoners suffered from overcrowding, severe shortages of water, food, and clothing, and rampant contagious diseases. The primitive barracks were constructed of thin wood planks and tarred fabric that did nothing to keep out the elements. Thanks to the region's very rainy weather, the grounds were drenched in mud, which prisoners vainly tried to manage with paths made of stones.

Hans continued to try to emigrate by any possible means. On November 14, he wrote a letter from Gurs, asking to be released so he could return to work in Ambazac (also in the Free Zone). Even though the letter included two references, from the town's mayor and from its chief of police, this appeal was denied. Then, in the spring, an inspector certified Hans' papers, indicating that he was likely to get a U.S. visa. That document also showed that Bruno had provided a blanket financial guarantee for him in the amount of 10,000 francs.

On May 14, 1941, Hans was shipped to Les Milles, a camp where Vichy authorities held detainees likely to emigrate in the near future, as well as those who would soon be deported. Hans seemed to be in the former, fortunate category. That August, he received a letter from American Export Lines in Marseille, stating that his ticket to the United States had been paid—by either Bruno or Max—and that he should present himself at their offices. Despite this, Hans was not allowed to leave. He survived in Les Milles for more than a year. In March 1942, he passed a physical exam that would have allowed him to join one of the official labor brigades, but there is no record of his enlistment.

Despite possessing a ticket to sail for the United States, Hans was trapped. His request for a U.S. visa was apparently denied. We were not able to determine why. Perhaps the reason was that the personnel at the U.S. consulate in Marseille had changed: Harry Bingham and Myles Standish—the empathetic consuls who had signed the papers allowing Flora and Georg to leave—were now gone, and the new staff was not as eager to help those who were trying to flee. At the same time, in the summer of 1942, the Vichy authorities were increasing roundups and deportations of foreign Jews.

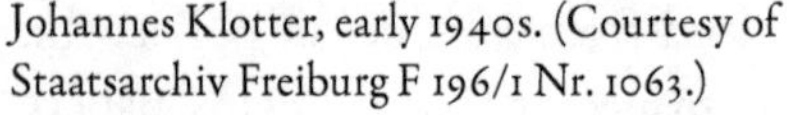

Johannes Klotter, early 1940s. (Courtesy of Staatsarchiv Freiburg F 196/1 Nr. 1063.)

Erna Klotter, late 1930s.

On August 12, 1942, Hans was deported to Drancy and from there to Auschwitz. Of the 1,000 people on the transport, 817, including all the children, were sent immediately to the gas chambers. We assume Hans was among them. Only five people from that transport survived until liberation.

Max had tried very hard to help Hans. After the war, when it became clear that all his efforts had failed, Max grieved the loss of his friend and carried the heavy knowledge that, had it not been for pure luck, he might have been murdered along with Hans in Auschwitz.

The surname Klotter was unfamiliar to me when I began paging through my mother's letters. As we researched further, I learned that Erna Klotter was born Erna Scheidt, and she was my grandfather Karl's niece, which meant she was my father and Max's first cousin. Her mother was not Jewish, and her father converted (at least in part to improve his chances of getting an orchestral conducting job), so she was baptized as a child. In 1915, she was admitted to the University of Heidelberg, where she studied philology and went on to earn a PhD in 1923, a remarkable accomplishment for a woman at that time. In 1929, she married Johannes Klotter, who was not Jewish, and they settled in Karlsruhe, where they were politically active in the Deutsche Friedensgesellschaft (German Peace Society, or DFG) and

Lore Scheidt, late 1940s. (Courtesy of Landesarchiv Baden-Württemberg, Abt. Staatsarchiv Ludwigsburg EL 350 I Bü 25934.)

the German Socialist Party (SPD). At a time when the Nazis were arresting Socialist leaders, Johannes and Erna risked their own safety to visit compatriots in prison and even smuggled messages to them.

The Gestapo started harassing the couple at home in the summer of 1933. Afraid they would be arrested, Johannes and Erna left Germany on October 1, 1933, and moved to Thônon, France, on the shores of Lake Geneva, taking Erna's widowed mother Lore with them.

A letter written by Max on July 4, 1939, indicates that he and Bruno were helping them financially, having already given them 5,000 francs that year. Flora reported bluntly on their dire circumstances in a June 1939 letter to Max, writing, "We found Lore very aged and Erna miserable-looking, much more needs to be done there. . . . Hans actually only has an 'alien's passport' without permission to exit and re-enter [France]—the only way to help is to somehow get him customers."

With France's declaration of war on September 3, 1939, Johannes, like other German men in France, was ordered to report to a camp and faced the sequester of their property and income, pushing the couple into an even more desperate financial situation. Johannes was detained on October 3, 1939. Letters from the Klotters show they were barely getting by and that the Scheidts continued to send them money. Erna wrote, "Dear Aunt Flora and Erna [Max's wife], I thank you from the bottom of my heart and most sincerely for the cash remittance, which really does us a world of good. Now we are beginning to drink milk in order to get back on our feet. Two weeks ago, our terrible *propriétaire* [landlord] absolutely did not want to wait any longer. He pressed and harassed the gentleman who is in charge of the *séquestre* to sell our furniture immediately."

More letters flew between Max, Flora, and Bruno, all trying to determine how much money they could provide to help them. On July 24, 1940, Flora frantically wrote to Bruno, "Today came a desperate letter from Johannes Klotter, who doesn't know where his wife and Lore are. I'm often nearly desperate about all of the misery in the world now."

Johannes located his wife and mother-in-law in Thuy in the nearby French Alps. They had retreated there after France's defeat, hoping that they would be safer in a more remote village. Bruno reported back to Max, "Their letters are ghastly and I'm not so optimistic about their future. But we certainly don't want to let them starve. Therefore, send another 300 francs as soon as possible on my behalf." On October 12, 1940, Johannes was interned again, this time in Loriol, and freed after a few months.

The Klotters appear to have lived undisturbed in the isolated village of Thuy, while it was under Italian control, from November 1942 until September 1943. But after Italy's surrender to the Allies, Hitler ordered his forces to invade the areas held by the Italians. Just five days later, on September 13, 1943, the Gestapo arrested Erna and Johannes. They were both taken to Annecy, where Johannes was interrogated, and then to Fort Montluc in Lyon. On October 8, 1943, they were transferred to Paris. Erna was sent to Drancy, and then, on October 28, to Auschwitz. The fact that her parents had converted to Christianity and that she'd been baptized didn't save her. In her transport of 1,000 people, 613 were immediately sent to the gas chambers. She was among them.

Johannes was sent from France to Germany, held in multiple prisons, and interrogated multiple times. He ended up in Karlsruhe prison on December 8, 1943, where the charges against him included escaping to France, fleeing from his military duty, antinationalistic activities, and listening to a foreign radio signal. Several weeks later, Johannes was told if he volunteered for the Wehrmacht, his record would be expunged. In the testimony he gave as part of his restitution claim, Johannes recalled that he answered, "Do you think that I am going to fight with enthusiasm for a country which I left because of its regime? After my wife and I have been arrested under degrading circumstances, separated from each other, and for four months I have been dragged through prisons and concentration camps, I cannot volunteer."

Because of his refusal to join the Wehrmacht, Johannes was deported to Dachau on March 22, 1944. He survived until April 29, 1945, when U.S. troops liberated the camp. He returned to France to search for his mother-in-law, and in mid-June, they were reunited. Lore had spent nearly two years barely surviving, alone in Thuy. She endured thanks to the generosity of her neighbors and because she sold her furniture and other belongings to eke out enough money on which to live.

Johannes stayed close to Lore for the rest of her life. He fought tirelessly for many years to get restitution for himself and for his wife Erna, hoping to use the money to support his bereaved mother-in-law. Johannes worked for a restitution commission and knew the system from the inside. In spite of this and after all they had endured, he was unable to get restitution during Lore's lifetime. He had to ask for financial assistance from Bruno, who willingly provided it. Johannes eventually received only a modest sum from Germany, though no amount could compensate for what he had suffered. Johannes did ask the German Red Cross to return his belongings from Dachau. Poignantly, he got back his wedding band, inscribed with his wife's initials and the date of their marriage.

Emil Lehrberger, Max and Bruno's uncle, was the youngest of my grandmother Flora's three brothers, born on June 25, 1880. He was the only brother who did not emigrate to the United States, largely because he was too young to go when his older siblings did. He lived in Darmstadt with a relative for some years and then joined Flora, Karl, and their family in Frankfurt. Like Karl and Max, Emil fought in World War I. He was a proud veteran of the Landwehr Infanterie of the 87th Regiment, and he was wounded in December 1914 and was left with only partial function in one leg.

On February 11, 1916, Emil married Lina Michel, and three months later, they welcomed a daughter, Rose. They lived a quiet life and ran a successful haberdashery business together. They must have endured the early years of Nazism relatively uneventfully, until *Reichspogromnacht*. Emil was arrested while on business in Bad Kissingen and was thrown into jail, where he remained until November 18, 1938. After Emil's release, he and Lina focused their efforts on trying to get out of Germany.

Emil Lehrberger, early 1920s.

Lina and Rose Lehrberger, 1916.

Lina and Emil's daughter Rose was able to emigrate from Germany and arrived in New York on January 6, 1939, from Le Havre, France. After my mother and father reached New York two months later, Rose lived with them for a short time. Emil and Lina remained in Frankfurt, struggling financially; their company had been de-registered on December 30, 1938, due to the law barring Jews from owning their own businesses. Flora sent her younger brother and his wife money whenever she could.

Bruno and Rose also did their best to support Emil and Lina financially and to help them escape Germany. We know that Bruno sent Emil $800 in the summer of 1939. In Emil's letters, he expressed hope they could eventually leave. He was selling his belongings to put together enough money to meet U.S. visa requirements and was leveraging his service in World War I to delay their deportation. Emil filed several applications for U.S. visas, always listing Rose and Bruno's support as a means of helping to meet financial requirements for approval. The U.S. government ignored Bruno's support, noting only that Rose worked as a housekeeper on the Upper West Side and could not provide the sufficient financial guarantees needed to sponsor them. As late as October 1941, Emil even tried to secure a visa and passage to Cuba—unfortunately, without success. After October 23, 1941, the Nazis banned emigration for Jews entirely, and Emil and Lina were trapped.

They remained in Frankfurt for another year, impoverished and desperate. They had to move several times and eventually lived as boarders with the father of one of Bruno's friends. Still, Emil clung to hope. He wrote to Rose that he was studying English in hopes of emigrating, and he even wrote portions of letters in English.

On September 15, 1942, Emil and Lina were deported to the ghetto-camp Theresienstadt. It was a way station for many German, Austrian, and Czech Jews en route to Auschwitz. Famous for its cultural life and its role as a centerpiece of Nazi propaganda, Theresienstadt was also an overcrowded ghetto, rife with disease, where tens of thousands died from malnutrition and illness. Emil was, like so many German Jews, simply unable to believe that his native country would betray him, especially because he had fought for Germany in the Great War, been wounded, and recognized as a veteran. Emil died in Theresienstadt on February 9, 1943. Lina was deported to Auschwitz on May 16, 1944. She did not survive, though we don't know the details or the date of her death.

Afterword

As we walked to dinner after our second visit to the Montessori school my cousin Ellien had attended, Ronald Sanders, our host, called our attention to this poem, etched on a plaque in the pavement. Hannie Voyles, an alumna of the school, wrote it about the indelible impact of witnessing her friends and their families being rounded up. Here is a translation from the original Dutch:

RAZZIA IN BEETHOVENSTRAAT,

AMSTERDAM 1943–1945

Violently
the trucks arrived:
They brought an end to
the children's world.

Eyes wide open
free of tears
they sat neatly,
the smallest up front.

There were parents,
no Jewish Council.
Death stood waiting for
the children in the street.

Now 65 years later
it still haunts me
how my friends disappeared
while I stood by.

Hannie Ostendorf Voyles
2006

Acknowledgments

In the nearly four decades since discovering my mother's trove of letters and documents, I have received invaluable assistance and encouragement from many wonderful individuals. Thank you all most sincerely for being a part of this journey. I could not have completed this project without you.

I am immensely grateful to the late Feli Gürsching, who was not only the first person to help with research but also the first to encourage me to delve deeply into my family history. She urged me to go beyond the basic facts and to write my family story with a broad audience in mind. In 2009, Feli encouraged my Swiss cousin Claudia Oliveri and me to visit Frankfurt and organized an impactful tour of archives and family sites for us. In 2016, despite already being very ill, Feli insisted on meeting Kat and me at the Historical Museum Frankfurt, where she introduced us to Jürgen Steen, a fellow historian. Without their help that day, we might never have solved some significant family mysteries. Feli sadly passed away four months later.

This book would lack many insights were it not for Hans-Peter Klein and Ingo Sielaff in Borken, Marie-Luis Folwaczny in Nordhausen, Mrs. Loether and Mrs. Wagner in Kitzingen, and Rosemarie Zepke in Würzburg. We thank them for welcoming Kat and me, sharing their town's Jewish history, and taking us to the local Jewish cemetery to find family tombstones.

On the first day of our first trip, by a pivotal stroke of good luck, Kat and I met Ronald Sanders in Amsterdam. I am deeply grateful to him for his long-standing dedication to preserving the memory of the Jewish children, including my cousin Ellien, who attended the First Montessori School in

Amsterdam. We are also indebted to Ronald for arranging many meaningful introductions for us, including Ellien's classmate, Betsy van der Meer, who shared invaluable memories; Betsy's daughter Cathy Jacob; and Stevyn Voyles Menegazzi, who gave us permission to translate and quote the poem written by her mother, Hannie Voyles.

Emanuel and Greet Lissaur warmly welcomed us into their home near Amsterdam and shared a family album with dozens of photos we had never seen of Ellien, Lilo, and Jessiah. I thank them for their generosity and honesty, offering us invaluable insight into the family and its dynamics.

My heartfelt thanks go to Thierry Marchand, our excellent travel companion to Bénerville and Lisieux and expert guide in Paris, who helped us untangle many puzzles surrounding historic events that took place in France and their effect on my family. Without his legwork and persistence, we would never have located La Ricoquette nor met our superb and sensitive hosts, Julia Schäfer and François Driesen. Spending time with them at La Ricoquette was exceptionally moving and meaningful. It was also Thierry who introduced us to key people and made arrangements for important visits throughout France. Thanks to Thierry, we met Jean-Bernard Challamel in Thuy, Jutta-Brigitte Millas in Marseille, Jean-Michel Urbajtel in Angoulême, and Guy Marchot, the author of the three-volume *Les Indésirables*, who provided historical information and researched family questions for us in regional archives. Each of them made important contributions to our understanding, and I thank them for their hospitality and assistance.

It was essential for me to visit the homes where my family's story began and unfolded, and, in this way, to begin to understand some of the pain that they carried. We thank the people who worked hard to organize these impactful visits for us: Christa Fischer in Frankfurt, Thierry Marchand in France, and Ronald Sanders in Amsterdam. And for graciously welcoming us, complete strangers, into their apartments, I sincerely thank all the present-day residents of my family's former homes.

Experts and professionals at museums graciously shared their knowledge and expertise. My family is forever indebted to the late Adelle Chabelski, who searched long and hard in her free time to locate Lilo's testimony in the remains of the dismantled Martyrs Memorial and Museum. Without Adelle's efforts, we would not have Lilo's heart-wrenching, first-person testimony. Beth Kean of the Holocaust Museum LA later tracked down Lilo's pictures that ended up at the museum. Rebecca Erbelding of the U.S. Holocaust Memorial Museum has been a fount of information and over the years patiently answered our seemingly endless questions. Batya Wolff of the Jewish Museum in Amsterdam was a wonderful guide and shared her resources and insights to help us answer several questions. And we thank Mirjam Wenzel, Eva Atlan, and Annika Friedman of the Jewish Museum Frankfurt for their encouragement and for sharing their knowledge of Jewish life in Frankfurt. Thank you also to Angela Jannelli who took the baton from Feli and continues her project, Bibliothek der Generationen at the Historical Museum Frankfurt, where my family history is preserved among many others.

I am very grateful to the entire team at Rutgers University Press, especially Alexander Hinton, Nela Navarro, and Natasha Zaretsky, the editors of the Genocide, Political Violence, Human Rights series, for their work in the field and for believing in this book. Thank you also for connecting me with Peggy Solic, who championed the book and expertly guided us through the editing process.

A vast project, such as this one, with a wealth of documents and letters in many languages, required the help of native speakers with a passion for history. I thank Christine Guenther for long ago agreeing to scan and organize the fragile letters and documents for me; the late Walter Karger who was invaluable in deciphering and translating many letters in old German script; Barbara A. Schmutzler for patiently checking and correcting German translations and offering excellent suggestions; Jeanette Patterson for translations of the French documents and letters; and Manon Hartogsveld and Pieter van Os for helping translate Dutch documents and the poignant poem by Hannie Voyles.

Over many years, David Black has been very forthcoming with insightful, practical advice and has introduced me to helpful contacts. I am also grateful to my cousins Jann Buckner, Barbara Grossman, Jay and Cathy Kaufman, Claudia Oliveri, Leslie Redd, and Vivian Scheidt, all of whom generously shared family stories that added depth to the book. In addition, I thank Patty Blum, Henry Ferris, James Gregorio, Marjorie Ingall, Anne Kelemen, Gary Ledet, Daniel Lee, Alexander Maro, Stefan Mentzer, Kavitha Rajagopalan, Michele Rosenberg, Dean Rotbart, Alexander Scheirle, Paul Steiger, Marc Stern, Erik Tozzi, and Alexi Zentner for their meaningful help at various stages.

This project and I personally have benefited enormously over the years from the knowledge and assistance of professors and leaders of NGOs, including Debórah Dwork (The Graduate Center, City University of New York);

Douglas Irvin-Erickson (George Mason University); Jocelyn Getgen Kestenbaum (Cardozo School of Law); Thomas Kuehne (Clark University); Max Pensky and Kerry Whigham (Binghamton University); Ernesto Verdeja (Notre Dame University); James Waller (University of Connecticut); Simon Adams (Center for Victims of Torture); Miriam Bistrovic, Renate Evers, Markus Krah, David Marwell, Frank Mecklenburg, and Billy Weitzer (Leo Baeck Institute); Tibi Galis and Owen Pell (Auschwitz Institute for the Prevention of Genocide and Mass Atrocities); Becca Heller (International Refugee Assistance Project); and Annie Polland (Tenement Museum).

Despite our passion for the project, both Kat and I came to the conclusion that telling the family story and bringing its individuals to life was an overwhelming task that required a professional. David Marwell kindly introduced me to Alexandra Zapruder, whose skill, insights, wealth of experience, and talent for storytelling are evident in this book, and I am very grateful. In addition, and very importantly, Natalie Holt was a key part of this endeavor, helping me organize my thoughts, writings, and notes through the years and tirelessly keeping this project organized and on track. And Christine Young worked with Natalie, Kat, and me on the edits, kept track of emails, and managed my other projects along with the book. Natalie and Christine, your feedback and passion for this project were invaluable. Kat and I thank both of you, and Alexandra, from the bottom of our hearts for your commitment and contributions to this endeavor.

I give special thanks to my partner on this quest, my travel companion and favorite sleuth, Kat Rohrer, for more than a dozen years of practical and emotional support on this daunting and difficult project. I came to rely on her knowledge and tenacity, amazing memory, and knack for finding a way where there seemingly was none. Her companionship and our shared experiences are central to this book and meaningful to me personally. We covered a lot of ground, both literally and emotionally, helped each other in the tough moments, and were able to find opportunities to laugh and enjoy each other's company. In the nearly sixty days of travel together over four years, we got to know each other well, forging a deep bond and lasting friendship.

I am most deeply grateful to my family, whose unwavering love and support have been at the heart of my journey. I am profoundly indebted to my late mother, Suse, for always being a loving, supportive, and nurturing presence in my life. I thank her for saving hundreds of letters and documents and for gathering her thoughts and strength near the very end of her life to tell me about the trove. I thank my first wife, Joanne, for the many years together, for our two sons, and for being part of my life when I was first grappling with the wealth of letters I had inherited. I thank my sons, Daniel and Peter, and their wives, Mattie and Joni, and my five amazing grandchildren, Joshua, Emily, Brian, Noah, and Harry. All of you have enriched my life in innumerable ways.

Finally, I owe an enormous thank you to my wife, Xiomara. She was enduringly patient and supportive over many years as I labored over the research, took long trips to investigate the story, and obsessed over the past, the work, the process, and the final product. She gave me the physical and mental space to fulfill this most important endeavor even when it meant time away from our life together, and I am very grateful. I also thank Xiomara for the gift of my second family, Marissa and Shayne, Nicole and Mike, and their sons, Luke, Mason, and Ocean. It has been one of the great joys to witness new generations of our families grow and thrive. In the end, this is a story about family. And it is my family—both past and present—who have given me the sense of purpose and determination to persist and to tell this story.

Notes

Foreword

1 See Roger W. Smith, "Human Destructiveness and Politics: The Twentieth Century as an Age of Genocide," in *Genocide and the Modern Age: Etiology and Case Studies of Mass Death*, ed. Isidor Wallimann and Michael N. Dobkowski (Syracuse University Press, 2000), 21.

2 R. J. Rummel, *Death by Government* (Transaction Publishers, 1994).

3 Quote accessed on August 24, 2025, at https://www.wickedlocal.com/story/watertown-tab/2013/04/25/second-gen-armenian-genocide-survivor/40373206007/.

Chapter 1 The Armoire

1 The Schames family had lived in Frankfurt's *Judengasse* since the sixteenth century. Samson Schames' mother, Sophie, and his sister, Luise, were both deported from Frankfurt in 1942. Sophie died in Theresienstadt and Luise perished in Lublin. Although Samson and his wife, Edith, were close family friends, nobody ever told me of their fate.

Chapter 2 Jewish and German

1 The Ephraim household must have been quite a crowded and tumultuous place, with thirteen children in total. Flora's three younger brothers—Emil, Meyer, and Emanuel—probably needed to make their own way at a young age. But where did they end up? Answering this question was made more complicated by the fact that, in some records, the family name was listed as Lehrberg, not Lehrberger. And we only discovered this—and them—when Kat accidentally left off the "er" at the end of Lehrberger in a digital search. Suddenly, records started popping up on her screen, including a passenger manifest from 1892. There on the list was a Meier Lehrberg and an Em Lehrberg. That's how Kat realized that the brother we'd thought was named Manuel was, in fact, named Emanuel. Thanks to this

confluence of mistakes and accidents, we learned that Meyer and Emanuel arrived together in New York Harbor on May 5, 1892. Emanuel was fifteen and Meyer fourteen. From the 1900 U.S. census, we discovered that Emanuel lived in Bainbridge, New York, with his uncle Mendell and aunt Bertha Lehrberger, both siblings of his father Behrmann Lehrberger. Emanuel changed his name to Manuel; he died a decade later, in 1902, in Schenectady, New York. As for Meyer, we tracked down his World War I draft card and found that he lived a long life in the United States, both in New York City and in Upstate New York.

2 My father had no middle name. He was simply Bruno Scheidt. Max, on the other hand, had been named Siegfried Max Scheidt. At some point, he dropped the very Germanic Siegfried as his first name and became Max S. Scheidt.

3 Lotte Appel, who was Jewish, married Max Lorenz, a non-Jewish, openly gay Wagnerian heldentenor in 1932. It was assumed to be a marriage of convenience. The couple was tolerated by the Nazis because Lorenz was considered one of the greatest musical interpreters of Richard Wagner, Hitler's favorite composer. In addition to the Berlin State Opera, Lorenz performed at leading opera houses across Europe and the United States. Recordings of him singing principal roles in Wagner and Strauss operas are available on YouTube, with accompanying slideshows of the dapper, handsome tenor. After Lorenz had an affair with a much younger man and was dragged before a court, Hitler felt that the star's sexuality could no longer be ignored. The Führer insisted that Lorenz be removed from the Wagner Festival in Bayreuth. But Winifred Wagner, the director of the festival, replied that the festival could not go on without him. Lotte had her own close call when the SS burst into the house she shared with Lorenz one night in an attempt to arrest her and her mother. She managed to reach Hermann Göring's sister by phone just in time, and the SS was ordered to stand down. In a letter dated March 21, 1943, Göring stated that Lorenz was under his personal protection, thereby enabling Lorenz, Lotte, and Lotte's mother to survive in Nazi Germany.

Chapter 3 German and Jewish

1 Michael Perlmann, "Genealogie der Familie Ballin," unpublished manuscript, 1913, 1–2.

2 Albert Ballin came from a humble background and fell in love with and married Marianne Rauert, a Christian. Albert did not convert, even when it might have been advantageous for his business and his standing in Kaiser Wilhelm II's court. Before and during World War I, Albert tried to use his influence with the kaiser to avoid German military conflict with the British, but his advice was ignored and his influence at court declined. On November 9, 1918, in the wake of Germany's catastrophic defeat and the kaiser's abdication, Albert took his own life with an overdose of sleeping pills. After his death, the Hamburg America Line launched the SS *Albert Ballin* in his honor. In 1957, Albert's portrait appeared on a German postage stamp. In 2007, almost a century after his death, the city of Hamburg opened the BallinStadt Emigration Museum, which preserves the city he created for emigrants and details the journeys of the tens of thousands of emigrants who passed through Albert's unique city on their way to a better life.

3 Albert Ballin's vision for BallinStadt was unique. In order to succeed, he knew he needed not only middle- and upper-class passengers but "between-deck" ones as

well. To entice them to sail on his Hapag steamers, he provided them accommodations and services in BallinStadt while they were waiting to depart.

4 The most celebrated student of the Schillerschule was Helene Mayer, who won the gold medal in fencing at the 1928 Olympics. Like her classmate, my mother Suse, Helene's father was Jewish. Helene moved to California in 1935 and attended Scripps College. Despite her ancestry, she decided to compete for Germany in the 1936 Olympics in Berlin, won the silver medal, and gave the Nazi salute on the podium. Helene later explained that action, saying she wanted to protect her German family who were in labor camps at the time.

5 Max Ballin was practicing in the Jewish hospital of Berlin when a colleague, an American doctor, presented him with a job offer in Leadville, Colorado. Max seized the opportunity, and his younger brother Friede went with him.

Chapter 4 An Imperfect Reprieve

1 Fred Uhlman, *Reunion* (Farrar, Straus and Giroux, 1997), 58.

2 Joseph Gritti came from a prominent Venetian family. One of his ancestors, Andrea, was doge of Venice in the sixteenth century, and his celebrated palazzo, the Gritti Palace, overlooks the Grand Canal. Joseph moved to Paris in the 1920s and established a food company, Maison Roland, in 1932. In August 1933, he became Bruno's partner in the similarly named Établissements Roland at the same address. Joseph's wife was a Moroccan Jew and famous soprano, performing leading roles at the Paris Opéra-Comique under her maiden name, Mathilde Saïman.

3 Dr. Lilian (Lily) Singer, née Popper (February 17, 1898–June 8, 1977), was born in Brünn (later Brno). She was a general practitioner, having passed her medical exams first in Czechoslovakia and then in Germany. Her lack of a German passport, however, meant she could not legally work there. As a result of her marriage to Max, Lily was able to practice in Germany. She eventually fled to London, where she again could not practice without first taking expensive courses and passing exams. Instead, in 1938, she accepted a job offer that sent her to a remote area at the southern tip of India, where she established a busy practice but led a lonely and difficult life as the region's only Western doctor. In 1951, she emigrated to the United States and settled in Cincinnati where she became a sought-after anesthesiologist, handling complicated cases. At her request, Anne Kelemen, her niece, buried her ashes in Israel.

4 "Jews are Beaten by Berlin Rioters; Cafes are Raided," *New York Times*, July 16, 1935.

5 The novel was translated from the original German into French by Albert Paraz. The Nazis did not permit publication of the book in Germany. It was to be published in German in Holland, but the outbreak of World War II prevented its publication. It seems the original German manuscript has been lost.

6 The reichsmark was the currency of Germany from 1924 to 1948.

Chapter 5 Rubble and Embers

1 Today, at the site of the Friedberger Anlage, there is an inconspicuous and inadequate memorial consisting of two pillars and a small plaque. Hanging high on the wall is a faded photo of the synagogue's beautiful interior. Below the photo

is a small sign that reads: *Bis 1938 stand hier eine Synagoge!* (Until 1938 a synagogue stood here!).

2 In March 1958, Georg filed a restitution claim for the family's stolen belongings and for the building he and his brothers owned in the center of Frankfurt. The file indicates that in 1932, the building was valued at 420,000 reichsmarks. On February 1, 1938, Georg and his two brothers were forced to sell it for only 115,000 reichsmarks. In addition, when they left Germany, they were required to pay the flight tax of 90 percent.

A detailed inventory dated January 12, 1939, lists Georg and Margarete's confiscated possessions: books, artwork, silver, a piano, a radio, and other furniture and household items. Despite his efforts to receive compensation for both the real estate and stolen possessions, Georg did not live long enough to get restitution. When it was finally provided in 1962, the amount was woefully inadequate: 500 deutschmarks (about $125 in at the time) for the silverware and 8,679 deutschmarks ($2,170) for the real estate.

Chapter 6 A Fateful Miscalculation

1 Oscar Heinrich Leopold Goldschmidt was born into an illustrious, wealthy Austrian Jewish family. He and Max became friends when they were living in Berlin. Like Max and Erna, Oscar and his family emigrated to Paris and, in November 1934, he founded Société d'Industries Opothérapiques. (Opotherapy is the treatment of disease using animal organs and extracts.) Max eventually became Oscar's partner in this company. Oscar and his family also rented a house in Bénerville in 1939 and frequently socialized there with Max and Erna. Oscar traveled to the United States for three weeks in May 1939, but he returned to France and was trapped there when war broke out in September.

Chapter 7 "Mein Lieber Bruder"

1 During the Phoney War, internees in some camps were given two options to get out of detention: one was to become a *préstataire*, a civilian serving in a noncombat work group, helping the French national defense; and the other was to join the French Foreign Legion in North Africa. In both cases, the pay was minimal and the work was at best unpleasant and at worst dangerous. Georg Münsterberger's son-in-law had chosen to join the French Foreign Legion to get out of the Braconne detention camp.

2 Max's imperfect English in this letter reflects his efforts to learn and practice his English in anticipation of getting a U.S. visa.

Chapter 8 "The End of Everything"

1 February 1941 was a fraught time of intense unrest in Amsterdam. Members of the militia of the pro-Nazi Dutch National-Socialist Movement (NSB) had begun terrorizing Jews and their businesses. Defensive measures were carried out by Jewish organizations, and there were violent confrontations between the groups. In one such incident, a member of the NSB was mortally injured. In another incident, thugs smashed the windows of an ice cream parlor owned by Jews; in

response, a group formed to protect the store. When German police raided the store on February 19, the resistance group sprayed ammonia in their faces. To try to put an end to this uprising, on the weekend of February 22–23 the German police stormed the Jodenbuurt (Jewish neighborhood), which had been demarcated with barbed wire and checkpoints several days earlier. The police rounded up about 400 young Jewish men, whom they deported to Buchenwald and then Mauthausen. (Only two of the men survived.) In response, the outlawed Dutch Communist Party organized a general strike, beginning February 25. The country's transport system, most public services, and major factory production came to a halt. The Nazis responded to the protest with rifles and hand grenades, killing nine and injuring several hundred strikers. After three days, they brutally stamped out the resistance, ending the strike. They then executed eighteen resisters, including three of the leaders. One owner of the ice cream parlor was executed on March 3, 1941, and the other died in Auschwitz.

2 The title of Ronald Sanders' book, *In verband met de vermindering van het aantal kinderen* (Due to the reduction in the number of children), mentioned earlier in this chapter, is a direct quote from the headmaster's cryptic note about the school's closure.

3 After the expulsion, Ellien attended an all-Jewish school for a short time. By September 1943, the Jewish schools were shut down entirely because most of the Jewish students and teachers had fled or been deported to concentration camps.

Chapter 9 "Caught in a Mousetrap on a Powder Keg"

1 Although a deadline of June 15 was mentioned in earlier correspondence, Erna was given additional time to enter the United States.

2 Walter Mehring, a popular satiric author in the Weimar years whose work was banned by the Nazis, put into words the experience of being trapped in Marseille: the sense of being penned up as if in a cattle stall, the yearning to escape, and the perilous journey to safety that lay ahead. His October 1940 poem, "Brief aus der Mitternacht VIII," translated by S.A. DeWitt with the title "Odyssey Out of Midnight VIII," opens:

> No word of this, I beg of you; we planned
> Escape to-night, against all countermand.
> The scheme was plotted in a drunken haze. . . .
> A ship embarks at midnight, and the craze
> For freedom fires us all. Imagine how
> The refugees will jam it, stern to bow
> Hard on a trackless course. Think how a breath
> Of this to the oppressor means our death.

3 Alexander Brailowsky (February 16, 1896–April 25, 1976) was a Russian-born French pianist considered one of the era's greatest interpreters of Chopin. He toured all over the world, was the first pianist to perform all of Chopin's 169 solo piano works as a cycle, and sometimes performed on Chopin's own piano.

4 When Georg and Flora decided to leave on the *Winnipeg* instead of taking the Spain-Portugal route, they told Max to give their steamship tickets from Lisbon to New York to his former partner Oscar Goldschmidt. Thanks to those tickets, Oscar and his family made their escape from Europe via Lisbon in July 1941.

5 Jews escaping the Nazis weren't the first refugees to sail on the *Winnipeg.* When General Francisco Franco came to power in Spain, his Fascist forces unleashed hell on those associated with the former democratic government and on Socialists, Communists, and artists of all kinds. Many fled to France, living in desperate squalor in camps near the border. In 1939, Chilean poet Pablo Neruda decided to save as many of the refugees as he could. He raised money, exerted influence on politicians to accept them in Chile, and gathered the resources to have the *Winnipeg* retrofitted to hold 2,200 passengers for the journey. He later wrote, "There were fishermen, peasants, laborers, intellectuals, a cross-section of strength, heroism and hard work. My poetry in its struggle had succeeded in finding them a country. And I was filled with pride." On August 4, 1939, the *Winnipeg* set sail for Chile from Pauillac, France. (Chilean novelist Isabel Allende told the story in her 2019 bestseller, *A Long Petal of the Sea.*) After the ship was seized in May 1941, it was sold to Canadian Pacific Steamships Lines of Montreal; it continued to carry refugees, as well as soldiers and cargo, between Liverpool and Halifax. On October 22, 1942, the *Winnipeg* was sunk by a German U-boat. Fortunately, another ship, the HMCS *Morden*, was nearby and could come to its rescue; all 192 aboard, including sixty women and children, were saved.

6 United States Holocaust Memorial Museum, accessed September 10, 2019, https://collections.ushmm.org/search/catalog/irn617447.

7 *New York Herald Tribune*, June 14, 1941.

Chapter 10 Nowhere to Turn, No One to Trust

1 The Schouwburg Theater was declared a "Jewish theatre" in 1941 by the Nazi occupation forces, who then turned it into a deportation center. Though more than 46,000 people were held there on their way to the camps, only eight photos of it survive. Five photos were taken in July 1942 by a non-Jewish Dutch teenager, Lydia Riezouw, from a window in her family's apartment on Plantage Kerklaan. One of Lydia's photos (later displayed at the Jewish Museum in New York City and around the world in a show called "The Illegal Camera: Photography in the Netherlands During the German Occupation, 1940–1945") shows her high school friend Grethe Velleman waving at Lydia's camera, smiling, oblivious to what was coming. Records show that Grethe (called Greetje) died in Auschwitz on September 30, 1942.

Chapter 12 Making Sense of the Present

1 Another close childhood friend who often joined my family on outings was Robert Rothenberg. Robert was from a similar background, the son of German-Jewish immigrants, and we shared hobbies of stamp collecting and tropical fish. We lost touch over the years but reconnected shortly after I sold the company. In the course of working on this book, we exchanged childhood memories, and Robert vividly recalled the games my father would play and the challenging questions he would ask to prepare us for the possibility of life outside the United States.

2 Stephen Slaton's mother died when he was thirteen, followed in quick succession by his father, just shy of Stephen's fifteenth birthday. Max and Erna were friends of his parents, and shortly before his death, Stephen's father asked them to be

Stephen's legal guardians. Though they did not know Stephen very well at the time, they agreed.

Stephen spent more and more time with Max and Erna. The three of them grew close, and he soon became an integral part of our family. Suddenly, Max and Erna had a son, and a brilliant one at that. I spent time with Stephen too, and we developed a close friendship; he was three years my senior and an inspiring role model during my teenage years. In 1959, at age nineteen, Stephen was formally adopted by Max and Erna and changed his last name from Slaton to Slaton-Scheidt, eventually dropping the hyphen and taking the surname Scheidt. After graduating from Princeton, Stephen won a Fulbright Scholarship and then attended Columbia Medical School. Stephen married Andrea Harris, and their children and grandchildren are part of our family today.

3 Apart from Kurt Lang, there were many immigrants who became essential long-term members of the company, including Mario Steinvurzel, the last person my father hired. Mario's parents had fled Europe for Argentina, where Mario grew up before coming to New York. Mario started in the import department but had a vision to expand Roland's reach. He moved into sales, became a vice president, and single-handedly developed markets in the Caribbean, Central and South America, where Roland became the leading brand. I trusted him, relied on his good decision-making, and he and I worked closely together for nearly five decades.

George Steiner was another key hire. He and his wife had fled Czechoslovakia during the 1968 Prague Spring, and George joined the company a few years after my father died. Like Mario, he got his start working in our import department. George eventually moved into purchasing, became a vice president, and oversaw the tremendous expansion in our product line. He was pivotal in paving the way with new and existing suppliers from countries all over the world, ensuring high-quality standards and negotiating good deals. He and I worked closely for nearly five decades. I trusted him and relied on him for thoughtful advice and to handle difficult situations.

4 It had always struck me as eerie that my father and my uncle Max died at almost the exact same age, mere weeks shy of their sixty-sixth birthdays. I was very happy when I celebrated my sixty-sixth birthday.

In Memoriam

1 Hans Schwab's wife, Marie Amon, also known as Bibiana Amon, was a frequent guest of Max and Erna's at La Ricoquette during the summer of 1939. Today, she's best remembered for her scandalous novel *Barrières*. The book was an enormous success in France, going through at least eight printings. (Erna mentioned in a letter to Bruno and Suse that she had enjoyed it.) Despite being separated from Hans, Marie tried to leverage her fame in France on Hans' behalf, pleading for his release from Lisieux in a letter to the Ministre de l'Intérieur on January 7, 1940. The book *Bibiana Amon: Eine Spurensuche*, written by the Viennese literary scholar Walter Schübler, was published in 2022.

Sources

This book aims to faithfully recount the lives of my family and those whose paths intersected with theirs—and with mine. Reconstructing the family history relied largely on letters, documents, photographs, testimony, and oral and written recollections. Additional material was generously shared by archives, and by descendants and friends of those involved. While memory naturally shifts over time, the accounts used to reconstruct this story are as true as recollection permits. Further historical context and inspiration came from over a decade of reading and research. The sources that follow reflect the wide-ranging and invaluable foundation behind this book.

Books

Amos, Elon. *The Pity of It All: A Portrait of the German-Jewish Epoch, 1743–1933.* Picador, 2003.

Appelbaum, Peter C. *Loyal Sons: Jews in the German Army in the Great War.* Vellentin Mitchell, 2014.

Badia, Gilbert. *Exilés en France: Souvenirs d'antifascistes allemands émigrés (1933–1945).* François Maspero, 1982.

Badia, Gilbert. *Les Barbelés de l'exil: Etudes sur l'émigration allemande et autrichienne (1938–1940).* Presses universitaires de Grenoble, 1979.

Ballin, Oscar. *Die Familie Ballin.* C. F. Hertel, 1913.

Birnbaum, Pierre. *Léon Blum: Prime Minister, Socialist, Zionist.* Translated by Arthur Goldhammer. Yale University Press, 2015.

Bohnekamp, Dorothea. *De Weimar á Vichy: Les Juifs d'Allemagne en République, 1919–1940/1944.* Fayard, 2015.

Brenner, Michael. *A Short History of the Jews.* Princeton University Press, 2010.

Browning, Christoper R. *The Origins of the Final Solution: The Evolution of Nazi Jewish Policy, September 1939–March 1942.* University of Nebraska Press, 2004.

Caron, Vicki. *Uneasy Asylum: France and the Jewish Refugee Crisis, 1933–1942*. Stanford University Press, 1999.
Epstein, Helen. *Children of the Holocaust: Conversations with Sons and Daughters of Survivors*. Penguin Books, 1988.
Feuchtwanger, Lion. *The Devil in France: My Encounter with Him the Summer of 1940*. Translated by Enrico Arosio. Feuchtwanger Press, 2007.
Friedman, Jonathan. *The Lion and the Star: Gentile-Jewish Relations in Three Hessian Towns, 1919–1945*. University Press of Kentucky, 1998.
Grandjacques, Gabriel. *La Montagne-Refuge: Les Juifs au Pays du Mont-Blanc*. La Fontaine De Siloé, 2007.
Helm, Sarah. *Ravensbrück: Life and Death in Hitler's Concentration Camp for Women*. Nan A. Talese/Doubleday, 2015.
Hoffman, Eva. *Lost in Translation: A Life in a New Language*. Penguin Books, 1990.
Jennings, Eric T. *Escape from Vichy: The Refugee Exodus to the French Caribbean*. Harvard University Press, 2018.
Kolb, Eberhard. *Bergen-Belsen 1943 bis 1945*. Vandenhoeck & Ruprecht, 1986.
Large, David Clay. *The Perils of Prominence: Jews in Weimar Berlin*. Leo Baeck Institute, 2001.
Lee, Daniel. *Petain's Jewish Children: French Jewish Youth and the Vichy Regime, 1940–1942*. Oxford University Press, 2014.
Levine, Emily J. *Dreamland of Humanists: Warburg, Cassirer, Panofsky, and the Hamburg School*. University of Chicago Press, 2013.
Lévi-Strauss, Claude. *Tristes Tropiques*. Translated by John and Doreen Weightman. Penguin Books, 2012.
Marchand, Thierry, and Gérard Bourdin. *Exils Normands: Les "ressortissants ennemis" internés dans les centres de rassemblement des étrangers de Normandie (1939–1940)*. Société historique de Lisieux, 2014.
Marchot, Guy. *Les indésirables: Les camps d'internés civils Français et étrangers, 1939–1946*. Association Philatélique du Pays d'Aix, 2020.
McClafferty, Carla Killough. *In Defiance of Hitler: The Secret Mission of Varian Fry*. Farrar, Straus and Giroux, 2008.
Mehring, Walter. "Brief aus der Mitternacht V" and "Brief aus der Mitternacht VIII." In *No Road Back: Poems by Walter Mehring*, translated by S. A. Dewitt, 38–45, 62–69. Samuel Curl, 1944.
Mogulof, Milly. *Foiled: Hitler's Jewish Olympian; The Helene Mayer Story*. RDR Books, 2002.
Moore, Bob. *Refugees from Nazi Germany in the Netherlands 1933–1940*. Martinus Nijhoff, 1986.
Perlmann, Michael. "Genealogie der Familie Ballin." unpublished manuscript, 1913.
Peschanski, Denis. *La France des camps: L'internement, 1938–1946*. Gallimard, 2002.
Röhl, John C. G. *The Kaiser and His Court: Wilhelm II and the Government of Germany*. Cambridge University Press, 1994.
Rummel, R. J. *Death by Government*. Transaction Publishers, 1994.
Ryan, Donna F. *The Holocaust and the Jews of Marseille: The Enforcement of Anti-Semitic Policies in Vichy France*. University of Illinois Press, 1996.
Saidel, Rochelle G. *The Jewish Women of Ravensbrück Concentration Camp*. University of Wisconsin Press, 2004.

Sanders, Ronald. *In verband met de vermindering van het aantal kinderen*. Lecturium B.V., 2008.
Schlotzhauer, Inge. *Das Philanthropin 1804–1942: Die Schule der Israelitischen Gemeinde in Frankfurt am Main*. Waldemar Kramer Verlag, 1990.
Schneeberger, Michael, Christian Reuther, and Elmar Schwinger. *Gedenkbuch Kitzingen*. Förderverein ehemalige Synagoge Kitzingen, 2011.
Semelin, Jacques. *The Survival of the Jews in France, 1940–44*. Oxford University Press, 2019.
Smith, Roger W. "Human Destructiveness and Politics: The Twentieth Century as an Age of Genocide." In *Genocide and the Modern Age: Etiology and Case Studies of Mass Death*, edited by Isidor Wallimann and Michael N. Dobkowski, 21–39. Syracuse University Press, 2000.
Strätz, Reiner. *Biographisches Handbuch Würzburger Juden 1900–1945*. F. Schöningh, 1989.
Uhlman, Fred. *Reunion*. Farrar, Straus and Giroux, 1997.
Wachsmann, Nikolaus. *KL: A History of Nazi Concentration Camps*. Farrar, Straus and Giroux, 2015.
Zucotti, Susan. *The Holocaust, the French and the Jews*. University of Nebraska Press, 1999.

Institutions

The following institutions provided data, articles, and other information:

Alliance Israelite Universelle, www.aiu.org
Ancestry, www.ancestry.com
Anne Frank House, www.annefrank.org
Association de Collectionneurs du Pays d'Ambazac, www.mairie-ambazac.fr/associations
Cambridge University Press, www.cambridge.org
Canadian War Museum, www.warmuseum.ca
Consistoire de Paris, www.consistoire.org
Encyclopedia Britannica, www.britannica.com
Facing History & Ourselves, www.facinghistory.org
Fondation Catherine Gide, www.fondation-catherine-gide.org
French Lines & Compagnies, www.frenchlines.com
Gedenkorte für die Opfer der NS-Zeit in Frankfurt am Main, www.gedenkorte-frankfurt-main.de
Gedenkstätte Bergen-Belsen, www.bergen-belsen.stiftung-ng.de
Généalogie à Thônes (Haute-Savoie) et dans les Aravis, www.genealogiethonesaravis.fr
The Herald Democrat, www.leadvilleherald.com
Historisches Museum Frankfurt, www.museumsufer.de
The Holocaust Encyclopedia, United States Holocaust Memorial Museum, www.ushmm.org
Holocaust Museum LA, www.holocaustmuseumla.org
Immigration and Ethnic History Society, www.immigrationhistory.org
International Society of Olympic Historians, www.isoh.org
Jewish Sites in Frankfurt, www.juedisches-frankfurt.de
Jewish Virtual Library, www.jewishvirtuallibrary.org

Joods Monument, www.joodsmonument.nl
Journal Officiel de la République Française (JORF), www.legifrance.gouv.fr
Jüdisches Museum Frankfurt, www.juedischesmuseum.de
Kulturamt Frankfurt am Main, www.kultur-frankfurt.de
KZ-Gedenkstätte Neuengamme, www.kz-gedenkstaette-neuengamme.de
Leer over de Holocaust, www.leeroverdeholocaust.nl
Leo Baeck Institute, www.lbi.org
Mahn- und Gedenskstätte Ravensbrück, www.ravensbrueck-sbg.de
Martyrs Memorial and Museum of the Holocaust LA (now defunct)
Merrimack College McQuade Library, www.merrimack.edu
The National WWII Museum, www.nationalww2museum.org
The New York Times, www.nytimes.com
Regesta Imperii, www.regesta-imperii.de
Simon Wiesenthal Center, www.wiesenthal.org
The Tenement Museum, www.tenement.org
Traces of War, www.tracesofwar.com
University of Chicago Press, www.press.uchicago.edu
Verzets Resistance Museum, www.verzetsmuseum.org
Winnipeg Free Press, www.winnipegfreepress.com
Wicked Local, www.wickedlocal.com
Yad Vashem, The World Holocaust Remembrance Center, www.yadvashem.org
Yivo Institute for Jewish Research, www.yivo.org

Archives

AUSTRIA

Österreichisches Staatsarchiv
Wiener Stadt- und Landesarchiv (MA 8)

BELGIUM

Algemeen Rijksarchief

FRANCE

Archives de Mémorial de la Shoah
Archives départementales de Bouches-du-Rhône
Archives départementales de Haute-Savoie
Archives départementales de la Guadeloupe
Archives départementales de la Haute-Vienne
Archives départementales de Martinique
Archives départementales de Paris
Archives des Pyrénées-Atlantiques
Archives municipales de Saint-Germain en Laye
Archives municipales de Saint-Laurent de Ceris
Archives nationales (AN)
Bibliothèque nationale de France (BNF)
La Contemporaine (bibliothèque, archives, musée des mondes contemporains)
Mairie de Bénerville-sur-Mer
Préfecture de Police de Paris

GERMANY
Arolsen Archives, International Center on Nazi Persecution
Borken Stadt Archiv
Bundesarchiv
Hessisches Hauptstaatsarchiv Wiesbaden
Institut für Stadtgeschichte Frankfurt am Main
Landesarchiv Berlin
Landesarchiv Hessen
Landratsamt Zwickau Kreisarchiv
Stadtarchiv Karlsruhe
Stadtarchiv Kitzingen
Stadtarchiv Würzburg

HOLLAND
Herinneringscentrum Kamp Westerbork
Nationaal Holocaustmuseum
Oorlogsarchief Rode Kruis
Stadsarchief Amsterdam

SWEDEN
Malmö stad Kulturförvaltningen

UNITED KINGDOM
British National Archives

UNITED STATES
Leo Baeck Institute Archives
National Archives and Records Administration (NARA)
USCIS Archives
USHMM Archives
Yad Vashem Archives
YIVO Archives

Index

Note: Page numbers in *italics* indicate figures.

About the Authors

CHARLIE SCHEIDT was born in New York City to parents who had escaped Nazi-occupied Europe. Growing up in a close-knit, German-Jewish refugee community, Charlie witnessed firsthand the traumatic effects of persecution and exile. Following his father's untimely death, Charlie stepped in to lead Roland Foods, the business his parents had founded, honoring their legacy and growing it into the leading imported specialty food company. After nearly five decades as CEO, Charlie retired and turned his focus to supporting universities and NGOs that advocate for refugee rights and work to prevent genocide. He and his wife split their time between New York City and Upstate New York, spending as much time as they can with their children and grandchildren.

KAT ROHRER is an award-winning filmmaker, born and raised in Vienna, Austria, who has produced and directed numerous narrative films, documentaries, and commercials. Kat's feature-length documentary *Back to the Fatherland* had theatrical releases in Austria, Germany, and the United States and has aired on TV in Austria, Sweden, Germany, and Israel. In 2023, Kat attended the Torino Next Series Lab and HerArts Film Lab with her upcoming projects, and in 2024, following its world premiere at the BFI Flare Film Festival, her latest narrative feature, *What a Feeling*, was screened at over thirty-five film festivals worldwide and played in theaters across Europe. She is currently in the early stages of developing a film inspired by this book. Kat splits her time between Vienna and New York City, creating stories that challenge cultural boundaries and explore identity and belonging.

www.InheritanceMemoir.com

Available titles in the Genocide, Political Violence, Human Rights series:

Nanci Adler, ed., *Understanding the Age of Transitional Justice: Crimes, Courts, Commissions, and Chronicling*
Bree Akesson and Andrew R. Basso, *From Bureaucracy to Bullets: Extreme Domicide and the Right to Home*
Jeffrey S. Bachman, *Genocide Studies: Pathways Ahead*
Jeffrey S. Bachman, *The Politics of Genocide: From the Genocide Convention to the Responsibility to Protect*
Andrew R. Basso, *Destroy Them Gradually: Displacement as Atrocity*
Alan W. Clarke, *Rendition to Torture*
Alison Crosby and Heather Evans, eds., *Memorializing Violence: Transnational Feminist Reflections*
Alison Crosby and M. Brinton Lykes, *Beyond Repair? Mayan Women's Protagonism in the Aftermath of Genocidal Harm*
Lawrence Davidson, *Cultural Genocide*
Myriam Denov, Claudia Mitchell, and Marjorie Rabiau, eds., *Global Child: Children and Families Affected by War, Displacement, and Migration*
Piergiorgio Di Giminiani, Helene Risør, and Karine Vanthuyne, eds., *The Futures of Reparations in Latin America: Imagination, Translation, and Belonging*
Daniel Feierstein, *Genocide as Social Practice: Reorganizing Society under the Nazis and Argentina's Military Juntas*
Joseph P. Feldman, *Memories before the State: Postwar Peru and the Place of Memory, Tolerance, and Social Inclusion*
Alexander Laban Hinton, ed., *Transitional Justice: Global Mechanisms and Local Realities after Genocide and Mass Violence*
Alexander Laban Hinton, Thomas La Pointe, and Douglas Irvin-Erickson, eds., *Hidden Genocides: Power, Knowledge, Memory*
Douglas A. Kammen, *Three Centuries of Conflict in East Timor*
Eyal Mayroz, *Reluctant Interveners: America's Failed Responses to Genocide from Bosnia to Darfur*
Pyong Gap Min, *Korean "Comfort Women": Military Brothels, Brutality, and the Redress Movement*
Fazil Moradi, *Being Human: Political Modernity and Hospitality in Kurdistan-Iraq*
Walter Richmond, *The Circassian Genocide*
S. Garnett Russell, *Becoming Rwandan: Education, Reconciliation, and the Making of a Post-Genocide Citizen*
Tatiana Sanchez Parra, *Born of War in Colombia: Reproductive Violence and Memories of Absence*
Victoria Sanford, Katerina Stefatos, and Cecilia M. Salvi, eds., *Gender Violence in Peace and War: States of Complicity*
Charlie Scheidt with Kat Rohrer, *Inheritance: Love, Loss, and the Legacy of the Holocaust*

Irina Silber, *Everyday Revolutionaries: Gender, Violence, and Disillusionment in Postwar El Salvador*

Amy Sodaro, *Lifting the Shadow: Reshaping Memory, Race, and Slavery in U.S. Museums*

Samuel Totten and Rafiki Ubaldo, eds., *We Cannot Forget: Interviews with Survivors of the 1994 Genocide in Rwanda*

Eva van Roekel, *Phenomenal Justice: Violence and Morality in Argentina*

Anton Weiss-Wendt, *A Rhetorical Crime: Genocide in the Geopolitical Discourse of the Cold War*

Kerry Whigham, *Resonant Violence: Affect, Memory, and Activism in Post-Genocide Societies*

Timothy Williams, *The Complexity of Evil: Perpetration and Genocide*

Ronnie Yimsut, *Facing the Khmer Rouge: A Cambodian Journey*

Natasha Zaretsky, *Acts of Repair: Justice, Truth, and the Politics of Memory in Argentina*

Julien Zarifian, *The United States and the Armenian Genocide: History, Memory, Politics*

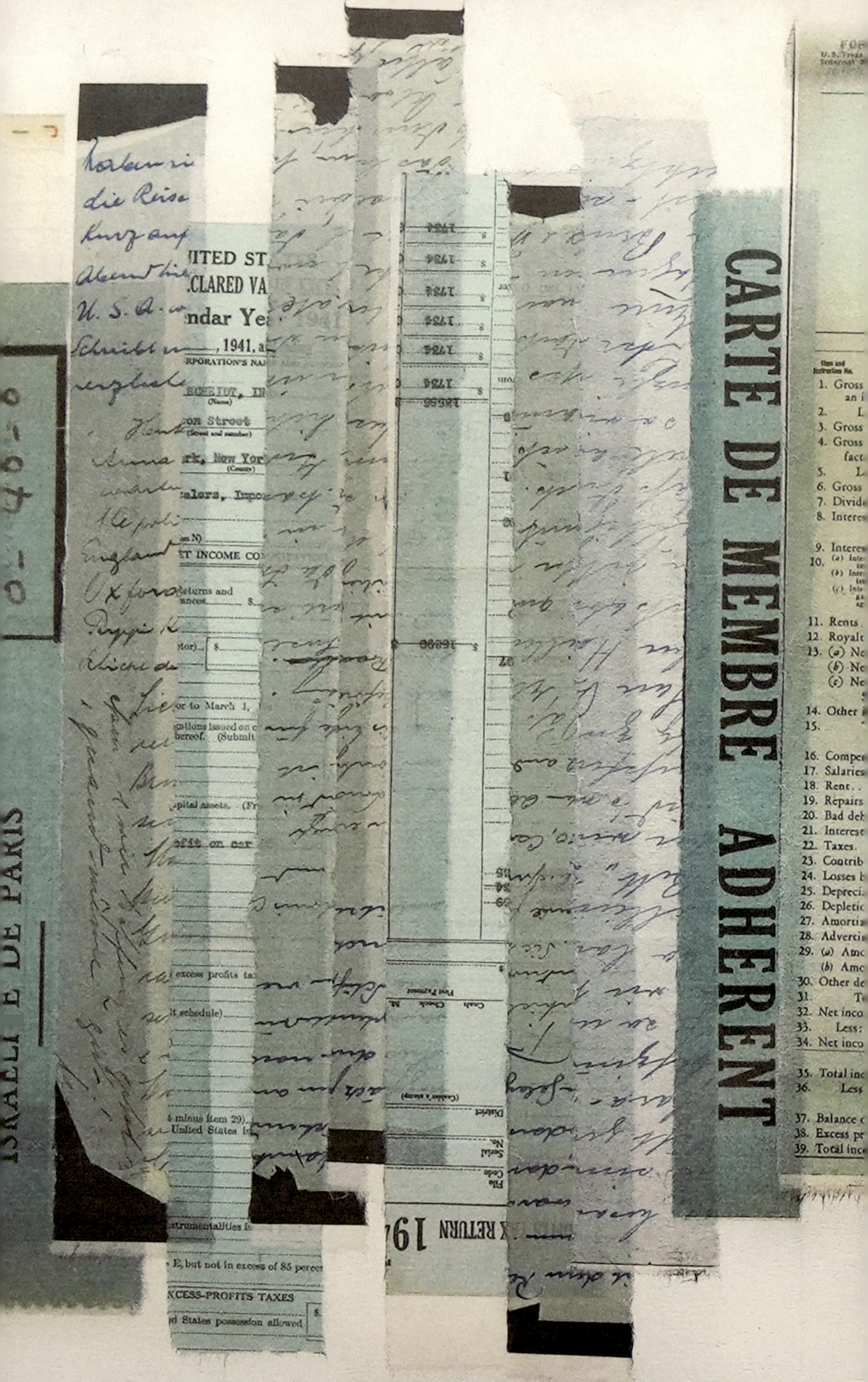
CARTE DE MEMBRE ADHERENT
ISRAELI E DE PARIS
ITED ST
CLARED VA
ndar Ye
1941
ET INCOME CO
EXCESS-PROFITS TAXES
E, but not in excess of 85 perce
d States possession allowed
19 X RETURN
1. Gross
2.
3. Gross
4. Gross
5.
6. Gross
7. Divide
8. Intere
9. Intere
10.
11. Rents
12. Royalt
13. (a) Ne
14. Other
15.
16. Compe
17. Salaries
18. Rent
19. Repairs
20. Bad deb
21. Interest
22. Taxes
23. Contrib
24. Losses
25. Depreci
26. Depletio
27. Amortiz
28. Adverti
29. (a) Amo
(b) Amo
30. Other de
31.
32. Net inco
33. Less:
34. Net inco
35. Total inc
36. Less
37. Balance
38. Excess pr
39. Total inc